A Comprehensive Guide to Religious and Spiritual Care for Sikh Patients in NHS Hospitals and Hospices

978-1-8382223-9-0

Satwant Kaur Rait

Published by

i2i

PUBLISHING

i2i Publishing. Manchester.

www.i2ipublishing.co.uk

Dedicated to

The Occasion of the 550th birthday of Guru Nanak, the founder of the Sikh Religion

Hospital and hospice patients, the main resource of this book

Table of Contents

Foreword

It is a privilege and a pleasure to write this foreword to an important educational book on Sikhism that also seeks to support and develop the provision of multi-faith chaplaincy across the healthcare sector. I have known the author since 2016 when she became the first Sikh Spiritual Care Volunteer at St. Gemma's Hospice in Leeds. Satwant is very experienced at providing generic pastoral, spiritual and religious care to patients of any religion as well as those with non-religious beliefs and values.

Her first book on this topic entitled 'A guide to being a Sikh chaplain' self-published in 2013 provided a foundation in order to inform those practising chaplaincy and their employing organisations. Here the author builds on these foundations producing a comprehensive and thought-provoking guide suitable for any organisation that provides chaplaincy services or pastoral, spiritual and religious care services.

The scope of this book is significant ranging from the discussion of Sikh philosophy and psychology, associated key ceremonies and festivals, to the development of Sikh Chaplaincy with an exploration of the key skills and competencies required. Satwant also explores generic pastoral and spiritual care and the impact on Sikhism and other minority faiths. The application of generic spiritual assessment tools merits further research to establish the credibility of these tools with particular emphasis given to cross-cultural validation to identify any Christian or other cultural bias inherent in these tools.

The author argues strongly regarding the importance of Sikh religious rituals and the impact on the care of Sikh patients, before exploring end of life and bereavement issues. Satwant demonstrates a passion for and a detailed knowledge of her subject coupled with a detailed insider's perspective of her philosophical and religious tradition of Sikhism. She also articulates the compelling need to develop chaplaincy or generic pastoral, spiritual and religious care services for minority faith groups in the UK.

I congratulate the author in producing such a comprehensive book and hope that it prompts deep reflection on the issues it raises.

Peter McEvoy
Spiritual Care Manager
St. Gemma's Hospice
Leeds

Acknowledgements

I am grateful to God who gave me the courage and energy to undertake this work against my adverse personal circumstances. This book is written in my husband's memory as his illness led me to enter this field. I hardly had any knowledge of this profession when I first started. My gratitude goes to Professor Rev. Dr Chris Swift, who was the Head of the Chaplaincy Department in Leeds Teachings Hospitals. Under his professional guidance, I learned and developed chaplaincy skills and developed a career in the field. He also gave me occasional support when I was struggling to make any decisions regarding this book. I am also grateful for the support given by Emma Tomlin, Professor of Religion and Public Life at the School of Philosophy, Religion and History of Science at the University of Leeds. My sincere thanks go to Peter McEvoy, the Spiritual Care Manager at St Gemma's Hospice, Leeds, who remained my active mentor throughout. His consistent help not only kept me going, but was also emboldening and invaluable. His perseverance pulled me through my most difficult moments. My heartfelt admiration goes out to Miss Jo Bewley, General Manager of Adult Therapies, who read this book over the weekend in her own time and gave encouraging feedback.

Manpreet Kaur Dhadda, a young Sikh and cultural sector professional, read the book and commented with an eye of a Sikh reader. Manpreet deserves appreciation for giving unbiased and constructive feedback on this work. I am indebted to my chaplaincy colleagues, in particular to Jo Jones, now Deputy Head of the

Chaplaincy department of LTH, who read and commented on the book with an eye of Christian chaplain. My gratitude also goes to Fr Benjamin Griffiths (LTH) who readily explained any Christian terminology which were not clear to me over the years. My appreciation goes to Delyth Birch, a bereavement councillor at St. Gemma's Hospice for commenting on my bereavement chapter. I am thankful to Avtar Singh Missionary, the chairperson of the Council of *Gurdwara* Management Committees UK based at Wolverhampton, and a TV presenter on the Sikh Channel, for his advice on dates and concepts in Sikhism. My thanks also go to Kathy (LBF) and her husband Paul for their support. I am grateful to those chaplaincy professionals whom I met in meetings, conferences, and trainings. They also tried to help and encourage me to complete this work, along with Joanna Mutlow, believing that it was worthwhile. I warmly acknowledge the support given by Albert Jewell, retired pastoral director of Methodist Homes for the Aged in the initial stage to prepare the framework. I also appreciate the goodwill gestures of those professionals who wanted to help but found it hard due to their work commitments and personal circumstances. I would like to acknowledge the most valuable contributions made by the patients of Leeds Teaching Hospitals, NHS Trust, and St Gemma's Hospice Leeds, by sharing their views without any hesitation. Their views enriched this book and became its main resource. This book may have my name on the cover, but it would not have been completed without the contributions of all mentioned above.

I am grateful for my family, who endured my long absences from their life, especially my grandchildren who politely requested me to visit them. They were regularly ringing me to ask of my well-being. They are my source of strength. I could not have managed without the IT support from my son and caring attitude of my daughter. Tanya Comber-Rait's input in finding the image for the cover page is much appreciated. Last, but not least, my friends were considerate, helpful, and supportive. They kept me amused when I was frustrated, distressed, and isolated, especially providing their support during Covid-19.

Background: Introduction and Research Methods

Introduction

A Comprehensive Guide to Religious and Spiritual Care for Sikh Patients in NHS Hospitals and Hospices

This book is about the care of Sikh patients, specifically focused on religious, pastoral and spiritual care. It is the revised and expanded edition of the author's previous book: *A guide to being a Sikh chaplain*, which was basic and limited. This comprehensive book covers the primary areas of spiritual care for the guidance of chaplains and volunteers. The main emphasis is on the care of patients in NHS hospitals, hospices and care homes. The contents of the book can also be applied to prisons and the armed forces. It is introductory in its content and easy to read due to the conscious decision to use plain language. This approach was deliberate as initially, the author herself had difficulty in grasping the terminology and concepts of Christianity and psychology when she first started to work as an honorary chaplain.

The aim of writing this book is to increase the capacity of the NHS to support and develop multi-faith chaplaincy and identify why religion and culture matter at all in healthcare. This research will also raise the profile of Sikh chaplaincy within the practical chaplaincy field and academia. It will help with raising awareness of chaplaincy, spiritual care needs, and improving the experience of Sikhs, particularly at the end of life, through research that identifies the needs of these stakeholders. Attending to the spiritual, cultural, and religious needs of patients is proven to enhance healthcare outcomes and make the experience better for the patient and their relatives, fulfilling the ultimate aim of the NHS. It will be a resource for chaplains, health and social care professionals, multidisciplinary teams, researchers and academics. Sikhs are mainly a faith community and religion plays a significant role in their lives. The main aim of this book is to draw the attention of healthcare professionals, in particular, chaplains and nurses, to the specific spiritual needs of Sikh patients and to suggest how to address those needs in different circumstances. It will also help in raising awareness of spiritual care in the Sikh community and may encourage them to demand the service. This guide is a pioneer in taking steps to close the existing gap within chaplaincy literature, and points out the areas for conducting further in-depth studies to create and enhance basic resources.

This book is semi-academic and practical in nature. The language used is simple. Jargon and technical vocabulary are avoided as much as possible to make it easily accessible. When any specialist vocabulary is used, the meaning is given within brackets in layperson's language. Certain Panjabi (language of the Punjab, where Sikhism was founded) words and concepts are introduced to make readers aware of specific terminology. Where it is necessary to make the meaning clear for readers, these are transcribed in English. The framework of the book follows the established pattern of current writing concerning chaplaincy and spiritual care. This lens will help non-Sikh chaplains to understand how and where Sikh spiritual care differs from the traditional pattern. This approach will help to improve the capacity of Sikh chaplains/volunteers and non-Sikh chaplains to provide an effective service, keeping in mind the values and traditions of Sikhs.

In the Western world, Sikhism is a widely used term for the Sikh faith, whereas Sikhs prefer to use *Sikhi* or the Sikh *Dharam*. The term *Sikhi*/Sikh *dharam* refers to a way of life, combined with spirituality. The term *dharam* encompasses and entwines religion and spirituality in all the religions of the Indian sub-continent including Sikh *dharam*. Religion has a different interpretation in the West, which treats religion and philosophy as distinct subjects. This book has used the terms Sikh religion or Sikh faith frequently, though the term Sikhism is used primarily.

Chaplains apply religion to their everyday work when they are giving religious care to patients. The essence of religious and cultural core values is used in spiritual and pastoral care. Religion influences the way the Sikhs should be cared for when they are ill and hospitalized. Christianity is the majority religion in the UK, with rich resources, and its terms are frequently used in chaplaincy. It is not always possible to translate those terms into the languages of the other faith communities. This led to finding the appropriate words and terms favoured in Sikh *dharam*. These words and terms often have a unique meaning and may be difficult to translate into English. The nearest English equivalents are given within brackets. If an English word or term is used, then the Panjabi word, in transcribed form, is given within brackets. It is not always possible to capture the full import (transfer) and every nuance (tone) of a statement or word when rendering it into another language, especially in languages between which a cultural and temporal chasm exists, as with Panjabi and English.

It is important to note that when the Sikh/Panjabi names are written in English, the reader may find different spellings of the same name, as writers often use transcription (representing phonemes) and not transliteration (accurately representing the graphemes) in normal writings. It has become a practice in the Western world to use 'Singh' and 'Kaur' as a surname; they are not a surname but a complementary element of the name. In this book, if authors have given their surname on the title page, then their surname is used for the purposes of references or bibliography. In case the author has given their forename and complementary name, then the prevalent practice of using 'Singh' or 'Kaur' as an entry point for references and bibliography is followed to avoid any confusion.

There is also the problem of variation of dates in Sikh history. Sikhs could not become a settled community; they have had to fight constantly for their survival and the maintenance of their identity since the inception of their religion (end of the 15th century) even until now. They suffered atrocities from their rulers and governments. They were displaced during the partition of India in 1947 and then in 1984 suffered genocide. During the process, Sikhs lost many of their original sources. Some Sikhs believe that constant efforts are being made to distort their history and religious literature in order to assimilate their religion into Hinduism. As Neuberger rightly states: 'There is great controversy amongst academic historians of religion who say that Sikhism is either an offshoot of Hinduism or that it is

Hinduism heavily influenced by Islam. In fact, neither is wholly true' (2004, p.53). Sikhs believe that their religion is distinct. It was founded amongst many other religions which undoubtedly have similarities with Sikhism, for example, monotheism is a commonly accepted belief among Christians, Muslims and Sikhs. The principle of 'Word' tends to have resemblances with Christianity. Love, compassion and helping others are common themes for almost all religions. It is a common practice among religions to refer to existing religions in order to clarify the logistics of its own values and traditions. Prime examples of this are the religions of the Abrahamic traditions.

Research Methods

The author has taken multiple approaches to collect the information relevant to the subject of the book. A literature search was conducted to find views of other academics on the subject, mainly those who have already written on Sikhism or caring for Sikh patients or who have the same or similar thoughts to that of the author. The hospital experiences of the patients, their concerns and demands that all reflected the needs of patients and their families, contributed to an audit of needs. Focus groups of Sikhs were organised to collect views on areas where they may not be familiar either with popular terms such as pastoral care or contested terms such as spiritual care. A quantitative approach (gathering numerical data) is taken to find the composition of patients, particularly with respect of age and gender, to find out their communication needs.

Structure of the book

There are ten main chapters of this book. The first three chapters give background knowledge to familiarise the readers with Sikhism and Sikhs. The next two chapters are on the background and historical perspectives to NHS chaplaincy in the UK, including multi-faith chaplaincy and the role and skills of healthcare chaplains. Chapters 6-9 focus on spiritual, pastoral, religious, end of life care and bereavement. Chapter 10 provides the book's conclusion.

Chapter 1 – Sikhism: the faith explored

The purpose of writing this chapter is to introduce Sikhism to non-Sikh readers in order to enable them to have a better understanding of the contents of this book. Chapter 1 covers Sikhism – the faith explored. It gives a background to Sikhism covering general and elementary information on Sikhism. It further explores the distinctiveness of this religion through its founder, Holy Scripture and place of worship. It demonstrates Sikh values, Sikh ethics and institutions, Sikh way of life, Sikh sects and denominations and Sikh migration. The contents are based on the Holy Scripture, where it is applicable, and Panjabi words are given in italics. It is useful to read this chapter to understand the Sikh words and concepts mentioned in the book more clearly.

Chapter 2 – Sikh ceremonies and festivals

This chapter covers life cycle rites and rituals for Sikhs: birth, initiation, naming, Sikh weddings, same sex marriages, and death. This also includes religious celebrations (*Guru's* anniversaries), Sikh symbols of identity, cultural festivals and the Sikh calendar to know the dates of their significant events.

Chapter 3 – Sikh psychology, philosophy and healing with faith

This chapter is on Sikh philosophy, psychology and healing with faith. It explores its metaphysics, cosmology, and ontology, covering the concept and nature of God, mapping out the spiritual path to achieve truthful living, and attaining liberation. It also explores the concept of grace, *hukam* (order), and *karma*. It touches upon the soul and Sikh belief after death. It covers the psychology of religion; religious behaviour such as prayers, recitation, invocation, supplication and *kirtan* (hymn singing); religious beliefs such as distinctiveness, togetherness, causes of pain and suffering, and their impact on health and healing.

Chapter 4 – Background to chaplaincy

There is a huge array of literature giving an insight into the development of Christian chaplaincy. This chapter focuses on the development of modern chaplaincy, as it exists in the National Health Service (NHS) since its foundation in 1948, including multi-faith chaplaincy. The National Chaplaincy Guidelines of 2003 and

2015 are evaluated as impacting on the development of Sikh chaplaincy. An Equality Analysis, review of the current guidelines, and the position and scope of Sikh chaplaincy in relation to chaplaincy provisions are further explored. The chapter also covers chaplaincy in Sikhism, health, and illness.

Chapter 5 – Role of a healthcare chaplain: skills and competencies

Chapter 5 outlines who a chaplain is, as well as the values, roles and responsibilities of a chaplain. It also draws attention to the knowledge, experience, skills and competencies that underpin the chaplain's role, drawing attention to what a Sikh chaplain or volunteer can contribute to chaplaincy services. Finally, it covers the shared skills and competencies needed to deliver religious, spiritual, and pastoral care. It also describes the chaplain's role as faith advisor for patients, hospital staff, and the NHS. It gives information on ward etiquettes and hospital management, information governance, culture, religious, spiritual, and cultural competencies and multi-disciplinary care.

Chapter 6 – Spiritual and pastoral care

This chapter combines spiritual and pastoral care due to their similarities and the shared skills and competencies that are necessary to deliver them. Spiritual care defines spirituality, its meaning, and importance. It explains the components of spirituality such as soul, spirit, and spiritual care for Sikh patients. It also precisely explains how spiritual needs are assessed, care plans are prepared, interventions are made, and their ultimate effects on patient experience. It explains pastoral care, its perception, provisions, and resources, explaining whose responsibility it is to deliver.

Chapter 7 – Religious care and rituals

This chapter covers religious care and rituals. It explains how to care for and treat the Sikh symbols of identity in healthcare. It discusses how Sikh religious rites and rituals such as birth, initiation, naming, marriage, and death are relevant to healthcare, particularly the end of life care, and how these can be conducted in healthcare settings to support patients and their families. It also describes religious care given to Sikhs through prayers, recorded music, and supplication, and the supportive effects. It further adds to the expectations from the chaplains as faith advisors. Chaplains play a crucial role as faith advisors to the NHS, healthcare professionals, patients, and their families on difficult matters arising from time to time, such as IVF, abortion, screening tests, and at present, the Covid-19/Coronavirus pandemic.

Chapter 8 – End of life care

This chapter explores end of life care, including death and dying, breaking life-changing news and its effect on the patient and family, and the stages in the process of dying and their application to Sikh patients. It explains further future planning for any seriously ill or dying patient, such as taking care of the legal aspects of finance and healthcare matters, the needs of the dying person, end of life experiences and physical signs of the dying person. It also covers how the dying patient and family are cared for in their final moments, and the role of hospices in this. Finally, it covers euthanasia and the Sikh view on euthanasia.

Chapter 9 – Bereavement

This chapter concentrates on bereavement, covering mourning and grief for adults, its effects and experiences, and coping mechanisms. Within the context of background information, the pattern, stages and theories of bereavement, Sikh customs and ritual of mourning and bereavement are explored in depth.

Chapters 8 and 9 are more relevant for hospices and care homes.

Chapter 10 – Conclusion

Overview

Finally, it is essential to give a complete but succinct overview of the book. It encourages readers to thoroughly read the introduction before reading any part of the book, as they will not be able to do it justice by reading chapters in isolation. The introduction has summed up the book and also the aims and purpose for writing it. It covers the target readership and scope of the guide. There are repetitions because of the nature of the book, especially keeping those readers in mind who may only need to read one of the chapters. In the concluding chapter, suggestions are made to make the service more accessible for Sikh patients. The references and bibliography cover the consulted books and material in producing this guide. The references quoted are from Western chaplaincy writers, where ideas are either similar or different. For Sikh explanations, the *Guru Granth Sahib* was used as the main resource. The views and the interpretations given regarding the Sikh faith are mine, which I have interpreted, and I take responsibility for them. Each individual will be different, and I recognise that for some in the Sikh community, there will be disagreements on practices. This is inevitable in any discussions on religion, but I hope that no comments or discussions cause any offence. The way the case studies are undertaken and recorded represent the views of the author and the author alone and should not be attributed to any other source. Minority faiths within the context of this book are those faiths that do not meet the standard criterion of thirty-five beds referred to in 2003 and 2015 chaplaincy guidelines.

References

Cobb, Mark (2005). *The Hospital Chaplain's Handbook: a guide for good practice*. Norwich: Canterbury Press.

Neuberger, Julia (2004). *Caring for dying people of different faiths*. 3rd edition. Abingdon: Radcliffe Medical Press.

Research Methods

Research Methodology

Qualitative and quantitative methods are used for research in this study in order to acquire the relevant information. A qualitative research methodology was adopted to conduct an in-depth study of spiritual care as practised in NHS hospitals and hospices. It was felt necessary to gain a deeper insight into the views of care receivers by using a methodology where participants could express themselves. Qualitative methods are also effective in identifying intangible factors, such as social norms, socio-economic status, gender roles, ethnicity, and religion. In this research it was mainly focused on extracting views on chaplaincy services. On occasions, quantitative methods are also used to find the composition of patients and also how many of them speak English. The findings are further supported through literature research.

There are three most common qualitative research methods: participant observation, in-depth interviews, and focus groups. Each method is particularly suited for obtaining a specific type of data:

- Participant observation is appropriate for collecting data on naturally occurring behaviours in their usual contexts.
- In-depth interviews are optimal for collecting data on individuals' personal histories, perspectives, and experiences, particularly when sensitive topics are being explored.

- Focus groups are effective in eliciting data on the cultural norms of a group and in generating broad overviews of issues of concern to the cultural groups or subgroups represented. (CCS)

Participant observation: This book is mainly based on the author's hands-on experience and patients' experience of stays in hospital and in other healthcare settings. It is mainly resourced through multiple approaches, such as by listening to patients' experiences, the questions asked by them, the stories related by them, their views on experiences and their feelings of hospital stay. The author's own experience of hospital and hospice services (as a service user when her husband was suffering from terminal cancer), and later working as a volunteer in hospital, hospice and Sir Robert Ogden Macmillan Centre are also relevant. It was easy for her to watch and observe them as she spoke their language and made sense of their body language and gestures. It was relatively easy for her to employ participant observation because of her language skills and intimate knowledge of the Sikh religious and cultural values and traditions. Her own standing in the community made through other writings was also helpful as *gurdwaras'* congregational members refer to her as neutral and trustworthy. Finally, the personal observations of the author of chaplaincy services in NHS hospitals, spiritual care in hospices, general discussions in chaplaincy meetings and management attitude provided food for thought.

Focus groups: A focus group is a group of individuals selected and assembled by a researcher to discuss and comment on, from personal experience, the topic that is the subject of the research (Powell and Single 1996). It is cost and time effective, providing an opportunity to interact directly with respondents, gaining data in their own words but allowing respondents to react and build on the responses of other group members in an open and flexible way (Stewart, Shamdasani and Rock 2007). The focus group on pastoral care of Sikhs was conducted as a part of the author's MA thesis which was published as a journal article. It was found in this group that participants did not know what exactly pastoral care is and what it concerns. It was also difficult for them to understand the word 'perception' and its application to pastoral care. The researcher had to explain to them in Panjabi, giving examples from Sikh religious and cultural traditions. Later, another focus group was organised on spiritual care. It is difficult for many Sikhs to understand the difference between religious and spiritual care. The educated Sikh patients equate spiritual care with non-religious care, part of Western thinking. The researcher asked them to define how they think of it as a Sikh. On the whole, it was found that most Sikhs were unaware of chaplaincy services and its coverage. The words used relating to chaplaincy services are derived from Christianity and this made Sikhs associate this service with Christian patients exclusively.

There are pros and cons of different research methods. The main difficulty faced by the researcher was that it was difficult to involve any professionals in these areas in focus groups. There were two volunteers who had little experience of chaplaincy work in the pastoral care focus group. As a result, the focus group was not as efficient in covering this subject in depth and struggled to have a critical and constructive discussion. They were struggling to grasp the meaning and perception of the term 'pastoral'. Along similar lines, members of the focus group on spiritual care were astonished why a researcher was asking certain questions. It was not making any sense to them, even after explaining the purpose of the research. The responses made by some participants matched with information given on the web. This led the researcher to have interviews with some members of the focus group and then further discussed topics with patients individually to secure meaningful information.

In-depth interviews: The interviews scheduled covered the areas of the focus group discussions. The interviews were conducted with those individuals who were anxious about participating in the focus group, or who had reservations about speaking openly due to the personal or sensitive nature of the information. This gave them an opportunity to relate their personal experiences in depth. This technique also proved helpful in collecting data on patients' experiences within healthcare settings in the sense of case studies. This needs time, empathy, active listening and making bonds with patients. It is a chaplain's skill to create a relaxed environment and warm vibrations to detect what a patient wants to tell; his/her body language, gesture, intonations and voice must support what the patient is relating. The author's personal circumstances enabled her to spend plenty of time with patients. In-depth interviews were also conducted with willing participants as a follow-up, to get a full grip of what they said, how they felt, and why.

It is hard for any volunteer to conduct an in-depth study, not only because of their status, but also because of the lack of professional support, basic published material and recognition of Sikhism in academic and healthcare settings along with the unfamiliarity of Sikh community about these services. It was also hard to find someone with whom to have a critical and constructive conversation, especially when professionals from other faiths are too busy with their own commitments to give time to volunteers from the minority faiths. Many of them may not have time and capacity to answer their queries.

Literature Research

Evidence comes from relevant literature and is augmented by personal experience. The initial search of literature found little focussed on religious and spiritual care of Sikh patients in depth. The literature search found chapters written on Sikhism and Sikh patients, guidance notes, and randomly basic information. The author tried to find what was already written on Sikhs applicable to healthcare chaplaincy services and divided her search into two categories:

1) General literature written on Sikhism in Britain

2) Specific pieces written by non-Sikh chaplains on chaplaincy services, keeping in view Sikh patients and Sikhism.

There are some written resources on Sikh chaplaincy and spiritual care as a distinct subject as found by the literature search. These are mainly written by non-Sikh chaplains interested in patient-centred care in their writings. References are found on Sikh patients and Sikhism as early as the 1980s, even well before the National Chaplaincy Guidelines of 2003, which triggered multi-faith chaplaincy and touched minority faiths for the first time on a strategic level, with political backing. Thereafter it became a trend to write whilst keeping in view the pluralistic nature of society. Every effort was made to refer to those resources where applicable in this book in order to acknowledge their valuable contributions based on their practical experience and acquired by talking to patients and their families. Since the majority of those writers are non-Sikhs, it is not easy for them to check the information against reliable sources. Their approach and contributions helped to introduce Sikhism in chaplaincy literature, a thoughtful advance. Although most of them did mention Sikhism, few manage to give an in-depth analysis.

It was thought necessary to mention the earlier works. Julia Neuberger wrote three books, one published as early as 1987 on *Caring for Dying People of Different Faiths*; secondly *Dying Well: A Guide to Enabling A Good Death,* published in 1999, and the third, *Caring for Dying People of Different Faiths,* in 2004 which was reprinted in 2005. She had practical experience of working in healthcare and her works have depth even in those earlier days, reflecting her understanding of caring for patients from diverse faiths and beliefs. She also covered humanism in the edition published in 2004. She has given a chapter on religious approaches to death with the perspectives of different religions and included Sikhism on pp. 42-45 in her 1999 edition. In her third edition, published in 2004, Sikhism was given on pages 53-61, covering their history and faith, the five 'k's, symbols of Sikh identity, Scripture, food restrictions, death and the afterlife and last offices. It is easy to read and its print is accessible for a wide range of audiences.

Culture, Religion and Patient Care in a Multi-Ethnic Society: a Handbook for Professionals, written by Alix Henley and Judith Schott, was published by Age Concern England in 1999. This book has a complete chapter on Sikhism on pages 571-584. It covers general information on Sikhism and gave a fair treatment to some areas useful for healthcare settings; for example: modesty, washing, cleanliness, visiting a Sikh home, and after death (touching the body, post-mortem, funeral and mourning). The rest of the book has good coverage on Islam, Judaism and Hinduism as compared to Sikhism. This is a useful book, easy to read, covering many aspects of minority faiths.

Death, Dying and Bereavement, edited by Donna Dickinson, Malcolm Johnson and Jeanne Samson Katz, was published in 2000. It has a chapter on 'Approaches to death in Hindu and Sikh communities in Britain' written by Shirley Firth in part 1 - Life and death (pp. 28-34). Firth gave basic knowledge of Sikh beliefs, covering the five symbols of Sikh identity. There was mention of caste, Holy Scripture, *gurdwaras* (Sikh place of worship), priesthood, *Karma* and reincarnation as given in religious theology. The information is based on the reliable source on Sikh religion written by Cole and Sambhi.

The rest of the chapter is not specific to Sikhs, but refers to Asians exploring talking about death, caring for the dying, the moment of death, ending or prolonging life, and after death. There is also a chapter by Shirley Firth: 'Cross-cultural perspectives on bereavement' in Part 4 – 'Bereavement, private grief and collective responsibility' (pp.338-346). This chapter not only concentrates on Sikhs but also covers other minority faiths, such as Buddhism, Hinduism and Islam. It covers preparing the body, funeral, mourning, finding meaning and problems of change. Shirley Firth also wrote on Sikhism, pp 161-163, in a chapter: 'Spirituality and Ageing in British Hindu, Sikhs and Muslims' in the book *Spirituality and Ageing*, edited by Albert Jewell in 1999. Gatrad et al produced an article entitled 'Sikh birth customs' in 2015. Carey and Davoren's article 'Inter-Faith Pastoral Care and the Role of the Healthcare Chaplain' have some implications on pastoral care for minority faiths.

Kalsi contributed on 'Change and Continuity in the Funeral Rituals of Sikhs in Great Britain' in *Contemporary Issues in the Sociology of Death, Dying and Disposal,* edited by Glennys Howarth and Peter Jumm in 1997 on pp. 30-43. Sheikh et al wrote an article on 'Diversity in Health and Social care' in 2004 presenting the findings of their national survey of hospital chaplaincy departments in England and Wales. Jhutti-Johal wrote an article on 'Understanding and Coping with Diversity in Healthcare' in 2013. Inderjit Singh (Lord) also wrote *Faith and Pastoral Care for Prisoners* for the Ministry of Justice, National Offender Management Service in 2013. The author wrote 'Pastoral Care for Sikhs' in *Abstracts of Sikh Studies* in 2017, pp. 22-37. These are the specific contributions found on Sikh chaplaincy and have been quoted and referred to in this book.

There are many NHS Trusts that have produced information on multi-faith chaplaincy which is also applicable to Sikh patients, for example, the South Devon Healthcare NHS Trust produced a guide on *Religious, Spiritual, Pastoral and Cultural Care* for the guidance of their staff. The Scottish Health Department (2002) and the UK Board of Healthcare Chaplaincy (2009) also produced information which is useful for multi-faith chaplaincy and is available online. The UK Sikh Chaplaincy Group produced a booklet titled 'Caring for a Sikh patient' (2010) including basic and limited information, more of a religious nature. Since then, some guidance notes have been produced by them, mainly on religious care.

This literature search tried to cover only published material that came to the author's knowledge during the process of her research. This is not a comprehensive list, there are other authors who may have touched this area. Her sincere apologies are given to those whose works have been missed.

There is hardly any in-depth single writing on Sikh chaplaincy giving comprehensive coverage. The author made a small attempt based on her practical experience when she had basic understanding of chaplaincy and its scope. Whatever she wrote was basic, elementary and based on patients' questions and their audit of needs. The book: *A Guide to Being a Sikh Chaplain*, published in 2013, was written with a purpose to encourage other Sikhs in the field to take it further and make contributions. This gave an opportunity to other authors and a base for researching on this subject in the hope of making some progress in resource building. During the period of her writing and afterwards, the Sikh Chaplaincy Group (based in London) became much more active in producing guidance notes on some areas of religious care, also adding the articles by other Sikhs and websites related to chaplaincy to their publication list.

An effort was also made to include Eastern and Western Sikh scholars on Sikhism in this book, where appropriate. Some writers are quoted in the book whose views seem relevant to the views expressed in this book. Along similar lines, many Western chaplaincy writers are referred to in the book, especially those who either supported or opposed the views expressed, in order to highlight the similarities and differences in the way spiritual care is provided to Sikhs in healthcare. Their details are not given here, though details of their work can be found in the references and bibliography.

There are rich resources on Sikhism produced in India. The author picked up Western writers whose works are particularly influential on this book. The writings of Cole and Sambhi on Sikhism are not only easy to read but also reflect the combined knowledge and skills of both authors. Sambhi contributed to the realistic and in-depth knowledge of Sikhism and Cole collated it in a scholarly way following the academic style of writing in English. Particular reference is made to *The Sikhs; their religious beliefs and practices* published in 1978 and another edition in 1985, and also to their unique work *A Popular Dictionary of Sikhism* published in 1990. All their publications are worth reading and can be used as reliable reference material. Their contributions are primarily on Sikh religion, traditions, and values in general, providing a firm base for background knowledge of Sikhism. This has rendered a good service to Sikhism in general, in the early days when multi-faith was not high on the agenda of British society. Though their contributions are not particularly aimed at chaplaincy and healthcare, they provide rich resources for in-depth knowledge on Sikhism. Much can be drawn from these resources and adapted to healthcare settings. A similar but complementary work was produced by the author in 2005: *Sikh Women in England: Their Religious and Cultural Beliefs and Social Practices*, based on women's experience and practice. Hollins' book *Religion, Culture and Healthcare* (2009) has references on Sikhism. Eleanor Nesbitt is another British writer who mainly writes on Sikh religion and her book on *Sikhism: A Very Short Introduction* became popular, published in 2005. She also contributed to Sikhism in *Ethical Issues in Six Religious Traditions*, edited by Morgan and Lawton in 2007, and in the *Oxford Textbook of Spirituality in Healthcare*, edited by Cobb, Puchalski and Rumbold in 2012. Mandair (2010) wrote *Sikhism* in *World Religions for Healthcare Professionals* edited by Sorajjakool, S., Carr, M.F., and Nam, J.J.

Nikky-Guninder Singh is of Sikh origin and an American writer, who wrote *Sikhism: An Introduction* in 2011. She has a deep understanding of Sikhism and possesses the ability to express her views in a scholarly and academic way. Her writings proved useful on spirituality for this book.

The sources quoted are referred to in this book along with other sources which have not been mentioned here, and the research is enriched by these sources. The upcoming book is a comprehensive and practical guide on religious and spiritual care for Sikh patients in NHS hospitals and hospices. It covers all the areas relevant to chaplaincy and has given the Sikh perspective in depth.

References

Powell, R.A., Single, H. M. (1996). Focus groups. *International Journal of Quality in Health Care* 8 (5) 1996.

Stewart, D. W., Shamdasani, P. N. and Rock, D. W. (2007). *Focus groups: Theory and practice*. 2nd ed. London: Sage Publications.

Websites

CCS (2020) Qualitative Research Methods [online] available at: www.ccs.neu.edu/course/is4800sp12/resources/qualmethods.pdf. [Accessed 19 April 2020].

Background chapters: Faith Explored, Sikh Ceremonies and Festivals, Sikh Philosophy: Health and Healing

Chapter 1

Sikhism – the faith explored

Introduction

The purpose of writing this chapter is to introduce Sikhism to non-Sikh readers in order to enable them to have a better understanding of the contents of this book and to grasp more clearly the Sikh words and key concepts mentioned. It gives the general background information on Sikhism and explores the distinctiveness of religion through its founder, Holy Scripture and place of worship. It demonstrates Sikh values, Sikh ethics and institutions, Sikh way of life, Sikh sects and denominations, and Sikh migration. The contents are mainly based on the Holy Scripture. Panjabi words are given in italics.

Background

The Sikh religion is considered to be the fifth largest world religion and fourth in terms of its adherents in the UK according to the last census (2011). The Sikh religion is the newest of the major world religions, being just over 500 years old and founded by *Guru* Nanak towards the end of the fifteenth century. He was born in 1469 in the village of Talwandi in north-west Punjab, now in Pakistan. *Guru* Nanak created a simple and practical religion and preached it in a language easily understood by ordinary people. His religious philosophy and expression are traditionally known as the *gurmat* (teachings of the *Guru*). Nine successor *gurus* developed and completed his mission. The *gurus* in Sikhism are the spiritual guides or teachers who enlighten, liberate and guide human beings on the path of truthful living and spiritual development leading towards salvation. The tenth *Guru* passed on *guruship* to the Holy Scripture, named the *Guru Granth Sahib*, thus ending the human lineage of *gurus* after his death. Since then, Sikhs accept their Holy Scripture as a living *Guru*.

Sikhs normally use the words '*Sikhī*', '*Gursikhī*', '*Gurmat*' and Sikh *Dharam* for Sikh religion. The word *dharam* has a broader scope than religion. There is no single word translation for *dharam/dharma* in the English language. According to Cole and Dusenbery (2014) the word *dharam* refers to one's duty in a general sense. Its broad definition suggests that it includes all that constitutes religion, moral duty and the way of life. *Dharam* also encompasses within its fold religion and spirituality. The religions founded on the Indian subcontinent integrate philosophy, spirituality and religion. It became common practice to use '-ism', an English and European suffix, in the names of most religions of the Indian subcontinent during the British rule in India. Sikhism is therefore a Western word which has become current and is readily used by Indian and Western Sikh authors and scholars (Nesbitt, 2005). In this study, the terms Sikh religion and Sikhism are used interchangeably for convenience and its popular use in the academic world.

3

Sikhism is a monotheistic religion. Sikhs believe in one and only one God and in the unity of God. It is an iconoclastic, socially motivated and pragmatic religion (Singh, 1985). It is against all kinds of oppression and exploitation (*GGS,* pp.140, 674). The Sikh religion respects other religions, believing in freedom of worship and against forcible conversion. It promotes simple living, harmony, human dignity, human rights, social justice, religious freedom, and religious tolerance. Its main areas of ethos are *naam japna* (remembering God and doing good deeds), *Kirt karna* (honest earning) and *wand chhakna* (sharing with the needy) (*GGS,* p. 1245). Its main beliefs are equality, *seva* (voluntary and selfless work) and donating to humanitarian causes. Sikhism emphasises devotion to God and submitting to God's Will (*hukam*-order). It is believed that everything happens under God's *hukam* (command) (*GGS,* p. 885). It recognises the basic needs of human life. In Sikhism, the world is real and meaningful. It believes in life after death, transmigration and *karma 'you get what you sow'* (*GGS,* p. 176). *Guru* Nanak's vision gave a new reality and made people challenge the existing meaningless rituals such as *shradhs,* feast for dead ancestors (*GGS,* p. 332), idolatry, renunciation (*GGS,* pp. 140, 684), making pilgrimages (*GGS,* p. 687), fasting (*GGS,* p. 873) and depending on horoscopes (*GGS,* p. 904). The GGS states that since the entire creation is a part of one being, all space and time are equally holy: only the faithless rely on dates and days (*GGS,* p. 843).

Sikhism stresses simple and truthful living (*GGS,* p. 62). Sikhism believes in the concept of *'karma',* literally meaning 'deeds' (Singh,

1971) and taking responsibility for one's own actions (*Bhai* Gurdas, *Var* 1, 8). Death is regarded as a gradual transition from the human state to another state, depending upon one's conduct (*karma*) in this world. Sikh belief in life after death is linked to the transmigration of souls. The soul is believed to be immortal although the human body is mortal and it has to end. There are 8.4 million *jonies* (forms of lives) and human life is the best of all forms as *Bhai* Gurdas has mentioned in his writing in *Var* 1 (Kaur, 2010, p. 21). The writings of *Bhai* Gurdas are known as '*Bhai Gurdas dian Varan.*'

Sikhism advocates full participation in life and establishes the primacy of family life (*GGS*, 587). It believes in fulfilling physiological and social needs. Religion should be practised by living in the world and coping with life's everyday problems and challenges. Family life (*GGS*, p. 522) is given preference over renunciation. The ethic of *kirt karna* (work ethos) provides Sikhs with financial security and safety, helping to enhance self-esteem. Sikhs can own property and acquire wealth only by honest means. For a Sikh, life is also to enjoy, eat, laugh, play and sing (*GGS*, p. 188). A constant reminder for a Sikh is to stay in tune with the Divine. The ultimate aim for any human being is to attain liberation and merge with the transcendent. The *GGS* has given different stages (*khands*) for developing a higher spiritual stage of life (*GGS*, pp. 7-8). Maslow (1943) proposed a similar pattern in his hierarchy of needs: physiological, safety, social belonging, esteem, self-actualization, and much later he explored a further dimension to reach the higher goal. The self only finds its actualization in giving itself to some higher goal outside oneself, in altruism and spirituality, which is essentially the desire to reach the infinite, highest level of human consciousness.

Distinct religion

Sikhs believe that their religion is distinct. The measures that apply to assess the distinctiveness of any religion are having its founder, holy book and place of worship. The Sikh religion clearly has all these markers as explained below:

Founder: Sikhism has its founder *Guru*, Nanak Dev (1469-1539). He gave a unique philosophy and way of living, place of worship and institutions that were developed and retained by the Sikh *gurus,* and to some extent, by Sikhs.

Sikh scripture: The Holy Scripture of Sikhs is known as *Guru Granth Sahib. Granth* means anthology. Its original form is referred to as *Adi Granth,* interpreted as the original or eternal scripture. 'The Adi Granth is a way of expressing the belief that Sikhism did not begin with the ministry of Guru Nanak but has its origin in eternity' (Cole and Sambhi, 1990, p. 32). They based this statement on the expressions in the *GGS* stating that the *bani* (hymns) came directly from God. It contains the compositions of six *gurus* written in their own lifetime, the writings of Hindu *bhagats* (pious men) and Muslims saints and *Sufis* (mystics) who echoed the same voice on matters such as the absurdity of religious rituals, the hatred of idolatry, and the caste system and gender inequality.

Bhai Gurdas, one of the devout early Sikhs, scribed this *Granth* under the supervision and guidance of the fifth *Guru* Arjun Dev and named it as *Adi Granth*. This *Granth* included the writings of the Hindu saints and Muslim mystics, who belonged to different castes (high and low) and came from different regions of India covering the period from the 12th to 17th century. The driving moral of *Guru* Arjun Dev was to affirm the fundamental unity of all religions, and the unitary character of all mystic experience. He also built a central place for the Sikhs called *Harmandar Sahib,* now popularly known as the Golden Temple, situated in Amritsar. According to the Sikh *Gurdwara Prabandhak* Committee (SGPC) records, the construction of *Harmandar Sahib* is from 1588-1601 and a famous Muslim *Sufi Mian* Mir laid the foundation stone in 1588. The *Adi Granth* was installed there in 1604 to give consistent guidance on the teachings of this religion. Later, the tenth *Guru* Gobind Singh dictated the second and the final version of this *Granth* to *Bhai* Mani Singh. He added the hymns of his father, *Guru* Tegh Bahadur (ninth *guru*), and possibly one couplet of his own, and finalised it in 1704. It is also known as *Damdami Bir* as it was written at *Damdama Sahib* in Punjab. He terminated the line of human *gurus* by bestowing *guruship* on the *Granth* and termed it as *Guru Granth Sahib* in 1708. 'After the tenth *Guru*, the human lineage of *Gurus* came to an end and the *GGS* was consecrated as the living '*Guru*' and became their continuing visible manifestation' (Singh, 1985, p. 32).

Guru Granth Sahib is not only the living *Guru* for the Sikhs, it also gives importance to *shabad* (word) and thus became the Sikh's eternal *Guru* (Banerjee 1983, MacLeod, 1997). It is a permanent, accurate and unalterable compendium of the spiritual teachings of Sikhism and Sikhs acknowledge it as the authorised version. *Guru Granth Sahib* is the only world scripture which was collected and put together during the lifetime of Sikh *Gurus.* The standard version has 1430 pages (*Angs*) and it became the focal point of every *gurdwara* and the basis for all Sikh ceremonies.

The *Granth* is written in a language spoken and understood by lay people. The *Gurus* believed that their aim and the use of language was to make religion accessible to the general masses in order for them to practice it with understanding. It is written in Panjabi, using the *Gurmukhi* script popularised by *Guru* Angad, the second *guru* of Sikhs, which could accommodate many languages and is far more accessible to the ordinary people. The language principally employed is the language of the saints (*sant bhasha*) generally known as *Hindvi*, a mixture of Western Hindi, Prakrit, Brij, and Panjabi that evolved during the medieval period. It also has expressions from the commonly used words of Sanskrit, Arabic and Persian. The hymns of regional saints added to the *Granth* allowed for variations and local dialects. Gopal Singh rightly remarked: 'Not only in subject-matter, or religious affiliations of its authors, but also in language, the *Granth* upholds the creed of synthesis as against exclusiveness of form, symbols and ideas' (1984, xix).

It is written in poetic form in *raags* following a definite metrical system. A *raag* in Indian classical music means a pattern of melodic notes, and there are 31 *raags* in the *GGS.* Music forms the basis of rhythms and classification of the hymns. The hymns are further classified according to the musical clef or key (*ghar*) in which each is to be sung. The *Granth* is arranged first according to the *raga*, secondly, according to the nature or metre of the hymn, thirdly authorship, and fourthly the key. The integral relationship between music and verse has been maintained throughout with scholarly rectitude and concern. Furthermore, a number (*mahalla*) which denotes the name of the composer *guru* from *Guru* Nanak onwards precedes each hymn. It extends from the first to the tenth *Guru*, referred to by their place in the order. What is more, each *guru* speaks in the name of the founder *guru* whose spirit permeates his successors. Nikky-Guninder Singh points out: '*Gurus* valued the aesthetic and epistemological power of Divine poetry: ambrosial word reveals the essence of existence; it comes with knowledge and contemplation' (2011, p. 24).

Other sources: The other main sources of the thoughts, beliefs and philosophy of Sikhism are the *Varan* of *Bhai* Gurdas (Singh, 1977), considered to be the key to *GGS*, the *Janamsakhi* narratives (stories related to the life of *Gurus*) and Sikh *Rehat Maryada* (Sikh Code of Conduct, 1950).

Sikh place of worship: The Sikh place of public worship is generally known as a *gurdwara*. It is made of two words *gur* (Divine) and *dwara*, a door/gateway or threshold to the *Guru*, originally termed as *dharamsal* (school of religious learning). *Guru* Nanak opened *dharamsals* to practice religion wherever he went (Singh, 1971). *Gurdwara* is central to the lives of Sikhs and plays a key role in their lives. They are bound to it both religiously and socially. It is open to the public seven days a week, from morning till evening, and can be visited by any person irrespective of religion, sex, race, caste, or colour, as long as they observe its protocol (Rait, 2010). The Sikh religion does not acknowledge priesthood, though for convenience, most *gurdwaras* do appoint *granthi* (priests), usually a male. A *granthi* or *bhai* acts as caretaker, and he is skilled in reciting *gurbani* and performing *kirtan* (hymn singing). *Kirtan* is the singing of devotional music generally accompanied by harmonium and *tabla* (a set of drums). *Gurdwaras* in England are found to be based on mainstream Sikhism, or caste, denomination and *sant* (saint) traditions. The Sikh *gurus* rejected caste. Sikhs have achieved equality in many areas of life. The main reason of creating caste based *gurdwaras* in the U.K. was to create a source of networking and forming close bonds to find suitable matches for their sons and daughters. Many Sikh families prefer to marry their sons and daughters within their own caste, thinking that it is easier for them to settle with those who know their own traditions. The new generations of Sikhs have begun to depart from this trend, giving preference to compatibility rather than caste.

Gurdwaras have now become more than a place of worship, as many *gurdwaras* provide accommodations for pilgrims or those visiting for other purposes. It is a place where all sorts of information is displayed for Sikhs. Many involved in service delivery use it as a pivotal point to make the community aware of their services in the UK, thus playing the role of a community hub. Sikhs also come to know the professional strength of their own community members and approach them for help when necessary. It also provides shelter in the case of disasters and calamities. Many *gurdwaras* provide facilities for drop-in centres, organised group meetings and nurseries. Most *gurdwaras* make arrangements for Panjabi language and religious teaching, including devotional music classes. Food is provided free of charge, known as *langar,* to anyone who visits the *gurdwara* as a part of the religious tradition. This has made *gurdwaras* a source of information, education, accommodation, food and fellowship.

Gurdwaras are easily visible from a distance because of the *Nishan Sahib* (Sikh flag) flown quite high outside all *gurdwaras*. It is the ensign of the *Khalsa Panth*, an expression of authority, and commands a high level of respect. It is made of cotton or silk cloth, saffron in colour and triangular in shape, with a tassel at its end. The flag is hoisted on a tall flagpole covered with fabric, and has the visible symbol of the *khanda,* which constitutes three symbols in one. This consists of a double-edged straight sword with concave edges placed in the middle of the symbol, representing the oneness of God and symbolising cutting evil both ways, surrounded by a circle with two curved swords. The two curved swords flanking the circle represent temporal (*miri*) and spiritual (*piri*) authority, introduced by the sixth *Guru* Hargobind after the inhumane tortures and persecution of *Guru* Arjun. The circle denotes no beginning and no end, signifying the continuation of life.

The essential characteristic of a *gurdwara* is that a copy of the *Guru Granth Sahib* is always kept in the main hall, which is opened, read and closed every day with great reverence. It is kept under a canopy and the *chauri* (which consists of a yak tail hair or artificial fibre set in a wooden or metal holder) is waved over the sacred book as a sign of authority. This is the highest spiritual authority for Sikhs. Sikhs are instructed to read, listen, understand and practice the teachings of the *GGS*.

Anyone entering a *gurdwara* needs to follow its protocol. Shoes must be removed and the head must be covered before entering the prayer hall as a mark of respect. It is important to wash hands after removing the shoes. On entering the hall, Sikh worshippers kneel, touching the floor with their foreheads before the *GGS*. Worshippers usually make a voluntary offering of money in front of the *GGS*. All people sit on the floor of the prayer hall. Women sit on one side and men on the other side; it is not a religious but a cultural dictate (Rait, 2010). Chairs are provided for those who find it hard to sit on the floor. Most *gurdwaras* follow a similar sequence. The *GGS* is opened daily at dawn, a practice called *prakash,* followed by obtaining the *vak* or *hukam* (refers to a hymn randomly selected from the *GGS* on daily basis) understood by devotees as the guiding message for the day. In the evening, the *GGS* is ceremoniously closed and this ritual is known as *sukhasan,* (position of rest for the night). There are other acts of worship carried out on a daily basis, such as *path* (recitation of hymns), *kirtan* (singing devotional hymns with musical instruments), *katha* (parables), *ardas* (supplication), and *bhog* (concluding ritual). Finally, it is culminated in the distribution of *karah prasad,* a mixture of flour, sugar and butter in equal quantity. It is a sacramental offering and is given to all devotees and visitors. The *karah prasad* should be accepted sitting down, with cupped hands raised high to make it easy for those who are serving it. It is then transferred to the palm of one hand and eaten with the other hand. It is normal to absorb the grease by rubbing the hands or taking a napkin to wipe away any grease from the hands.

There is a separate *langar* hall where food is cooked in the communal kitchen and served. It is free food for all those attending the *gurdwara.* It is served in all *gurdwaras,* being an essential part of the Sikh religious tradition. It is not only courteous but also binding to eat sitting in *pangat* (rows), which is a symbol of equality and fulfils a human need. The food served is lacto-vegetarian (including milk and milk products), and is cooked with love and care, following strict hygienic procedures. The main source of income for a *gurdwara* is donations from the *sangat* (congregation). Sikh volunteers (*sevadars*) run and manage the *gurdwara* who offer their services free of charge, with love and dedication.

It is an essential institution for Sikhs because of the congregational nature of the religion and the importance given to *sangat* (congregation) by the Sikh *gurus.* The *gurus* made it clear that attendance at communal worship is a necessary part of the spiritual life of a Sikh. It is also integral to the lives of Sikhs as all the life cycle rites such as birth, initiation, naming and wedding ceremonies take place in the *gurdwara*. In the UK, it became a tradition that the last journey of death also departs finally from a *gurdwara*. There are a number of other functions and religious festivals taking place all around the year, such as *gurpurabs* (anniversaries and special events in the lives of the *gurus*) and Sikh patriots, *sangrand* (the first day of the lunar month) and festivals such as *Vaisakhi, Diwali, Hola Mahalla* and *Maghi*.

The *gurdwara* promotes the Sikh religion, its values and traditions. It serves as a pivotal point for the local community. It is a source of information, education, support, refuse, food and a social network. Sikh elders, singles and the infirm are increasingly using *gurdwaras* during the week, as they feel lonely and isolated in the UK. One can argue that the usage of the *gurdwaras* saves a lot of government funding spent on community provisions such as drop-in centres and lunching facilities. The Sikh community creates and maintains its social, cultural, intellectual and political links through the *gurdwaras*. In the UK, it is usual to have a larger congregation on Sundays as it is a weekly holiday, though it is not a fixed day of worship. In India, Sikhs often go every day to the *gurdwaras* before going to work or starting their daily routine.

Sikhism is a distinct religion, having some unique traditions and rituals from other religions. *Gurdwaras* should remain open for the *sangat* every day of the week, an essential feature of the Sikh traditions, the *GGS* is revered by the Sikhs and they treat it as a living *guru,* having two ceremonies *parkash* (opening) and *sukhasan* (position of rest for the night) every day in the morning and evening. Many Sikhs like to visit the *gurdwara* before they start their day. It is also a community hub mainly used during weekdays by elderly, single Sikhs and those feeling low, being isolated and lonely. There are some rituals pertinent and distinctive that take place in *gurdwaras*, for example, bowing in front of the *GGS*, touching the pages of the *GGS* while reading, waving *chaur sahib* over the *GGS*, touching musical instruments to perform *kirtan*, serving *karah Prasad* and preparing and serving *langar*. Coronavirus had a huge impact on the gurdwaras and these rituals. The UK government invited faith leaders to discuss the implications of this virus and prepared the guidelines, which Sikhs rigidly followed.

Sikh Values

Equality: Equality is of paramount importance in Sikhism. Gender equality in particular was close to the hearts of the *gurus* due to the social inequalities of their periods. The structure of Indian society was patriarchal and male supremacy was reinforced and perpetuated in the name of religion. It was further justified by the Laws of Manu, the most authoritative and the best-known legal text of ancient India (Buhler, 2009). Child marriage and female infanticide were practised. *Gurus* disagreed with the views of Manu on the status of women and clearly stated the position of women suggesting that men and women were equals in this new community (*GGS*, p. 605). *Gurus* assigned to women a superior place as they give birth to kings and emperors (*GGS*, p. 473). The

Sikh *Gurus* encouraged women to participate in religious and public life. The third *guru* Amar Das divided his spiritual domain into 22 provinces called *manjis,* each managed by a devoted Sikh. He also established local organisations to spread the *guru's* message (Singh and Singh, 1989). Women played an active part at a local level. This gave them opportunities to gain confidence. Nikky-Guninder Singh (2011) argues that equality is accorded to women because the *GGS* contains feminine symbolism and gives women a permanent role in both the sacred and secular realms.

The *Gurus* took a firm stand against these derogatory practices that undermined women at that time, such as the *purdah*, veil (*GGS*, p. 484) and *sati* (*GGS*, p. 787). *Gurus* discarded the necessity of giving dowry (*GGS*, 79) and denounced female infanticide (Sikh *Rehat Maryada,* 1950). *Gurus* condemned taboos against female pollution, menstruation and sexuality (*GGS*, pp. 140, 472). *Gurus* also condemned the practice of *sutak (*keeping a woman aloof after childbirth roughly for a period of 40 days for the reason of pollution) and a need for ritual purity (*GGS*, p. 472). *Gurus* disapproved of polygamy and favoured monogamous marriage. Widows were allowed to remarry.

Complete equality among all is declared as the fundamental principle by the Sikh *gurus*. They rejected the caste system and its rigid hierarchical codes. The validity of caste inequality is denied, as there is no fundamental difference among people in terms of physical constitution and the laws of nature (*GGS*, pp. 349, 1128). Sikhism gives importance to the good deeds of a person rather than his/her social status (*GGS*, pp. 272, 931). All human beings, regardless of gender, caste, race, status or birth are judged only by their deeds. Equality became the very basis of Sikhism, though Sikhs need to make concerted efforts to achieve it. The *gurus* gave them a framework, putting an onus on the Sikh community to develop and act upon them candidly.

Sikh ethics: There are three ethical principles of Sikhs. *Kirt Karna* (earning a living by honest and approved means) puts an onus on having a strong work ethic (*GGS*, pp. 1245-6) and honest earning. The Sikh *gurus* disapproved of money earned by deception, begging and unfair means. *Naam japna* (remembering the Divine) means doing good deeds and leading a truthful life (*GGS*, pp. 266, 1376). This also includes *naam simran* (reciting the *naam*) which enhances concentration and also reminds Sikhs to practice the *gurus'* teachings. According to Cole and Sambhi (1985), it is the transforming of personality through practice. *Wand chhakna* means to share with the needy and less fortunate (*GGS*, p. 1245). 'A Sikh is meant to give tithe (*daswandh*), one-tenth of his/her income to the service of the *panth*' (Cole and Sambhi, 1990, p. 60) but also for humanitarian causes (Rait, 2010).

Sikh institutions: Sikhism has evolved three important institutions i.e. *seva*, *langar* and *sangat*. *Seva*, voluntary service (*GGS*, p. 25) is an essential part of Sikh life. It is a deed of love and selfless service for fellow human beings. It is considered the highest ideal in Sikh ethics. It is the duty of every Sikh to do *seva* for humanitarian causes. It helps in cultivating humility, overcoming the obsession with the egoistic self, extends beyond self-centredness and is rewarding (*GGS*, p. 26). *Langar* (*GGS*, p. 967) is an integral part of the Sikh religion introduced by the founder *Guru*. The second *guru* Angad Dev maintained the practice of the communal kitchen managed by his wife, *Mata* Khivi, well known for serving delicious dishes to the congregation (Singh and Singh, 1989). The third *guru* Amar Das developed it further and institutionalised the practice for bonding the community together. It asserts the principles of social equality and the importance of human needs. *Sangat* (*GGS*, pp. 835, 1244-45) is an essential institution for Sikhs because of the congregational nature of the Sikh religion and the importance given to *sangat* (congregation) by the Sikh *Gurus*. They gave the *sangat* a status higher than that of a *guru*. A Sikh should keep the company of *sadh sangat* (good people) and pray in the *sangat*. It helps to not only overcome social, religious and gender barriers but also in forming spiritual and social bonds. Participation with like-minded people is a catalyst for moral and spiritual development. The Sikh *gurus* put all these ideas into practice in order to achieve their vision.

Sikh way of life: Sikhism is also a way of life. Sikhs are expected to develop and practice the five virtues considered essential to become a true Sikh. These are compassion (*daya*), humility (*nimrata*), love (*pyar*), contentment (*santokh*) and being truthful (*sat*). They must resist the five vices or evils, lust (*kam*), anger (*krodh*), greed (*lobh*), attachment (*moh*) and ego (*hanker*). A Sikh should stay away from backbiting (*GGS,* p. 674). Truth is the highest of all virtues, but higher still is truthful living (*GGS*, p. 62) strongly advocated for leading a Sikh way of life. Sikhs recite and meditate on *gurbani* as a constant reminder of truthful living. *Seva* (voluntary service) is a prerequisite to develop humility and to get rid of ego. Self-centredness (*manmukh*) combined with ego makes a person selfish and materialistic. Developing virtues can help to become a '*gurmukh*', one who is God-orientated and spiritually aware. Keeping the Divine in mind does not advocate withdrawal from daily life or renouncing the world. A Sikh should value the importance of family living and the role of family to pursue a spiritual life in order to attain liberation. The Sikh code of conduct specifically prohibits the following four acts called *kurahits* (bad acts):

- Cutting, shaving and trimming hair for both men and women.

- Eating *halal* meat (ritualistic slaughter by slow bleed) is strictly prohibited. Sikhs may eat meat but only that from an animal slaughtered in one stroke (*Jhatka*).

- Adultery

- Use of intoxicants and narcotics (Sikhs should not consume spirits, tobacco, hemp, opium) as they are harmful for the body and mind and affect relationships (Takhar, 2005).

Covid-19 Coronavirus pandemic

Education: Educating congregation members is an added advantage particularly during any national or local health scares or pandemics such as Covid-19. It is a good idea to display posters of safety measures in English and Panjabi in the *gurdwara's* entrance hall, *langar* hall, and stairs, easily visible and in readable fonts. It will also be beneficial if the *gurdwara's* video in the *langar* hall can demonstrate hand-washing techniques and explain the safety measures in Panjabi for those who are not able to read or understand some technical words. The Sikh community is obliged to do *seva,* (voluntary work). A committee of volunteers who are knowledgeable of healthcare should be assembled to advise and answer any questions from members of the congregation and should be present in the *gurdwara's* entrance and around the halls.

Worshippers: Those visiting *gurdwaras* should greet each other without contact, saying '*Gur Fateh*' or '*Sat Sri Akaal*' (Sikh greetings) with folded hands. It is important to stick to safety measures such as washing hands, keeping a safe distance of two metres, sneezing and coughing by covering the mouth with tissues, and disposing of them immediately after use. It is to the advantage of everyone to wear face masks as a preventative measure. If anyone thinks they have any symptoms of this virus, such as fever, cough, shortness of breath and tiredness, self-isolation is absolutely necessary, avoiding contact even with family members and definitely avoiding attending the *gurdwara.*

Cleanliness: This is of the utmost importance and everyone needs to be extra vigilant and careful to observe it. All surfaces should be disinfected, including the *diwan* hall, kitchen, and *langar* hall, before and after every *diwan.* This also includes tables, doorknobs, light switches, counter-tops and phones. Good practice is to keep bathroom, sinks and toilets very clean, and keep sanitisers close by to clean after every use. The visitors should be advised to bring their own head coverings to be on the safe side. If gurdwaras are providing head coverings, these should be kept in a clean container, and used head coverings should be left in another container labelled 'used'. These should be washed and disinfected thoroughly before using again. Hand sanitiser and soap should be kept on each sink.

Rituals: When Sikhs bow in front of the *GGS* they touch their forehead in front of it, and place both hands on the rug to maintain balance. There is every possibility that other visitors performing the same ritual may have already touched the area. In order to resolve this, Gulshan, a prominent religious preacher suggested on the Akaal Channel on 21st May 2020 to stand in front of the *GGS*, put your hands to your sides and politely bow your head. The other alternative is to sit on your knees and bow towards the *GGS* without hand touching. The next compulsory ritual is to serve and receive '*karah prasad*' which is a must for every Sikh, as it is considered to be a sacred food. There was a suggestion that *karah prasad* should be put in plastic bags and left near the *langar* hall entrance to pick. This was disputed by some religious Sikhs on the basis that there is a special way of distributing and receiving of it as mentioned earlier in the chapter. They suggest that the distributor should wash their hands thoroughly and distribute in the Sikh way. The distributors do not touch the hands of the receiver and suggest that it is a safe measure. There is another suggestion by the American Sikh Coalition to use a scoop or spoon. Sikhs also have to be careful as how to touch *chaur* *sahib*, pages of GGS, instruments used for performing *kirtan* and performing *prakash* and *sukhasan* ceremonies. They can resolve this either by sanitizing hands or by the use of gloves.

Langar is an essential part of Sikh prayers, and everyone who attends the *gurdwara* is obliged to sit in the *pangat* to consume the food. In the preparation of *langar,* all the safety measures should be observed, and washing and sanitizing hands are absolutely necessary. Distribution of food is generally done by big spoons (*karchhis*) and chapatis can be served by tongs. It will be safer if volunteers preparing *langar* can use food-grade gloves. It is safer if all volunteers can wear face masks and make sure that they do not have any symptoms of Covid-19. Washing and sanitizing hands after every move is absolutely necessary. Tissues and trash bins should be easily accessible and visible.

Sikhism has not yet been assimilated in many service provisions and delivery and policy makers may not be fully aware of the importance of some Sikh traditions and rituals and Sikh politics. Some suggestion are made above and there is a scope for further expansion for those involved with *gurdwaras* through the council of *gurdwaras* management committees and other prominent organisations. Sikhs should be mindful that the measures are not to distort their religion, but to adapt to a lifestyle in a most difficult period, which is not only affecting one religion or one country. It is a worldwide phenomenon and flexibility as well as understanding is needed under the circumstances. At the same times, it is necessary to preserve the pertinent rituals without compromising but within a reasonable adjustment.

Sikh sects and saint preachers

The Sikhs are a numerically small community and it has further shrunk with internal divisions. There are some sects developed originally from the reform movements which gave importance to the living *guru* departing from the mainstream Sikhism and have developed other traditions contrary to Sikhism over the years. The most important are *Namdharis, Narankaris,* and *Radhasoamis. Namdhari* was a Sikh reform movement began by *Baba Balak Singh* (1785-1862) that originated in the nineteenth century. It contributed enormously to the revival of Sikhism. *Namdharis* are initiated Sikhs, strictly vegetarians and believe in the living *guru. Narankari* literally means one who believes in the formless God. It was a spiritual regeneration movement founded by *Baba Dyal Singh* (1783-1855). They sing *shabads* (devotional songs) from the *GGS* and do not perform *Ardas* or distribute *karah prasad.* They serve food to the congregation at the end of their *diwan* (congregation gathering). *Radhasoami* literally means union of the soul with God. Their main emphasis is on the attainment of spiritual unity with God through 'naam simran' and they give importance to *satsang* (congregation of faithful people). They do not believe in any religious rituals. Shiv Dyal Singh started the movement in 1861. According to their beliefs, the *satguru* (true teacher) is the light-giver. They believe in the living *guru* who will teach the meaning of *naam* (God's word) in order to attain spiritual unity with God. They are vegetarians, practice *shabad* yoga meditation, and abstain from alcohol and drugs.

There are many saint preachers and organisations that tried to spread the message of the Sikh *gurus* and brought many followers within the Sikh fold. It is not possible to mention them all. As an example, three are mentioned here due to their popularity in the West. The 3H organisation stands for healthy, happy and holy founded by Harbhajan Singh Puri, popularly known as Bhajan *Yogi* in 1971. It had its origin in North America attracting a number of white Americans who became initiated Sikhs and follow the Sikh code of conduct strictly. Both men and women wear turbans, usually white. They are strictly vegetarians and place considerable emphasis on meditation, what they call kundalini Yoga. This is also becoming influential on the UK Sikhs. *Guru* Nanak *Nishkam Sevak Jatha* is a popular organisation founded by *Baba* Puran Singh *Kerichowala.* He migrated to East Africa from India in the 1930s and settled in an East African town called Kericho. He revived Sikhism there and preached the message of the Sikh *gurus.* Many East African Sikhs became his followers. He later came to Britain in the early 1970s and attracted a large number of followers in the Midlands and eventually spread in other cities of Britain. These Sikhs are initiated, lacto-vegetarian and abstain from alcohol and any other intoxicants. They meditate on '*naam simran'.* They do not allow women to participate in the continuous reading of the *GGS. Akhand Kirtani Jatha* is another organisation that emerged during the early 20th century. They believe in wearing the *keski* (small turban) under the turban. This group is strict in its beliefs and attaches great importance to *kirtan.*

These reform movements and sects saved the Sikh religion from decline and made timely contributions. The principle of a continuous succession and a presence of supreme spiritual authority forever in the living *guru* mainly distinguished them from mainstream Sikhism. Many of these sects digressed from their original aims and deviated from mainstream Sikhism, which has divided the Sikh community, creating many factions.

Sikh migration

Sikh migration to the UK started in 1854 with the arrival of Prince Duleep Singh. Since then, artists and students came for studying, and rich Sikh tourists came for travelling and shopping. The first *gurdwara* was opened in 1911 in Putney, London with the donations of *Maharajah* Patiala. The Sikh regiments came frequently to parade during gala State occasions. A contingent of wounded Sikh soldiers was brought to London during the First World War for treatment, rest and rehabilitation. Many Sikh soldiers discharged after the First World War chose to stay in Britain. *Bhatra* Sikhs were the earliest Sikh presence in Britain. The British Nationality Act of 1948, passed in response to India's independence, gave the citizens of the Commonwealth their right to settle and work in Britain. The main migration started in the 1950s, caused by not only a shortage of industrial and agricultural employees in Britain, but also the chaotic aftermath of the 1947 partition of India. East African Sikhs started migrating to the UK in the 1960s because of Africanisation and the policies of Idi Amin. Sikhs frequently assisted their relatives and friends in making their way to Britain to find jobs in factories and foundries. With the post-war boom and the liberalisation of immigration policies, Britain became the host for the largest Sikh diasporic community.

Sikhs in the UK can be grouped as direct migrants from India, twice migrants (migrated from India to another country and then the UK) from East Africa, Malaysia, or Singapore, asylum seekers from Afghanistan, and British-born Sikhs. This creates a mixture of cultures within Sikhism. The values, behaviour and attitudes of UK-born Sikhs have changed considerably due to indigenous influences of media, education, culture and societal expectations. This indicates that Sikhs are not a homogenous community. There are different cultures, traditions and behaviour patterns within the Sikh community depending on their cultural heritage (Bhachu, 1985) and degree of religious adherence. There are also variations of practices in the religious groups, mainly led and influenced by historic saints and religious leaders who claim to be associated with the Sikh faith. In spite of this, Sikhs maintain and sustain their cultural and religious values. Their global presence makes them known as a diasporic community. Diaspora, the Greek-derived word used to denote the Jewish dispersal, is now widely used for the faith communities' residence in countries other than their own historical homeland, whether or not their emigration and settlement resulted from traumatic events.

Conclusion

In conclusion, it can be said that Sikhism has developed into a cohesive and powerful religion, retaining and responding to the diversity within it, in spite of its struggle and sacrifices for survival. Sikh history is full of persecutions and atrocities tolerated by devoted Sikhs. New generations growing up in the Western world are keenly studying and trying to understand the depth and reality of their religion. Western Sikh scholars are trying to grasp an in-depth understanding of the real message of the *Guru Granth Sahib* in order to present it through their writings to those interested in Sikhism in a language they understand. This effort is much needed, as many Sikhs do not grasp and practice the *Gurus'* teachings in its entirety. The Panjabi culture is deeply ingrained in the older generation and they failed to explain their religion and culture to their children growing up in Western countries. They have done well in upholding certain values, such as building and developing Sikh *gurdwaras*, sharing with the needy, voluntary service (*seva*), maintaining a strong work ethic, and investing in their children's education. They have to be careful with others, particularly when helping to grasp and understand the Sikh teachings and adoption of the Sikh culture. Sikhs are failing due to a lack of real understanding of Sikh culture and religious values. The Sikh *gurus* gave them framework and the onus is on Sikhs to further develop and promote their teachings. Sikhs themselves can avoid many malpractices if they embrace their real values and practice them. Some examples include gender equality (regarding the practice of female foetus aborting) though Sikhs have taken steps to stop it, also the caste system is still ingrained in Sikhs (*gurdwaras* based on caste). Many Sikhs use alcoholic drinks, as reflected by a Sikh survey conducted by SikhNet, which is totally against Sikhism. *Gurus* discarded the dowry system, yet Sikhs are still giving their daughters dowry beyond their means. As a Sikh, it is important to introspect. It is also encouraging to see that many Sikhs growing up in Western countries have become keen to keep their identity, where some may be not so keen to keep their external identity (explained in chapter 2).

References

Banerjee, A. C. (1983*). The Sikh Gurus and the Sikh religion*. Delhi: Munshiram Manoharlal.

Bhachu, P. (1985). *Twice migrants: East African Sikh settlers in Britain*. London: Tavistock.

Buhler, G. (2009). *The laws of Manu*. Carolina: Biblio Bazaar.

Cole, W. O. (1985). *The Sikhs: Their religious beliefs and practices*. London: Routledge and Kegan Paul.

Cole, W.O. (2014) In: Singh, P., Louis E. F. (eds) *The Oxford handbook of Sikh studies*. Oxford: Oxford University Press. pp. 250-261.

Cole, W. O. and Sambhi, P.S. (1990). 'Sikh interactions with other religions.' In: *A popular dictionary of Sikhism.* London: Curzon Press.

Dusenberry, V. (2014). 'Punjabi Sikhs and gora Sikhs.' In: Singh, P. Louis E. F. (eds) *The Oxford handbook of Sikh studies. Oxford*: Oxford University Press. pp. 560-560.

Guru Granth Sahib. (n.d.). Amritsar: *Shiromani Gurdwara Prabandhak* Committee (Standard version of 1430 pages in Panjabi).

Kaur, G. (2010). *Gurbani di kunji varan Bhai Gurdas steek, Var* 1. Delhi: Arsee.

McLeod, W.H. (1997). *Sikhism.* London: Penguin.

Maslow, A. H. (1943). A theory of human motivation. *Psychological Review,* 50, 4, pp. 370-96.

Nesbitt, E. (2005). *Sikhism: A very short introduction.* Oxford: Oxford University Press.

Puratan Janamsakhi (1885). Amritsar: Wazir-i-Hind Press.

Rait, S. K. with Bhogal, I. S. (2010). *Understanding Sikhism.* Ripon: Plug and Tap.

Sikh *Rehat Maryada* (1950). Amritsar: *Shiromani Gurdwara Prabandhak* Committee.

Singh, G. (1984). *Sri Guru Granth Sahib*: *translated and annotated*. New Delhi: World Sikh Centre Inc.

Singh, G. (1971). *The religions of the Sikhs*. New Delhi: Allied Publishers.

Singh, H. (1985). *The heritage of Sikhs*. Delhi: Manohar Publishers.

Singh, M. (*Bhai*) (1635*). Puratan Janamsakhi Guru Nanak Dev ji*. Amritsar: Chattar Singh and Jiwan Singh.

Singh, N. G. (2011). *Sikhism: an introduction*. London: I.B. Tauris.

Singh, T. (1964). *Sikhism: Its ideals and institutions*. Calcutta: Orient Longmans.

Singh, T. and Singh, G. (1989). *A short history of the Sikhs*, 1 (1469-1765). Patiala: Punjabi University.

Singh, V. (*Bhai*) (ed) *Varan Bhai Gurdas* (1977). Amritsar: *Khalsa Samachar*, 1977.

Takhar, U. K. (2005). *Sikh identity: An exploration of groups among Sikhs*. London: Ashgate.

Further references

Most books written on Sikhism cover the following topic. It was difficult to mention them all in the main text. The books which were consulted to write this chapter are listed here:

Place of worship

Cole, W.O. and Sambhi, P. S. (1978). 'Protocol.' In: Cole, W.O.and Sambhi, P. S. (1978) *The Sikhs: Their religious beliefs and practices*. London: Routledge & Kegan Paul.

Rait, S. K. (2010). 'Sikh place of worship – *gurdwara*.' In: Rait, S. K. with Bhogal, I. S. (2010) *Understanding Sikhism*. Ripon: Plug and Tap. pp. 7-9.

Rait, S. K. (2010). 'Sikh scripture.' In: Rait, S. K. with Bhogal, I. S. (2010) *Understanding Sikhism*. Ripon: Plug and Tap. pp. 15-20.

Singh, N. G. (2011). 'Worship and gurdwaras.' In: Singh, N.G. (2011). *Sikhism: An Introduction*. London: I.B. Tauris. pp: 79-85.

Websites

Office for National Statistics (2011). *2011 census,* [online]. Available at: https://www.ons.gov.uk/census/2011census [accessed 18 Oct. 2019].

Oxford Sikhs (2019). *Sikh population around the world,* [online]. Available at: http://www.oxfordsikhs.com/SikhAwareness/Sikh-Population-Around-The-World_159.aspx [Accessed 13 Oct, 2019].

SikhNet. (2020) *The unspoken alcohol problem among UK Punjabis*. Available at: www.sikhnet.com › news › unspoken-alcohol-problem-... [Accessed 22 June 2020].

SriGranth.org (2006) *Siri Guru Granth Sahib Ji* [online]. Available at: http://www.srigurugranth.org/index.html. [Accessed 18 Oct. 2019].

Chapter 2

Sikh ceremonies and festivals

Introduction

Every religion has its own rites and rituals, ceremonies and festivals, along with prescribed rules to perform them. Sikhism is no exception to this. This chapter covers the rites and rituals of Sikhs which are tied to their life cycle rites, such as naming, initiation, marriage, and death, and how these are conducted in the Sikh way of life. Information is also given on controversial topics such as same-sex marriages, and what direction is taken by Sikhs. The main source and focus of all Sikh rites and ceremonies is the *GGS* and these are generally conducted in *gurdwaras* in the presence of the congregation. This chapter also includes the importance of religious celebrations (*Gurus'* anniversaries), Sikh symbols of identity, and religious and cultural festivals and how they are celebrated. The Sikh calendar is explained to make it easy for Sikhs to remember the dates of their festivals. How this information can be used in healthcare by chaplains and Sikh volunteers is given in the chapter on religious care.

Life cycle rites and rituals for Sikhs

The main aim of Sikhism is to give guidance on how to lead a noble and virtuous life. Family and the institution of marriage is important for Sikhs. The third *Guru* Amar Das made some reforms in the matters of marriage and death ceremonies (Banerjee, 1936). *Guru* Ramdas, the fourth Sikh *guru,* instituted simple ceremonies and rites for birth, marriage, and death.

Naming ceremony: The naming ceremony takes place in the *gurdwara* a few weeks after the birth of a child. The family visits the *gurdwara* when the mother is well enough to go out. This is the first visit to the *gurdwara* at which the child and the family receive religious blessings as part of the congregation. The name of the child is taken from the first letter of the *vak* (first word of the edict of the *GGS* read after its random opening) from the left-hand page and read to the parents. They will then decide upon a name beginning with the first letter and the *granthi* (Sikh priest) will announce it publicly, adding the suffix of *Kaur* (lioness/princess) for a girl and *Singh* (lion) for a boy. Every child receives a name made up of two elements: the first element of the name is the given name determined by the process in which the *granthi* opens the *GGS,* and the second element is the suffix, which signifies affiliation to the Sikh religion and is indicative of gender. It is to be noted that *Singh* and *Kaur* are complementary elements and not a surname (Rait, 1984) as considered and used in this country. Adding a surname is against the principles of Sikhism as it specifies caste or position in society. It is also against the principles of equality, though Sikhs living in the UK tend to add their surname to obey the tradition and legal obligations of the country they live in. Practically all children receive their name in this traditional manner with one exception. If the family is unable to attend a *gurdwara*, a close friend or relative may go to the *gurdwara* on behalf of the family and get the first letter of the name using the same procedure.

Initiation: Some initiated families believe in initiating the child and ask for it soon after the birth. This rite is generally performed in a *gurdwara* as this requires the presence of five initiated Sikhs to prepare the *amrit* (holy water) in the presence of the *GGS* and put a few drops in the mouth of the child and a few drops are sprinkled over the eyes and on the hair. It is a normal practice that a Sikh who has reached the age of accountability ought to be initiated (baptised). The *amrit* is given to the person who wishes to undertake this ceremony. At the ceremony, hymns are recited from the Sikh scripture, prayers are said, and the principles of Sikhism are affirmed.

Marriage Ceremony: The Sikh marriage ceremony is known as *Anand Karaj* (*Anand* means bliss and *Karaj* means ceremony) which achieved legal recognition in 1909 when the *Anand* Marriage Act was passed. In Sikhism, marriage is not a civil contract; it is a sacrament and has spiritual meaning.

> *Marriage is thus both literal and metaphorical. On the literal level, it is a union of two people; and on the metaphorical level, it is a union of the microcosm with the macrocosm. Fully in tune with the Divine, husband and wife begin to live sensuously in this world.* (Singh, 2011, p. 26)

Anand Karaj is performed according to *guru-maryada* (compulsory rituals in the presence of the *GGS*) thus establishing a permanent relationship between the two persons. It should take place in the *gurdwara* before midday. Any *granthi* or *amritdhari* Sikh man or woman who has undergone traditional initiation ceremony and practices the prescribed Sikh code of conduct (*SGPC*) in daily life can perform this ceremony. Sikh weddings have a definite pattern consistently followed by the Sikhs. This pattern includes the welcome of the groom and his family and friends (*GGS,* p. 764). A short invocatory prayer is performed and a *milni* (introduction) takes place when the close relatives of the bride are introduced to the relatives of the bridegroom. Each meets the other with a small gift and exchange garlands of flowers outside the *gurdwara.* Refreshments are served after the *milni* and before the actual wedding ceremony.

The two obligatory rituals are the *karmai* (the engagement) and *viah* (the wedding ceremony). The engagement takes place before the wedding. The groom's eldest sister puts a *palla* (long scarf) around the groom's shoulders so he holds it open in his lap. The bride's father then fills the *palla* with handfuls of dried fruit and presents the gift to the groom. He feeds the groom with a sweet called *ladoo,* followed by the rest of the family and friends who will give money known as *sagan.* The *granthi* then sings a short hymn followed by *Ardas* (invocation).

Guru Ramdas's composition 'Lavan' (*GGS,* p. 773-4) are used as marriage verses and serves the basis for the Sikh wedding ceremony. *Lavan* (circling) are performed by sitting in front of the *GGS* and walking around it. *Anand Karaj* is performed by reciting *lavan,* four stanzas from the *GGS* with *kirtan* (singing devotional music with instruments) in the presence of the bride, the bridegroom, their families, relatives, friends and congregation. The couple is asked to move in front of the *GGS.* The groom comes forward and takes his place. The bride then joins the congregation and sits at the left side of the groom attended by a sister, sister-in-law or a friend. They sit down cross-legged after due genuflections. Whoever is conducting the marriage then asks the couple and their parents to stand whilst he or she prays that God bless the marriage. The bride and groom publicly assent to the marriage by bowing towards the *GGS.* When they sit down, the bride's father performs the *palla frowna* ceremony. He ties the end of his daughter's *dupatta* (wide headscarf) to the muslin scarf which hangs from the groom's shoulders. This is a 'giving away' ritual, which signifies that the bride's father is giving his daughter away to the groom, and is then followed by the singing of a short hymn.

The officiator then reads *lavan,* which are sung by *ragis* (religious musicians) as the couple walk slowly around the *GGS* with the groom leading in each case in a clockwise direction. They sit and bow in front of the *GGS* after every *lav.* The first *'lav'* emphasises the importance of married life lived in the service of God and the pursuit of truth (*GGS*, p. 773-774). The second *'lav'* is an indication of the joy of finding a marriage partner and the joy experienced by the soul in realising the presence of God within them (*GGS*, p. 774). The third *'lav'* refers to the detachment towards worldly matters and moving towards a life of spiritual living preoccupied by love for each other and God (*GGS*, p. 774). In the fourth *'lav'* the couple reaches the state of complete oneness, a state of balance which knows no separation and mistrust. They feel and think alike. They are now one soul in two bodies (*GGS*, p. 788). It is the total surrender of the soul in God's love and the perfect love between husband and wife. This also concludes that human love is superseded only by Divine love (*GGS*, p. 774). The couple are then declared 'man and wife'. The scriptural *lavan* launches the couple together in their spiritual passage. Cole comments that '*Lavan* presents a reversal of the *varna ashram dharma* (stage of renunciation) process affirming that the path to *moksha* is one of deepening love, not increasing asceticism' (1995, p. 124).

The service ends with the concluding hymns of the singing of the first five and last stanzas of the *Anand* (*GGS*, p. 917) followed by the *salok* '*Pavan guru…*' (*GGS*, p. 8) and *Ardas,* which is joined by the whole congregation who stand. Finally, *vak* is read. At the end, the officiating person explains to the couple the duties of married life according to the *Guru's* teachings and makes them aware of their mutual obligations as husband and wife to the family and the community.

Finally, *Karah prasad* is served to the congregation as a symbol of hospitality and blessing. The bride's father and mother come forward carrying sweets, which are offered to their daughter and son-in-law. Other family members and guests bless the couple with a small token of money (*sagan*) for their blissful happy married life.

Registration Ceremony: Most *gurdwaras* have facilities for civil marriage. The *gurdwara's* management committee nominates a registrar from the congregation at the time of election. He/she registers the marriage in the *gurdwara* for the convenience of Sikhs. The registrar will ask the bride and groom to stand for conducting the ceremony and will provide them with a legal document (marriage certificate).

Langar is served in the *gurdwara* after the marriage ceremony. It is a blessed lacto-vegetarian meal (no fish or eggs). The families may add some extra dishes to mark the special occasion and it takes place in the *langar* hall or adjoining community centre hall. Some Sikhs prefer to hire halls outside the *gurdwaras* for serving the lunch.

Homosexuality and same-sex marriage is a contemporary issue, having the statutory support of equality laws in the UK. In practice, homosexuality has not been a matter for open discussion in Sikhism until recently. Sikh religious teachings, as enshrined in the *GGS,* do not seem to refer to homosexuality explicitly, in spite of its firm stance on equality. Sikhism endorses marriage and family life and belief in the laws of nature. The main purpose of marriage is to have a family and work together towards spiritual growth. Marriage has a religious, spiritual and social significance. Sikhs generally resolve any issue for which they could not get an answer in the *GGS* by referring it to the religious authorities in India SGPC and *Akal Takht* for a final decision (Sikh Code of Conduct, p. 20). The response to this issue was made on 16th January 2005 when it came into the public domain in Canada. The custodian of the *Akal Takht Sahib,* Joginder Singh Vedanti issued an edict (*sandesh*) denouncing same sex marriage and urging the worldwide Sikh community not to allow such marriages to take place at any *gurdwara*. Homosexuality was described as 'against the Sikh religion and the Sikh code of conduct and totally against the laws of nature'. It advised the Sikh MPs in Canada not to support laws permitting same-sex marriage (Coh, 2005). It is also evident from the major newspapers across India that reported on the decision of the Shiromani Gurdwara Parbandhak Committee (SGPC) to not honour Ontario Premier Kathleen Wynne during her visit to the Golden Temple, because of her support for same-sex marriage and being openly lesbian. SGPC president Avtar Singh Makkar even said: "Offering her (Wynne) a *siropa* (an honour) would be against Sikh ethics". However, some Sikhs are beginning to accept homosexuality, and they point out that the *Gurus*' teachings do not expressly forbid it. They quote that it is the union of two souls and the soul is genderless given the Sikh belief on equality (SikhNet, 2013). Jhutti-Johal commented that the 2005 dictate about same-sex marriages has been adhered to, because any move away from marriage between a man and a woman is viewed as an attack on morality, and a deviation from the religious teachings contained within the *GGS* (2011, p. 86).

Death: Death is the cessation of life when all functions of the human body cease; whosoever is born must die one day is the universal principle. All shall take their turn (*GGS,* p. 474). There is no fixed time and place for death. When someone dies, relatives and friends are informed, and they visit and sit with the family in order to console and support them until the funeral. Sikhs living in this country follow this country's funeral arrangements and practices.

After the funeral, everybody returns to the *gurdwara* for the *bhog* (finishing rite of the recitation of the *GGS*) and *langar* is served to all, indicating the normality of life.

Sikhs believe in *bhana manana* (accepting the Will of God) and see death as part of the natural process and an opportunity for the merging of the soul with its creator. They recite *gurbani* and pray for the peace of the departed soul (*GGS*, p. 923). It is contrary to Sikhism to place the dying person on the ground and make an excessive show of grief by lamenting, crying loudly and wailing. However, shedding tears is a normal and natural expression of grief. Sikhism recommends that spiritual and emotional consolation in grief must be found through singing or listening of s*habad kirtan* and by reciting *gurbani* (*GGS*, p. *923*).

Sikhism does not restrict the way in which a dead body is disposed of. Sikhs generally cremate the body at death, though it is not a religious dictate (Singh, 2009, p. 85). Other methods, like burial or consigning in water, can also be used if convenient under the circumstances (Gulshan, 2005, pp.186-187). The Sikh *Rehat Maryada* (The Code of Sikh Conduct and Conventions) suggests the body should be cremated. It has not overruled the other options when it suggests: 'However, where arrangements for cremation cannot be made, there should be no qualm about the body being immersed in flowing water or disposed of in any other manner'. Sikhs dispose of the body the same day before sunset in India. If the person dies late near sunset, then the very next day. The author asserts that this happens due to the hot weather and lack of facilities to preserve the deceased body. Here in Britain, Sikhs tend to accept the indigenous way of going through a funeral director, and depending on the availability of a date, and longer if a post-mortem is required.

They arrange for the bathing facilities and provide any help needed. The immediate family of the same sex generally wash the body of the deceased, and dress them in clean clothes, not necessarily in new clothes as many Sikhs practice, also ensuring that the deceased has all the symbols of faith if initiated. Like males, a female's family have a choice to dress her according to their choice and the age and status of the deceased.

All the religious rituals before and after the funeral should be discussed by the family with the *gurdwara's* management committee where the funeral service is booked. *Gurdwaras* often differ in the help and support provided by them additional to religious ceremonies, such as the preparation and serving of *langar*. In any case, families have to arrange for a *romalla* (a square cloth to cover the *GGS*, ready made available in Indian fabric shops) and flowers. It is customary to donate clothes and utensils to the *gurdwara*, although many Sikhs prefer to donate money instead. It is important to note that it is a cultural dictate. The belief that the deceased needs these in his/her journey is a simulated idea.

The body is generally brought in a coffin by the hearse to the family home after bathing. The family members pay their last respect and the *granthi* performs the *Ardas* for the deceased soul before leaving the house. The coffin is then taken to the *gurdwara,* where the *granthi* sings hymns from the *GGS* emphasizing detachment and performs the supplication. In the UK, *gurdwaras* have developed a local tradition of giving the deceased a religious clothing (*saropa*) by the *gurdwara's* management committee, which is put on the head and around the body of the deceased. The community members pay their last respect by walking around the coffin. The body is taken from the *gurdwara* to the crematorium. The sons and brothers of the deceased carry the coffin. At the crematorium, there is a short service. A *granthi* leads the mourners in the reading of *Kirtan Sohila* (*GGS,* p. 12-13) and this is followed by Sikh supplication (*Ardas*) and a homily for the departed soul. Traditionally, it is the duty of the eldest son, accompanied by other sons and close relatives, to light the pyre while other attendees recite '*Gur Mantar*' (*vaheguru* - wonderful Lord). In the absence of a son, one of the male relatives performs this ritual in line with the Panjabi culture. In Sikhism, it is not necessary that only the son can perform this. The daughters have as much right as sons. It is a long-standing cultural tradition which is still continued in the Sikh community. In the UK, an electric switch is pressed, and some crematoria allow members of the family the privilege of assisting a coffin as it goes into a furnace. It is normal for the mourners to return to the *gurdwara* after the funeral. One can see at the return to the *gurdwara* many women washing the corner of their headscarf, a practice derived from having a shower to remove any bits and pieces of debris that fly during the funeral on an open wood log pyre in India. It is not a religious practice and there is no need and purpose of this here in Britain.

The mourners go to the prayer hall in the *gurdwara* after the funeral for *path bhog* (finishing ceremony of the recitation of the *GGS)* which is normally a *sadharan path* (a non-continuous recitation of the *Granth)*. It is generally kept by the family at their residence or a local *gurdwara* for the peace of the departed soul. Usually, the reading of the Holy Book marks the culmination of ten days of mourning. This is now combined with the funeral in this country and may not necessarily meet this criterion of mourning days. The service generally includes special hymns '*allahnia de path*' (*GGS*, p. 578) and prayers such as six stanzas of *Anand Sahib*, including supplication and *vak* with eulogy (tribute). *Karah Prasad* (sacred sweet signifying God's blessing) is distributed. After the *bhog*, there is a turban ceremony if the head of a family has died. The tying of the turban signifies that the responsibility for the family is now with the eldest son, who becomes the head of the family according to the tradition prevalent in the Panjabi culture. After the *bhog* ceremony and other programmes all the mourners have *langar*, generally organised by the *gurdwara*, marking the return to the normality of life. It symbolises the continuity of social life and its normal activities as opposed to isolation from human contacts, fasting and other ritual manifestations of grief. The family and the relatives of the deceased usually make gifts to the poor, to the *gurdwara* or to a charity. All this suggests: 'Rituals around the time of death provide a framework for managing the situation and can give comfort and continuity, reminding people that this has happened to others before them' (Henley and Schott, 1999, p. 97). The younger generation and those who do not have connections with *gurdwaras* need support at this time.

The ashes are collected after three days or as soon as possible. Sikhs consign (*parvah*) ashes in running or flowing water. There are designated places for consigning the ashes in the UK cities where Sikhs live. The *granthi*/chaplain accompanies the family on this last ritual. Some Sikhs take ashes to Kiratpur in the Punjab to consign.

Sikhism does not believe in the ritual of performing *shradhs* (*GGS*, p. 332). It is a ritual performed once a year to feed ancestors by feeding *priests* and making donations in the memory of ancestors (*pitr*) to maintain the continuous bond between the living and dead. Sikhism also rejects rituals like '*diva*', keeping an oil lamp lit for 360 days after the death, in the belief that it lights the path of the deceased. Sikhism also restricts erecting memorials, and the veneration of monuments erected to honour the memory of a deceased person or of cremation sites. There are certain other rituals prevalent in the Punjab that are contrary to the approved Code of Sikhism, being a ritual-less religion. These are *Adh Marg*, the ceremony of breaking the pot used for bathing the dead body amid doleful cries halfway towards the cremation ground. *Pind* is the ritual of donating lumps of rice flour, oat flour, or solidified milk (*khoya*) for ten days after the death. *Budha Marna* is a ceremony of celebrating the death of an old man by waving a whisk over the hearse of an old person's dead body and decorating with festoons and balloons (Sikh *Rehat Maryada,* 1950). Sikhism does not approve of breast-beating, organised lamentation by women and *phuri* (sitting on a straw mat in mourning for a certain period).

Sikh calendar

Sikh festivals and religious days were fixed according to the *Vikrami* calendar, based on 12 astronomical lunar months and 365 solar days. The difficulty in using this calendar was that the dates could never be fixed and tend to fluctuate every year, thus creating confusion for many Sikhs. In order to find the solution, the Sikh calendar was introduced and named as the *Nanakshahi* calendar after *Guru* Nanak. The year of this calendar starts with the birth of *Guru* Nanak in 1469 and is based on the mechanics of the solar (Gregorian) calendar. The *Shiromani Gurdwara Prabandhak* Committee adopted this in 1998 and it was implemented in 2003.

This calendar offered the solution and set fixed dates for Indian months and most Sikh holy days except *Guru* Nanak*'s* birthday, which still coincides with the full moon in the lunar month of *Katik.* According to this calendar, dates set for Indian months are *Chet* (March 14), *Vaisakh* (April 14), *Jeth* (May 15), *Harh* (June 15), *Sawan* (July 16), *Bhadon* (August 16), *Asu* (September 15), *Katik* (October 15), *Maghar* (November 14), *Poh* (December 14), *Magh* (January 13) and *Phagan* (February 12). The calendar was also able to fix the dates for *Guru* Gobind Singh's birthday (5 January), *Vaisakhi* (14 April), *Guru Arjan's* martyrdom (16 June), *Parkash utsav* of *Guru Granth Sahib* (1 September) and *Guru* Tegh

Bahadur's martyrdom (24 November). Sikh *gurus* gave *Diwali* and *Holi* a religious face and the names changed accordingly. The calendar did not fix the dates of these Sikh festivals. Their dates are still set by the *Vikrami* calendar. Sikhs celebrate *Diwali* as *Bandi Chhor Divas* (prisoner's release day) and Holi as *Hola Mahalla* to demonstrate their martial skills in simulated battles. These are both set a day after the Hindu festivals.

There is no doubt that the *Nanakshahi* calendar had the advantage that most dates of Sikh religious celebrations would remain constant by the Gregorian calendar (Appendix 3). Pal Singh Purewal, the designer of this calendar, believed that having a unique calendar was vital for the integrity of the Sikh religion. Nesbitt comments: 'Establishing a separate calendar defied Hindu tendencies to subsume Sikhism in Hinduism, and it put Sikhs on par with Hindus, Muslims and other "world religions"'. (2005, p. 129)

Sikh *gurpurabs* and festivals

Sikhs celebrate *gurpurabs* (*gurus*' anniversaries) and festivals. The dates for some of the Sikh festivals are calculated according to the lunar calendar. The day of the full moon is called *puranmasi,* when the month comes to an end, and on the following day is *sangrand,* when the next month begins.

Sikh *gurpurabs*: *Gurdwaras* celebrate the anniversaries of their *gurus*, called *gurpurabs*. The word *gurpurab* literally means the religious festival commemorating the birth and death anniversaries of their ten *Gurus;* some are celebrated more elaborately than others. The most important are seen to be the birthday of *Guru* Nanak, the martyrdom of *Guru* Arjun *Dev*, the martyrdom of *Guru* Tegh Bahadur, and the birthday of *Guru* Gobind Singh. The *Parkash* of *Guru Granth Sahib*, historical events, and the martyrdom of Sikh heroes are also celebrated. All *gurpurab* ceremonies start with *akhand path* (continuous recitation of the entire *GGS*), which normally begins on Friday morning and finishes on Sunday morning. *Granthis* (readers of the Holy Book) and Sikhs that are participating work in relays, and the recitation takes approximately forty-eight hours. Sikhs take pride in organising huge processions with colourful floats carrying the Holy Scripture and depicting the different aspects of Sikh life. Scriptural hymns are sung joyously. In India, it is called a *prabhat pheri* as it takes place in the early hours before sunrise. On the first day of each lunar month (when the sun enters the new Zodiac sign), *Sangrand* is celebrated. It is observed with a special service organised in *gurdwaras* and the new month is announced with the reading of the relevant portion, '*Barahmaha*' (hymns relating to twelve months) from the *GGS* (pp. 133-136). Many *gurdwaras* start *sadharan path* on this day and hold *bhog* on the next *Sangrand*. *Langar* is served on all occasions.

Sikh festivals: Sikhs celebrate many Indian festivals. The Sikh *gurus* gave some of these festivals an added religious interpretation. Among those are *Vaisakhi, Diwali, Holi* and *Maghi*. Sikh festivals have both religious and social significance. Sikhs also celebrate cultural festivals of the Punjab, *Basant Panchmi, Lohri, Rakhi/Rakhri* and *Teeya.*

Religious festivals

Vaisakhi (Baisakhi) is the most important Sikh festival, named after the second lunar month, *Vaisakh.* It normally falls on the 13th of April though once every thirty-six years it occurs on 14th April. The date is now fixed, being based on a solar calendar on 14th April. *Vaisakhi* is widely celebrated by Sikhs all over the world and initiation ceremonies are held in *gurdwaras. Akhand path* is performed and *langar* is served for all three days in every *gurdwara* anywhere in the world. Religious processions are carried out in many cities of Britain by the Sikh *sangat* (congregation). It is a summer harvest festival in India and is celebrated by farmers all over the Punjab. *Vaisakhi* may also be interpreted as a festival of renewal; the previous agricultural cycle has ended and a new one is about to begin. The third Sikh *guru* Amar Das first institutionalised this as one of the special days when all Sikhs would gather to receive the *Guru's* blessings at Goindwal (Punjab) in 1567.

The most important reasons for celebrating *Vaisakhi* by Sikhs is that it is the day of birth of the *Khalsa* and it also marks the Sikh New Year. *Guru* Gobind Singh gathered thousands of Sikhs at Anandpur *Sahib* (Punjab) on this day. He gave a call for the devoted Sikhs who would be prepared to die for their faith. Five Sikhs answered his call whom he initiated and created the *Khalsa Panth* (order) on *Vaisakhi* day in 1699. He ordered them to wear five symbols and made it compulsory for initiated Sikhs to wear, giving them a unique identity.

The Sikh symbols of identity

Sikh identity is considered essential, and it is religiously binding to become a complete Sikh and a member of the *Khalsa Panth* by being initiated. It is important to know the symbols of Sikh identity. The Sikh symbols of identity are known as the 'five Ks', all beginning with the letter 'k'. It gave them not only a unique and distinctive appearance but also signified their full commitment to the faith and submission to God, reminding them of their personal pledge to fight against oppression and injustice. Formal initiation into the Sikh faith is traditionally one of the most important and sacred ceremonies of Sikhism and is open to both men and women. Every Sikh ultimately strives to become initiated. These symbols have meaning and special significance for Sikhs. The Sikh symbols of faith are *kes* (uncut hair), *kangha* (wooden comb), *kirpan* (sword), *kacchera* (cotton knee length undergarment) and *kara* (steel circular band). These have special significance and meaning for Sikhs.

Kes is symbolic of an acceptance of God's Will, and Sikhs believe in maintaining what God has given to them and not to cut or shave hair from any part of the body. They also believe that hair is there for a purpose and considered to be a sign of spiritual and moral strength. It is to move beyond the concerns of physical appearance towards spiritual maturity. It is a visible symbol of Sikhs which helps to spot a Sikh from a distance as the aim of the *Guru* was to create an easily identifiable community.

Turban (*Dastar, pag, pagri*) does not come under the 'five Ks' but forms an important part of the dress for initiated and *keshadhari* Sikhs. Sikhs wear a turban to cover their unshorn hair and it is mandatory. For Sikhs it is a sign of dedication, self-respect, courage and piety. The turban signifies high moral values and according to Dickenson et al (2000) is a sign of identity. It is also a symbol of honour in the Punjab, not only in the Sikh faith, but also in Indian cultural tradition. At one time, most Panjabis used to wear it irrespective of their religious association. The turbans come in many styles and colours though some colours may express a political association such as dark blue for '*Akalis*' (organisation for Sikh rights). The colours are also indicative of a particular occasion, such as pink for marriage. The colour and style of the turban is significant for different religious groups. For women, it is optional.

Kangha: This is a small wooden semi-circular comb and a symbol

of personal care and cleanliness, orderly spirituality and discipline of the mind (Cole and Sambhi, 1978, p. 128). It points out to maintain personal care since the body is one's vehicle for enlightenment.

Kirpan (sword) is made of two words '*kirpa*' (compassion) and '*ann*' (honour). It is difficult to find an exact expression in English and the nearest is ceremonial sword. It is a symbol of freedom from oppression and servility. It signifies dignity and self-respect. Its obvious meaning is of self-defence and individual freedom. *Guru* Gobind Singh created *Khalsa*, who are a community of soldier-saints. *Kirpan* reminds them of their duty as a soldier to fight for social justice and defend the vulnerable. The *kirpan* indicates readiness to defend the faith, the poor and the oppressed (Cole and Sambhi, 1978, p. 128; Neuberger, 1987, p. 17). It is a small or long curved symbolic sword, which can be anything from a few inches to three feet long. Initiated Sikhs wear *kirpan* all the time, in bed, in the shower and everywhere else. It is worn under or over clothing, covered by a sheath (*gatra*) on the right shoulder and under the left arm, at waist level. Most Sikhs wear a small *kirpan* and some wear a brooch or pendant with a *kirpan* shape. In the West it is common to consider *kirpan* as a dangerous weapon. Neuberger comments:

> *Sadly, it has been all too common for nursing staff to try and remove the kirpan from Sikh patients at night on the grounds that it is dangerous. This causes immense and unnecessary distress, and often discourages Sikh patients from seeking help when they need it. Particularly in the case of dying patients, no such restrictions should be applied by the staff. If for any really good reason the kirpan does have to be removed, then it must*

be kept within the sight of the patient, and the issue discussed with the patient and his family (2004, p. 56).

Kara is a round thin circular band of steel like bangle, rather than gold or silver, because it is not an ornament or bracelet. Some Sikhs also wear a heavier rounded iron *kara* which indicates their stronger commitment. Most assimilated Sikhs wear *kara* to maintain their Sikh identity even though they are neither initiated nor *keshadhari*. It is circular in shape, which is a reminder of infinity and so of God. It is a symbol of responsibility and allegiance to God, reminding Sikhs that God is eternal, with no beginning and no end (Rait, 2010, p. 4). It is considered as a symbol of divine unity and infinity (Cole and Sambhi, 1978, p. 128). *Kara* is worn on the right wrist as a reminder to use the hands only for good purposes. Neuberger states: 'Left-handed people wear the bangle on the left wrist'. She further adds that 'in origin the *kara* was supposed to protect the military Sikh from the bowstring cutting into him but now it is supposed to represent the unity of God by virtue of its circular shape' (2004, p. 55). It is also a visible symbol of belonging to Sikhism.

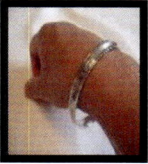

Kacchera are specially designed underpants (more like shorts, or drawers), fairly long, reaching down to the knees and tight at the bottom. They are a symbol of chastity, and signify modesty, moral restraint and continence (Cole and Sambhi, 1978, p. 128). They were particularly useful and comfortable garments for Sikh warriors to wear in the past when they were riding horses to fight in war battles.

Bandi chhorr divas is celebrated on the following day after *Diwali*. Sikhs celebrate this festival because of its religious association with Sikh history. The sixth *guru* of the Sikhs, *Guru* Hargobind, was released in 1619 from the Gwalior Fort, where the Mughal king Jahangir imprisoned him for his failure to pay a fine imposed on his father, *Guru* Arjun Dev. There were also fifty-two Hindu imprisoned princes, each of them innocent of any crime. The *Guru* accepted his release only when the other fifty-two princes were also released along with him. He was told that as many princes as could pass through the narrow passage holding on to his cloak would be freed. The *guru* ordered a cloak to be brought, which had long tassel-like ends, and so the princes were able to leave holding on to his cloak. Sikhs call this day *Bandi chhorr divas*. On this day, the *Guru* arrived in the city of Amritsar where a tumultuous welcome was given to him. On this night, the holy city of Amritsar and the Golden Temple was lit to greet the *Guru*. Since then, this tradition is carried out every year and it is celebrated with great rejoicing for three days. The lit city of Amritsar is worth seeing on this occasion. On this day, fireworks are displayed, and prayers and celebratory events are held across the world. The main theme is the triumph of light over darkness. It is also symbolic of concern for others as well as for ourselves that should guide the actions of all Sikhs. Traditionally in India, houses are autumn-cleaned for the visit of the goddess Lakshmi, but Sikhs clean their houses before moving the beds indoors as the cold nights begin with the inception of winter. Houses are decorated; candles, *divas* (earthen oil lamp) and electric bulbs illuminate *gurdwaras* and homes. Family and friends share sweets and exchange presents.

Hola Mahalla is celebrated instead of Holi, a Hindu festival which is the day after the Spring Equinox. The festival marks the beginning of the spring season and usually falls in the month of *Phagan* (February-March) around March 17. On this day, in 1680, *Guru* Gobind Singh decided to perform mock battles and military exercises in the presence of the Sikh community, stressing the desirability of strength along with the purification of their souls to be able to withstand evil. Since then, Sikhs observe *Hola Mahalla* every year by performing military manoeuvres, displaying weaponry and having processions signifying the importance of social discipline. Anandpur (a city in the Punjab) remains the principal location of this festival. *Gurdwaras* hold *diwan* (religious programme) and relate the significance of this day.

Maghi falls around 14 January and is named after the Indian lunar month *Magh*. It is connected with the battle of Mukatsar where *Guru* Gobind Singh found forty men from *Majha* (a region of Punjab) who had deserted him during the siege of Anandpur. Their women folk were so ashamed of them that they would not let them enter in their homes. The men then returned to reinforce the *Guru*'s small army and died fighting for him. The *Guru* was deeply moved and tore up the paper in front of *Bhai* Maha *Singh* (one of the *gursikh* fighting the battle) on which they had written their *betaba* (disclaimer) as a sign of forgiveness and reconciliation. He embraced each one of them, as they lay dead or dying, and called them the 'Saved Ones'. This *mela* (festival) of *Maghi* is celebrated in their memory at Mukatsar (Punjab) and many Sikhs go there every year. Sikhs visit *gurdwaras* and listen to *kirtan* on this day to commemorate the martyrdom of the 'Forty Immortals'.

Cultural Festivals

Sikhs live in and share the Panjabi culture, which is a fusion of Hindu and Muslim traditions. The Punjab has been predominantly an agrarian society and some of its celebrations are tied to agricultural cycles and seasonal traditions.

Basant Panchami is a spring festival usually falling in early February and associated with the colour yellow. On this day Panjabis wear bright yellow attire as if emulating the bright yellow mustard-seed blossom in the fields. They eat *jarda* (yellow sweet rice) and the youngsters fly kites on their rooftops.

Lohri is a popular seasonal festival which falls in winter, normally mid-January. Bonfires are made and families gather around the fire throwing sesame seeds, peanuts and corn. It is traditional to cook mustard leaf *saag*, corn meal *chapaties*, *halwa* and rice pudding. Children go around the neighbourhood collecting money and sweets. Parents give gifts to their married daughters and sons-in-law and their families. In Britain, *Lohri* is celebrated in *gurdwaras* as it falls on *Sangrand*, though traditionally it is celebrated in homes, especially if the son is married or a son is born in the family. Sikhs are gradually bending towards celebrating a daughter's birth, reflecting their belief in gender equality.

Rakhri is another cultural festival linked to historical fact when women needed protection from the invaders in medieval India. It falls in mid-August. A *rakhi* is a band which is tied around a brother's right wrist by his sister as a reminder that he is her protector. The brother gives her generally money or maybe clothes and jewellery depending on his financial situation as a reassurance. The family shares sweets.

Teeyan is the Panjabi name of the festival of '*Teej*' and is a much-awaited festival for women. It is a cultural and seasonal festival dictated by the onset of the monsoon, which falls in the Indian lunar month of *Sawan* (July-August). It signifies happiness, prosperity and well-being. Newly married women and young unmarried girls gather together to celebrate the beginning of the rainy season. Married women go to their maternal house to participate in the festivities. It is traditional for women to spend the whole month of *Sawan* in Hindi and *Saun* in Panjabi with their parents. Whether or not a married woman goes to her parents, brothers give '*sandhara*', a gift that includes a Punjabi suit/*saree*, *ladoos* (Indian sweet), bangles, henna and a swing to his sister. It gathers momentum when *gidha* (clapping) and dancing begins with the traditional Punjabi folk *geet*/*boliyan*. The festival lasts from a few days to four weeks. The food traditionally associated with *Teeyan* is rice pudding, *malpua* (sweet, creamy and fried like a pancake), *halwa* (sweet pudding made of semolina), *phulke* (very thin large *chapatis*) and *gulgulay* (sweet made of wheat and jaggery) which is suitable and unique for the weather.

Conclusion

The celebrations of Sikh ceremonies and festivals have social and religious connotations. They have a special significance in the lives of Sikhs. Sikh ceremonies remind them of Sikh teachings and the requirement of their faith to live a purposeful life. The celebrations of *gurpurabs* and festivals are the time for introspection in order to assess that Sikhs are leading their life according to Sikh teachings and principles. The aim of *Akhand path* is to bring them close to the words of their Holy Scripture by listening, understanding and putting them into practice. Sikhism encourages human beings to enjoy their life. The Sikh faith by no means denies cultural activities, as it is a part of human life to have a balanced life. The Sikh calendar has not only enforced Sikh identity, but also helped in fixing permanent dates for some of Sikh ceremonies and festivals, helping Sikhs and non-Sikhs to take these dates in mind in planning for religious festivals and cultural events.

References

Banerjee, I. (1936 and 1947). *The evolution of the Khalsa*. 2 volumes, Calcutta: A. Mukerjee.

Coh, M. R. (2005). Reject gay bill, Sikh MPs told: Warning from top religious authority says marriage backers will be shunned. *Toronto Star*, 28th March 2005, p.A.1.

Cole, W. O. (1995). *The Sikhs: Their religious beliefs and practices*. Eastbourne, UK: Sussex Academy Press.

Cole, W.O. and Sambhi, P. S. (1978). *The Sikhs: Their religious beliefs and practices*. London: Routledge & Kegan Paul.

Dickenson, D., Johnson, M. and Katz, J. S. eds. (2000). *Death, dying and bereavement*. London: Sage Publications.

Gulshan, G. S. (2005). *Darpan Sikh Rehat Maryada* (Panjabi). Essex: Khalsa Pracharik Jatha (U.K).

Guru Granth Sahib. (n.d.). Amritsar: *Shiromani Gurdwara Prabandhak* Committee (Standard version of 1430 pages in Panjabi).

Henley, A and Schott, J. (1999). *Culture, religion and patient care in a multi-ethnic society: a handbook for professionals*. London: Age Concern.

Jhutti-Johal, J. (2011). *Sikhism today*. London: Continuum International Publishing Group.

Nesbitt, E. (2005). *Sikhism: A very short introduction*. Oxford: Oxford University Press.

Neuberger, J. (1987). *Caring for dying people of different faiths*. London: Austen Cornish Publishers in association with the Lisa Sainsbury Foundation.

Neuberger, J. (2004). *Caring for dying people of different faiths*. 3rd ed. Abingdon: Radcliffe Medical Press.

Rait, S. K. (1984). *Dictionary of Punjabi name elements*. Leeds: School of Librarianship.

Rait, S. K. with Bhogal, I. S. (2010). *Understanding Sikhism*. Ripon: Plug and Tap.

Sikh Rehat Maryada (1950). Amritsar: *Shiromani Gurdwara Prabandhak* Committee.

Singh, G. (2009). *The Sikh faith: a universal message*. Amritsar, Singh Brothers.

Singh, N.G. (2011). Sikhism: *An Introduction*. London: I.B. Tauris.

Websites

Purewal, P.S. (2020). *Purewal's page* [online]. Available at: http://www.purewal.biz [Accessed 14 Feb.2020].

SikhNet (2013). *Same-sex marriage and LGBT issues part II of II,* [online] Available at: https://www.sikhnet.com/news/same-sex-marriages-lgbt-issues-part-ii-ii [Accessed 31Mar. 2020].

Further references

Most books on the Sikh religion cover these undermentioned topics. It was difficult to mention them all in the main text. Those which were consulted for this chapter are listed here:

Life-cycle rites and rituals

CGMC (2020). *The Anand Karaj marriage ceremony in Sikh religion*, [online] Available at: http://cgmc.org.uk/wp-content/uploads/2016/anandkaraj.pdf. [Accessed 11th June 2020].

Cole, W.O. and Sambhi, P. S. (1978). *The Sikhs: Their religious beliefs and practices*. London: Routledge & Kegan Paul.

Kalsi, S.S. (2007). 'Rites of passage'. In: Kalsi, S.S. (2007) *Sikhism*. London: Bravo Ltd. pp. 102-116.

Rait (2010). 'Equality'. In: Rait, S. K. with Bhogal, I. S. (2010) *Understanding Sikhism*. Ripon: Plug and Tap. pp. 31-36.

Rait (2010). 'Rites of passage'. In: Rait, S. K. with Bhogal, I. S. (2010) *Understanding Sikhism*. Ripon: Plug and Tap. pp. 47-50.

Singh, G. (1987). 'Lavan'. In: *The religions of the Sikhs*. New Delhi: Allied Publishers. 185-187.

Singh, N.G. (2011). 'Ceremonies and rite of passage'. In: Singh, N.G. (2011) *Sikhism: An Introduction*. London: I.B. Tauris. 85-99.

Gurpurabs and festivals

Cole, W.O. (1986). 'Sikh Festivals: *Vaisakhi, Diwali* and *Hola Mahalla'.* In: Brown, A. (ed.) (1986). *Festivals in world religions.* London and New York: Longman (on behalf of the Shap Working Party on World Religions in Education). pp.234-244.

Kalsi, S.S. (2007). *'Diwali, Baisakhi, Hola Mahalla* and *Sangrand'.* In: Kalsi, S.S. (2007). *Sikhism.* London: Bravo Ltd. pp. 86-89.

Rait, S.K. (2005). 'Sikh festivals'. In: Rait, S. K. (2005). *Sikh women in England: Their religious and cultural beliefs and social practices.* Stoke on Trent: Trentham Books and University of Leeds: Department of Theology and Religious studies. pp. 43-45.

Rait, S.K. (2010). 'Vaisakhi, Diwali, Hola Mahalla, Maghi'. In: Rait, S. K. with Bhogal, I. S. (2010). *Understanding Sikhism.* Ripon: Plug and Tap. pp. 50-54.

Singh, G. (1978). *The Sikh festivals.* Edgeware: The Sikh Cultural Society of Great Britain.

Singh, T. and Singh, G. (1989). 'Hola Mahalla.' In: Singh, T. and Singh, G. (1989). *A short history of the Sikhs.* Vol. 1 (1469-1765). Patiala: Punjabi University. pp. 66-67.

Sikh identity

Nesbitt, E. (2007). *A guide to Sikhism*. University of Leeds: Centre for Philosophical and religious studies.

Oberoi, H. S (1994). *The construction of religious boundaries: culture, identity and diversity in the Sikh traditions*. Delhi OUP, Chicago: University of Chicago Press.

Rait, S.K. (2010). 'Sikh identity - Five Ks'. In: Rait, S. K. & Bhogal, I. S. (2010). *Understanding Sikhism*. Ripon: Plug and Tap. pp. 3-7.

Singh, T. and Singh, G. (1989). *Khalsa*. In: Singh, T. and Singh, G. (1989). *A short history of the Sikhs*. Vol. 1 (1469-1765). Patiala: Punjabi University. pp. 64-68.

Chapter 3

Health and healing – impact of Sikh philosophy and psychology

Introduction

This chapter explains the nature of Sikh philosophy and psychology as influencing health and healing. It draws distinctions between religion and *dharma*. Sikhism is a monotheistic religion, explaining the nature and qualities of God. This chapter further explores the purpose of human life, how to develop truthful living and a spiritual path for liberation, mapping the five realms, and the importance of congregation. It also explores the concept of grace, *hukam*, and *karma*. It touches upon the soul and Sikh belief after death. It covers the psychology of religion, religious behaviour and religious beliefs and their impact on health and healing. It explains the causes of pain and suffering and how faith is proven to be therapeutic.

Philosophy

Philosophy is 'the study of the theoretical basis of a particular branch of knowledge or experience', according to the definition given in the Oxford English dictionary. It is the pursuit of wisdom by intellectual search and logical reasoning, and a way of thinking. Religious philosophy is a rational study of matters concerning religion. Religion and philosophy are distinct subjects in the West.

The word 'dharam' captures both philosophy and religion in Eastern religious traditions founded on the Indian subcontinent, including Sikhism. Religion puts an emphasis on one's beliefs at the core of religiosity, even in the absence of empirical evidence. Philosophy on the other hand tackles concepts like metaphysics, the search for ultimate truth, knowledge and life itself.

Sikh Philosophy

Every religion has its philosophy and theology. It prescribes a working philosophy and principles in order to educate and guide its followers. *Guru* Nanak was not a philosopher but a deeply religious man. He travelled widely and met saints belonging to various religions and traditions. His philosophy developed from his spiritual adventure in search of truth. He had the experience and came face to face with the Supreme Reality (*Bhai* Gurdas *dian Varan, Var* 1). Sikh philosophy is a philosophy of action, deed and consequence. It covers metaphysics, cosmology and ontology. In simple words, it covers the existence of God, the creation of the universe, the nature of the human soul, life after death, *karma* theory and the importance of *Naam* and word. The main source of Sikh philosophy is *Guru Granth Sahib* (GGS), the Holy Scripture of Sikhs. *GGS* also contains the hymns written by various saints who raised their voices against the degrading practices prevalent in different societies and religious traditions.

Sikh philosophy accepts the existence of God. There is one and only one God *Ek-on-kar* ੧ੳ (*Mool Mantar, GGS,* p.1) making

Sikhism a monotheistic religion. Nikki-Guninder Singh argues that the Sikh monotheistic vision is different from that of the West being a non-dualist (advaitvadi). 'In the Sikh belief, there is no opposition between the one and many, nor is there any dualism between unity and plurality' (2011, p. 61). The *Guru Granth* claims, 'From the One issue myriad and into the One they are ultimately assimilated' (*GGS*, p.131). It affirms the belief of One God and the unity of God. 'God is eternal and without God there is no other at all' (*GGS*, p. 760). The *GGS* holds that no argument is needed to prove the existence of God.

The concept of God is explicitly stated in the *Mool Mantar*. It is 'a typical terse composition, which almost defies translation' (Cole and Sambhi, 1990, p. 111). They paraphrased: 'This being is One; the Truth; immanent in all things. Immanent in creation. Without fear and without enmity. Not subject to time. Beyond birth and death. Self-manifesting. Known by the *Guru*'s grace'. God is a transcendent being, eternal and self-existent. God is beyond space, and beyond time. 'For millions of aeons the timeless was by Himself. There was no substance, nor space nor time, nor day or night, no stars or galaxies. God was in His trance.' (*GGS*, pp. 1035-1036). In Sikhism God is addressed as a male and all devotees as females. The *Gurus* repeatedly describe the nature of God as wondrous, infinite, unknowable, indescribable, ineffable, and immeasurable by human categories of thought and perception.

It is a Sikh belief that God created everything at the time of creation. For thirty ages, there was only void (*GGS*, p. 555). God is said to be like a juggler who created the world by His magical power (*GGS*, p. 1061). From an empirical point of view, God appears to possess many qualities (*sargun*), and from a transcendental point view, God is indeterminate (*nirgun*) (*GGS*, p. 287). Being devoid of qualities, God is beyond human knowledge and comprehension, but God becomes *sargun* 'with attributes' for the purpose of revelation. The Divine is invisible (*alakh*), formless (*nirankar*) and immaculate (*niranjan*). According to Sikh doctrine 'From God's absolute existence, God assumed the immaculate form: from the formless, God assumed the supreme form' (GGS, p. 940). God, the Supreme power, pervades all places and interspaces. The One is the giver of all - there is no other at all (*GGS*, p. 45) which makes God omnipotent, omniscient, omnibenevolent and the only reality. Human beings are part of God and God resides within humans (*GGS*, p. 1153) and permeates in the whole of creation.

Truth is supreme and it is equated with God. Sikhism stresses upon truth and truthful living. The next question is how we can attain truthful living leading to the path of salvation. *GGS* has given clear direction for leading a truthful life as described in chapter 1. *Japuji* has also outlined the spiritual path leading to liberation (*Pauria* 34-37, *GGS*, pp. 7-8). This spiritual path is mapped in five realms (*khands*) of spiritual progression. '*Dharam khand*' is the first realm of righteous living, which is the basis of human life. *Dharam* (duty) develops from compassion and compassion from humility, and love being the source for leading to contentment and being truthful. Nikky-Guninder Singh (2011) observes that spiritual progression commencing with the stage of *dharma* (duty) and peaking in *sach khand* (literally the stage of truth) is that state of ultimate union between the human being and God, a blissful tranquil state beyond birth and death.

The second realm of '*Gyan khand*' gives importance to knowledge and wisdom of spirituality. There exists diversity in God's creation. There are innumerable gods, saints, kings and demons. There are different types of food, and languages. God is all-powerful and limitless. God created five elements and many forms of birth. Sikhism mentions the four: *andaj* (egg), *jeraj* (womb), *utbhuj* (earth, soil and seed) and *setaj* (sweat and secretion) (*GGS*, p. 835). There are planets, solar systems and galaxies. Spiritual wisdom reigns supreme in the realm where mystical melodies, sublime visions, wonder and bliss prevails.

The third realm is *Saram* (humility) *khand*. Those who reach this realm of spiritual happiness speak elegantly. It is uniquely formed, having no parallel whatsoever. It is impossible to depict what is happening there. If someone tries to describe it, they have to repent later. The intuitive consciousness, intellect and concentration of the mind are sharpened here to match those of genius and realised ones such as *Gurus*, holy men, genius men/women in their own fields and leaders working for humanitarian causes.

The fourth realm of *Karma* is the expression of Divine might. No one other than warriors and powerful heroes reside there, whose minds are filled with *Naam* (God) and they are absorbed in the praises of God. They are beyond death and deception. Their beauty is beyond narration. The saints of all worlds, whose minds are imbued with the true Lord live there in bliss.

The fifth realm 'Sach khand', is described as the realm of Truth where formless God resides. Having created the creation, He watches over His creation bestowing happiness with a gracious glance. There are continents, planets and galaxies. There are worlds upon worlds in which live innumerable creatures. As He commands, so they exist. There is no limit and no end to God's creation, it is too vast to describe. God rejoices by watching and contemplating over His creation. It is beyond human description.

Sikhism also emphasises developing and practising the five virtues: *sat* (truth), *daya* (compassion), *santokh* (contentment), *nimrata* (humility), and *pyaar* (love) which are essential for truthful living. The barrier in developing these qualities lies in five evils, *kam* (lust), *krodh* (anger), *lobh* (greed), *moh* (attachment) and *hanker* (ego) and must be resisted (*GGS*, p. 843). It is important to recite and meditate on *gurbani* as a constant reminder of the Divine and to do *seva* (selfless service) in order to develop humility and control the ego. Self-centredness (*haumai*) combined with ego leads a person into delusion and worldly attachment. The good and evil is judged in God's court based on one's actions and deeds. It is important for humans to acknowledge God's power as nothing can be achieved without His Grace. At the same time, humans should recognise their own duty. Those who are able to develop the five virtues are happy, peaceful and mentally healthy.

Guru Nanak's 'Japji' celebrates cosmic order and Divine Will, a concept he called hukam (Divine order/Will). It is through the Divine Will that everything exists, and to hukam everything should submit (GGS, p. 885). The hukam of creation reveals God, and so too does shabad, the word, in the sense of divine revelation, and naam, the name. Naam is central to Guru Nanak's teaching and philosophy, as it means not only the word or utterance through which truth is revealed but is itself the compression or encapsulation of divine reality. Naam is for Guru Nanak the total divine self-expression, rather than merely God's title or epithet (label), and on its power, human life depends (Singh, p. 2011). She further adds that Guru Nanak urges naam simran not so much as a theological rationale but as a constant spiritual practice, and not spiritual practice in isolation from life's ordinary activities and preoccupations, but as the grounding for these: 'Highest is the truth, but higher still is truthful living' (GGS, p. 62). In fact, 'word' is given much importance as it has come directly from God, remains forever and is unalterable.

Sikhism believes in the concept of 'karma', which literally means deeds (Singh, 1971), and taking responsibility for one's own actions (Bhai Gurdas, Var 1, 8). Human beings are judged by their actions and deeds. They get their next life according to their deeds, determining whether or how they will be born again, but it is also stressed that human efforts must be blessed by the grace of God and the Guru. God's grace can transcend karma, and mindfulness of divine grace is a way of weakening the ego (Singh, 2011, p. 27). Sikh belief in life after death is linked to the transmigration of the soul. According to this, death is regarded as a gradual transition from the human state to another state, depending upon one's conduct (*karma*) in this world.

The soul is believed to be immortal although the human body is mortal and has to end. *GGS* mentions that there are 8.4 million *jonies* (form of lives) and human life is the best of all forms. Sikhism gives importance to the *Guru* and the company of *sadh sangat* (congregation) as a means of enriching spiritual knowledge. It is clear that the Sikh way to liberation is through *karam* (actions, deeds), *bhakti* (devotion) and *gyan* (knowledge). One can also achieve it with God's grace.

> *The Sikh philosophy as embodied in the Guru Granth Sahib is chiefly a philosophy of action, deed and consequence. It explains the genesis of the world and the ultimate nature of reality. It is a science of reality and the art of union with reality. It gives a vision of truth, and it opens up new paths for the mind of man.* (Mansukhani, 1965, p. 249)

GGS offers spiritual guidance not only to Sikh adherents but also to all human beings. It advocates the monotheistic belief of the single Divine power and fraternal unity of all human beings. Reciting and listening to it is soothing.

The purpose of human life is to look after Divine creation and to do good deeds to achieve truthful living, with the ultimate aim of attaining salvation (*mukti* - merging with God). It is important to understand that human life is transitory and a passing phase, and that this world is illusory (*GGS*, p. 147). In *GGS*, *Guru* Nanak says that all are suffering in this world (*GGS*, p. 954). Whatever appears pleasant is really a source of pain at the end (*GGS*, p. 1328). This suffering is not only caused by human passion but also by the forgetfulness of the name of the Creator (*GGS*, p. 135). It is not only cessation of the passion, which releases from sufferings, but also God's grace. Sikhs believe that God is their ultimate support in their times of need.

Religious psychology

Psychology is the branch of science dealing with behaviour, acts or mental processes, and with the mind, self or person who experiences these things (English and English, 1958). Loewenthal explains this in a simple way by suggesting that psychology is the study of behaviour, thought and feeling (2010, p. 1). Western psychologists view it presumably on their scientific findings and empirical studies. Every religion has an inbuilt psychology to appeal to and influence the human mind, though religion has not been included in traditional theories of psychology until recently. In this respect, it may become important to consider how religious psychology is defined. Religious psychology is the study of religious behaviour, thought and feeling.

Sikh religious behaviour

Religious behaviour is a behaviour holding religious values and beliefs, and one's actions are tied with religious practices. Sikhism is a religion embedded in spirituality. It covers behaviour that is spiritually valued and considered healthy and therapeutic. Being a way of life, it relates how to lead one's life, detailing daily routine, honest earning, and ways to develop truthful living and what to eat and wear. It also covers religious behaviour such as prayer, *kirtan*, invocation, *Ardas* and recitation of *gurbani*. It suggests different levels of spiritual growth to attain salvation. Sikhs are generally religious, which has a number of implications on chaplaincy including spiritual assessment.

Prayer is the most distinctively religious of all forms of behaviour and is believed to be helpful. It is a mechanism to connect with God through devotion, love, and sincere concentration. Concentration refers to presence, connecting, and participating. Connected (Rettie, 2003) is the emotional feeling that you are not alone, that you are in touch with someone. Prayer has three functions (1) enables true I/Thee relationships; (2) it allows for meaning to exist in a situation; and (3) it enables an individual to be responsible in the 'here and now' (Gould, 1993). 'Prayer is a basic spiritual practice that enables people to pause before God and be mindful of the divine presence. Prayer can be expressed in words and action as well as in silence and stillness' (Cobb, 2005, p. 124).

The methods used for prayer in Sikhism are reading, reciting, hymn singing (*kirtan*) and invoking through supplication (*Ardas*) to be in tune with the divine and to plea for His constant support. Sikhs pray alone and in congregations. It is a sacred rite in which the devotee makes an effort to be connected with God. Sikhs pray daily in the early hours. The *Gurus* suggested concentrating on *Naam* (name of God) in the early hours before dawn (*GGS*, p. 611). These serene moments are the best time to connect 'I with Thee' through *samadhi* or meditation. It is performed when asking for help, in thanksgiving, dedication and confession. Prayer is also an important part of performing life-cycle rites, thus forming a significant part of Sikh religious behaviour.

Praying aloud in the congregation is a construct of presence. Sikhism believes in the presence of God in the congregation as it is seen as a school for learning goodness (*GGS,* pp.1316-7). It can be experienced by being present and joining in *kirtan* or listening to what is being sung. Sikhism puts emphasis on praying in congregations and attending congregational prayers. The collective prayer is considered the most productive.

It is acknowledged that prayer provides the potential to be supportive (Royal College of Nursing, 2011). Despite its disputed place in clinical practice, recent research has suggested that in life-limiting illness, most patients and practitioners view prayer as spiritually supportive (Balboni et al, 2011). If the listener and patient are both people of same faith, the final prayer at the end of a visit may recognise and affirm that conviction by its choice of language.

Kirtan is the process of singing the verses of the *GGS* accompanied by musical instruments. It is a normal part of Sikh prayers. Many congregation members love to join in singing hymns, a forceful way of connecting with the Supreme power by singing

God's glory. In this process, true meaning is revealed directly to the *surat* (consciousness and awareness) through cosmic vibrations. The body's energetic vibrations from our voices bind us to the spiritual light (Lal, 2020).

Invocation is a kind of petition and a modest way of asking a favour from the supreme power. Sikhs mainly use supplication (*Ardas*), recitation of certain specific hymns of *Gurbani* (verses from *GGS*) and other religious sources for invocation related to their life circumstances. God is the supreme power and all humans are God's children. Asking for help in difficult circumstances should not be considered a selfish act but an act of faith, love, loyalty and humility.

Ardas (supplication) is one of the most commonly used ways of invocation in *Sikhi* (Sikh way of life). It is a request to ask for or plead for a desired thing for oneself or others (on behalf of someone, the congregation or for the whole of humanity). It is also a way to show one's gratitude to the Creator. It is a Sikh belief that *Ardas* performed from the depth of one's heart and with devotion is more likely to be answered.

Recitation: The recitation of the name of God is an antidote of suffering, pain and grief (ਦੁਖੁ ਕਾਟੈ ਹਿਰਦੈ ਨਾਮੁ ਵਸਾਈ - By keeping the *naam* in mind, pain withers away). It gives strength to bear the burden of sufferings. It is a common practice within the Sikh community to recite certain prayers such as *Japuji*, *Sukhmani Sahib*, *Benti Chaupee* either alone or in a group. *Japuji* (composed by *Guru* Nanak) is one of the *banis* (religious verses) which is prayed every morning. It is the most used *gurbani* in various Sikh rituals. It is strongly believed that *Sukhmani Sahib* (*bani* written by *Guru* Arjun) gives solace to the mind. It is mostly recited when a person is feeling low, anxious, deeply entrenched in sorrow, remorseful, or is tired of life in order to get consolation and peace of mind. It is normal practice in many Sikh homes to recite this *gurbani* for the harmony and peace in the family and the well-being of humanity. The *Benti Chaupee* (written by *Guru* Gobind Singh) can be read at any time during the day to provide protection, positive focus and energy. Some people also recite to thank God for what God has given to them. Some religious minded patients recite their favourite hymns from the *GGS* or recite *Mool Mantar* (root formulae) to experience the feeling of tranquillity.

Religious belief

Religious belief refers to the contents of beliefs about religious matters concerning God, the Divine, the Supernatural or other related topics. 'Religious belief is different from religious behaviour. This includes different types of human activity with different antecedents' (Loenthal, 2010, p. 58). They may look similar but are definitely distinct.

Sikh religious beliefs

Sikhs believe in one God and in the unity of God. According to Sikh beliefs, God is the creator and the whole creation is God's play (*Lila*)

(*GGS*, p. 11). The Creator is connected to its own creation by being omnipresent. It also establishes a relationship between God and God's creation, the soul (divine spark) and the Divine, as well as human beings and the cosmos, in a logical and coherent way, ensuring harmony for a healthy existence. Religious beliefs dictate how to become a virtuous human being, the importance of human life, nurturing of the soul, caring for God's creation (humans, nature and environment) and doing good deeds. Human life is a mixture of happiness, comforts, challenges and sorrows. Sikhs should live in reality accepting the Will of God, and there is no place for meaningless rituals, astrology, black magic and evil spirits to get rid of adverse situations in Sikhism.

Distinctiveness: Religious symbols and identity are signs of distinctiveness. Every religion has its own identity and unique symbols which are revered and valued. Religious identity is chiefly based on ideology, making adherents distinctive or different from others. Beit-Hallahmi (1989) has suggested that all religions aim to create members with a high level of ego-involvement, with a strong religious identity. In the Sikh faith, a high level of humility and spirit to fight for social justice and against exploitation is cultivated. Recent studies conducted in religious psychology have largely ignored the Sikh religion, consequently there is little researched and written in this respect. The tenth Sikh *guru* in 1699 instituted the *Khalsa* (men and women with the spirit of faith and valour to fight for justice and human rights) and made them visible by prescribing them to wear the five articles of faith (described in chapter 2). This unique identity makes Sikhs stand out from the crowd. There are also symbols and insignia unique to Sikhism. These are:

Ek-on-kar ੴ, the Sikh *Khanda* ☬, and the *Nishan Sahib* ◢ .

Togetherness: Being together provides an opportunity to know each other and develop social relations that can provide a source of support. Carl Jung acknowledged the importance of togetherness and being with others in psychology (1934, pp.220-227). Maslow proposed five basic needs required for self-actualisation in his 'Hierarchy of Needs' in 1943, and the human need to belong was one of them.

The Sikh *Gurus* put an emphasis on being together to create an accessible support mechanism for Sikhs which is considered healthy in human psychology. The congregational nature of Sikhism and *sangat* (gathering of spiritual people) indicate the importance of togetherness. *Langar*, an integral part of Sikh traditions is eaten sitting together in a *pangat* (row), which provides opportunities to get to know each other socially and emphasises the importance of togetherness on equal basis. *Langar* is prepared on the premises in *gurdwaras* gives added opportunities to create stronger social bonds among *sevadars* (volunteers) and the members of congregation. This regular being in touch with each other gives individuals the confidence to share, learn and appreciate each other's views, concerns and skills contributing to strong bonds.

Sikh rituals, rites and festivals also offer opportunities for togetherness. Initiation (*Amrit*) creates a strong bond within religious congregation. *Gurpurabs* (anniversaries of the *Gurus*), religious, and cultural festivals offer them the chance to be together religiously and socially. Lifecycle rites (birth, initiation, marriage and death) provide further opportunities to get together. These positively affect health and healing.

Gurdwaras are open all hours of the day, seven days a week. Many Sikhs and families as well as the elderly, single, and those in need of company are often seen gathering in *gurdwaras* during weekdays, not only having spiritual time, but also enjoying social time. Some *gurdwaras* also provide facilities for organised activities. It helps to not only address isolation and loneliness but also make them active through socialisation and physical activities. Their information needs are often met through the information network available in gurdwaras, which also serve as a support mechanism for the Sikh community.

Causes of pain and suffering

Patients often ask questions when they are seriously ill: "Why am I suffering?", "I do not think I have done anything wrong, God is still punishing me". Life is a mixture of happiness, comfort, pain, sorrow and suffering. According to Sikhism, pain and suffering are the result of *karma* from this present and the previous life. God ordains suffering and comfort, as He ordains, so do we receive (*GGS*, p. 1). Everything becomes painful when one forgets the Lord (*GGS*,

p. 394). Pain is the application of natural law, but pain is also a cure (*GGS*, p. 1240). Sikh *Gurus* repeatedly emphasised that *haumen* (individualism and self-centredness; ego, pride) is at the root of problems from which the individual and society suffer. Self-concern creates ego (*haumen*) which becomes one of the causes of suffering and pain.

Healing with faith

Sikhs use their faith as an important tool and support mechanism for treatment and health recovery. There are number of *sakhis* (parables) available in Sikhism as to how illnesses are cured by using religious resources. Religious people normally do not surrender to illness but remain obliged to God's *hukam* and leave it to 'Him' to take care of them. It is believed in the Sikh community that this happens only when the devotee wholeheartedly surrenders to the supreme power and has a deep faith in Him. It is difficult to give any concrete data due to the lack of research on healing with faith or investigations made on the therapeutic or healing power of Sikh religious resources.

Religion: There is a common assumption by religious people, including professionals, that religion has a positive effect on health. Practicing Sikhs and *amritdharis* believe in the healing power of faith considering it serving as a therapeutic process. It helps patients understand and resolve their concerns by increasing awareness of their inner world and its influence over relationships, both past and present (Koenig, 2001). This is one of the reasons that religion and spirituality are increasingly considered an integrative part of holistic care. These instill and encourage positive qualities, such as love, kindness, compassion, honest earning and sharing with the less fortunate, contributing to greater well-being and are beneficial for health. Koenig at al rightly pointed out: 'The faithful have for centuries taken these pronouncements as truth based upon the highest authority' (2001, p. 54). Those who have faith in God believe that faith cures not only diseases, but also takes care of surgical and other serious cases. Many patients, while relating their stories, mentioned that their life was prolonged because of their faith when they had limited time to live. Religion contributes in many ways to health and well-being propounded by the research of Koenig.

Gurdwara: *Gurdwaras* play an important role in reducing social isolation, which is especially a problem for the elderly, single and infirm. Gurdwaras provide venues for getting together and free food for the socially isolated. The social life plays an important part in human well-being. The presence of congregational members becomes added support for them. There is often sincere mutual love, concern, and respect among members of the faith community. This social bond can become an informal health-promotion network where problem sharing and solving is also discussed and explored. Many *gurdwaras* organise activities to help in reducing social isolation. The caring attitude of *gurdwaras*' volunteers, especially for the elderly, frail and those in distress, are more likely to establish amicable relations with them to feel happy and supported.

Healthy lifestyle: It is not surprising to know that many religions direct their adherents towards a healthy lifestyle. Sikhism is a way of life and those who follow it have a healthier way of living. Some of its teachings include 'speak no evil, think no evil, see no evil, hear no evil and do no evil', which helps in purifying one's mind and deeds. 'Early to bed and early to rise' (*GGS*, p. 305; Darragh, A. 2012), meditation and prayers are recommended for mental health and a peaceful existence. *Guru Granth Sahib* states:

> *One who calls himself a Sikh of the Guru, the True Guru, shall rise in the early morning hours and meditate on the Lord's Name. Upon arising early in the morning, he is to bathe, and cleanse himself in the pool of nectar. Following the Instructions of the Guru, he is to chant the Name of the Lord. All sins, misdeeds and negativity shall be erased* (*GGS*, p. 305). *By hearing the naam, the mind is comforted and pain withers away.* (*GGS*, p. 1240)

Prayer is the most frequently mentioned religious method of coping with stress (Cinnirella and Loewenthal, 1999) and this is frequently applied in Sikhism. The person who is praying devotedly surrenders to God and is believed to bring consolation and hope, as well as the relief of tensions, worries and fears. Prayer provides a feeling of support and closeness to God, which gives peace of mind. It is normally comforting and may help to provide guidance. Prayer also helps in coping with negative feelings, low moods and tragic events supported by an Australian study suggesting prayer as one of many possible strategies for coping with negative feelings (Parker and

Brown, 1982). Prayers and contemplation affect cognition and emotions, and this in turn may have effects on mental and physical health and wellbeing. Shapiro and Walsh (1984; Brown, 1994) also support this view by recognizing the positive cognitive and emotional effects of contemplation and meditation. Sikhs believe that God is benevolent, and answers to the prayers of His devotees through divine intercession when they are performed with love and devotion. Many Sikh patients have related the stories of their answered prayers. Prayer entails a 'dynamic sense of harmony within and without that heals conflict and loneliness' (Johnson, 1956).

Music: Music is considered to have a soothing effect on the body, mind and spirit. The Holy Scripture of Sikhs is written in *ragas*, which makes it musical, and verses are often sung in a process known as *kirtan* (singing of devotional music). In the words of Harbans Lal (2018):

The physical body of the singer experiences the essence of each word through the lightening energy in the brain and the calming vibrations in the body, all caused by the sound currents. They keep the mind to stay focused on the Word. They heal the physical body and cleanse inner thoughts. The sound waves of the Gurmat Raags connect the mind, body and spirit by alignment of the physical, emotional, mental and spiritual entities. They implant in the psyche the basis for both spiritual and mental growth.

There are a number of spiritual poetic compositions in the *GGS* and some of them are considered to be healing in themselves. Singing those rhythmic hymns may have a healing effect, but certainly give the singer peace of mind. Some religious-minded patients chant them frequently for the relief of their symptoms and to reduce illness. It seems to facilitate understanding of pain by 'mindfulness' and living in the moment.

Human needs: Sikhism recognizes the importance of human needs and Sikhs are allowed to fulfil their physical, mental and spiritual needs. Possessions are not denied in Sikhism, but greed is. They can own property, have savings only through honest earning, get married (as Sikhism promotes the institution of marriage), and have family, promoting support mechanisms. Sexual behaviour is strictly regulated in Sikhism in order to lessen the possibility of contracting and transmitting sexual diseases for practising Sikhs. Sikhism also includes self-help, self-reliance and community participation. They can enjoy recreational activities along with developing their spirituality. Sikhism promotes a balanced life by living in a family and facing life's challenges. Sikh *Gurus* repeatedly emphasised that *haumen* (individualism and self-centredness; ego, pride) is at the root of problems from which the individual and society suffer. One should free oneself from the evil manifestation of *haumen* i.e. five evils and replace them with virtuous qualities. Sikhism insists on good deeds and actions, encouraging Sikhs to do virtuous deeds. Sikhism believes in transmigration when a person gets to the next life according to the actions (*karma*) in their present and previous life, further encouraging them to do good deeds. Those who do good deeds, are devoted to God, and care for God's creation tend to have a healthy, content and fulfilled life in this world, and it is believed that their soul merges with God after death. The Sikh belief is that a contented and benevolent state of mind contributes to a healthy mind and body, and is less prone to anxiety, depression and tension.

Diet: Sikhism has laid down rules on dietary habits, including the consumption of food and drink. Sikhs from a strong religious background who frequently attend *gurdwaras*, pray, and read the Holy Scripture are far less likely to eat meat. This will help to save them from illnesses such as heart problems and high blood pressure. Sikhism prohibits drinking alcohol, smoking tobacco or experimenting with drugs and nicotine which are extremely harmful for the liver and mental health including anxiety, low mood and depression.

Conclusion

Every religion has its own unique philosophy and psychology that makes it distinctive. *Philosophy* of *religion* is the *philosophical* study of the *meaning* and nature of *religion*. It includes the analyses of *religious* concepts, *beliefs*, terms, arguments, and practices prescribed for the *religious* adherents. Religious psychology plays an important part in people's lives because of their love, devotion, belief and behaviour. Religious teachings inspire and empower its devotees with virtues and values to promote human flourishing, a common good, harmony, love, compassion and humility. Religion brings peace, contentment, and a caring and sharing attitude. Feeling the support and presence of someone even though that someone is invisible (God), gives strength and hope. The sufferer, however, finds solace in the name of God, and finds strength to face the pain and the grief. The faith becomes more important when someone is sick, suffering or dying. It directly and indirectly influences health, peace of mind and self-satisfaction. It is also healing. There is a need and scope for further research in the area of healing with the Sikh faith.

References

Balboni, M. J., Babaer, A., Dillinger, J., Phelps, A., George, E., Bloc, S., Kachnic, L., Hunt, J., Peteet, J., Prigerson, H., VanderWeele, T. & Balboni, T. (2011). "It depends": viewpoints of patients, physicians, and nurses on patient-practitioner prayer in the setting of advanced cancer.' *Journal of Pain and Symptom Management.* 41, 5., pp. 836-47.

Beit-Hallahmi, B. (1989). *Prolegomena to the psychological study of religion.* Canterbury, New Jersey, London, England, and Ontario, Canada: Associated University Presses.

Brown, L. B. (1994). *The human side of prayer.* Birmingham: Religious Education Press.

Cinnirella, M. and Loewenthal, R.M. (1999). 'Religious influences on beliefs about mental illness in minority groups: a qualitative interview study.' *British Journal of Medical Psychology*, 74. pp. 293-303.

Cobb, M. (2005). *The Hospital Chaplain's Handbook: a guide for good practice*. Norwich: Canterbury Press.

Cole, W. O and Sambhi, P. S. (1990). *A popular dictionary of Sikhism*. London: Curzon Press.

English, H. B. and English, A. C. (1958). *A comparative dictionary of psychological and psychoanalytical terms: A guide to usage*. New York: Longmans Green.

Gould, S.J. (1993). In: Nelson, J. M. (2009). *Psychology, religion and spirituality*. New York: Springer Science and Business Media.

Guru Granth Sahib (n.d.). Amritsar: *Shiromani Girdwara Prabhabd hak* Committee. (Contains 1430 pages written in Panjabi, Gurmukhi script).

Johnson, P. E. (1956). *Psychology of religion*. 2nd ed. Nashville, Tennessee: Abington.

Jung, Carl (1934). Modern man in search of a soul. New York: Harcourt Brace & Company.

Koenig, H. G. (2001). *Healing power of faith: how belief and prayer can help you triumph over disease*. New York: Touchstone.

Koenig, H., McCullough, M. E. and Larson, D. B. (2001). *Handbook of religion and health*. Oxford: University Press.

Loewenthal, K. M. (2010). *The psychology of religion*. Oxford: One World Reprint.

Mansukhani, G. S. (1965). *The quintessence of Sikhism*. 2nd ed. Amritsar: *Shiromani Gurdwara Prabandhak* Committee.

Parker, G. B. and Brown, L. B. (1982). Coping behaviour that mediate between life-events and depression. *Archives of General Psychiatry*. 39, pp.1386-1391.

Rettie, R. (2003). *Connectedness, awareness and social presence*. Sixth International Presence Workshop, Aalberg.

Shapiro, D. H. and Walsh, R. N. (eds.) (1984). *Meditation: Classic and contemporary perspectives*. New York: Aalberg.

Singh, G. (1987). *The religions of the Sikhs*. New Delhi: Allied Publishers.

Singh, N.G. (2011). *Sikhism: An introduction*. London: I. B. Tauris.

Websites

Cherry, K. (2017). The 5 levels of *Maslow's hierarchy of needs*. [online] Available at: https://www.verywellmind.com/what-is-maslows-hierarchy-of-needs-4136760 [Accessed 21 Jan. 2017].

Darragh, A. (2012). *About ageing, diet, sleep, and exercise*. [online] Available at: http://podcast.rasset.ie/podcasts/2012/pc/pod-v-11041244m49slivelinescams-pid0-2689176- audio.mp3 [Accessed 31 Jan. 2018].

Lal, H. (2018). *Boundless Scripture of Guru Granth Sahib.* [online] Available at: https://www.searchgurbani.com/guru-granth-sahib/ introduction [Accessed 2 June 2018].

McLeod, S. (2017). *Maslow's hierarchy of needs,* [online] Available at: https://www.simplypsychology.org/maslow.html [accessed on 21 Jan.2017].

Maslow, A. Hierarchy of needs. [online] Available at: psychology.about.com/od/theories of personality/hierarchy needs.htm. Cached page [Accessed 21 Jan. 2017].

Philosophy. Available at: https://en.wikipedia.org/wiki/Philosophy# Indian_philosophy [Accessed 21 Jan.2017].

Royal College of Nursing (2011). *Spirituality in Nursing Care: a pocket guide.* [online] Available at: http://www.elament.org.uk/ media/1205/spirituality_in_nursing_care-_rcn_pocket_guide.pdf [Accessed 21 Jan. 2017].

Search *Gurbani* (2018). *Vaaran Bhai Gurdas.* [online]. Available at: https://www.searchgurbani.com/bhai-gurdas-vaaran/pauri-by-pauri [Accessed 19 Oct. 2018].

Main chapters

**Chaplaincy, chaplains, their skills and competencies,
spiritual, pastoral and religious care, end of life, bereavement
and conclusion**

Chapter 4

Background to Sikh chaplaincy

Introduction

There is a huge array of literature giving an insight into the development of Christian chaplaincy, from its beginning to the modern age. This chapter concentrates on the development of modern chaplaincy, as it exists in the National Health Service (NHS) since its inception in 1948, including multi-faith chaplaincy and the position and scope of Sikh chaplaincy in relation to chaplaincy provisions. It reviews the National Chaplaincy Guidelines 2003, 2015, Equality Analysis, review of the current guidelines and the report: *Fit for the Twenty-First Century?* as these impact on minority faiths. It also covers the development of Sikh chaplaincy including its inheritance from the times of Sikh *gurus*.

Modern NHS Chaplaincy

The term chaplaincy is closely associated with a chaplain, the priest or person in charge of a chapel (Christian place of worship). Chaplaincy, as the term implies, refers to everything pertaining to the work of chaplains, their theology, spiritual care, pastoral practices and professional identity. It clearly suggests that the term has a Christian orientation and connotation. This has also been the dominant religion in shaping the work of chaplains in the NHS.

Chaplaincy as situated in the NHS may be a modern construct, but it is not a new concept in British society. It has been a part of the healing and caring process for many centuries in the UK, though the role and status of chaplains has changed over time, influenced by the role of the church, religion, sovereignty and government. The chaplain has remained the central figure in providing religious and pastoral care for the vulnerable, sick and poor (Swift, 2009). Many people other than chaplains, for example nursing staff, family, friends, and hospital visitors, often provide care when someone is in hospital. The uniqueness of chaplains is that they are qualified and professionally trained to do this work, and they are encouraged to develop through ongoing training, supervision, reflection and Continuous Professional Development (CPD).

Healthcare chaplaincy is a well-established and accepted service embedded in the NHS. It has been publicly funded since its founding. It became part of holistic care in the NHS following the assurance of the 're-housing' of religion in the NHS (Church of England, 1951, p.3). Their new position in the NHS and anticipation of conforming to the norms and expectations of the health service removed chaplains from local churches, giving them their own identity. In spite of this, Christian churches have always remained influential in the work and development of chaplaincy services in the NHS. Later, with the efforts and writings of some eminent chaplains and social academics, it began to move towards professionalism (Autton, 1966 and Wilson, 1971) in order to give the profession a unique identity. The concept of a 'holistic' approach to patient care brought in an added dimension to chaplaincy work later in the form of spiritual care (term as used here is for non-religious beliefs). Following the election of New Labour in 1997, chaplaincy organisations began to do far more to articulate the work and contributions of chaplains to healthcare, making the case for establishing chaplaincy with the status of a valuable profession (Swift, 2009).

Chaplaincy in the NHS has been an almost exclusively Christian activity mainly dominated by Anglican priests for a considerable time. As Todd argues: 'The role of Anglican chaplains has often been seen as an aspect of the role of the established Church, extending the ministry of the parish church into hospitals, workplaces, industry and so on' (2011). Todd is right in highlighting the influence of the Anglican Church and its expectations from Anglican priests from the very beginning and it is still trying to keep the same hold. However, the demography of Britain has changed since 1948. It has become multi-faith and multi-cultural though, in fact, it is not a secular state. Secondly, the NHS could never have become autonomous in making its own decisions by detaching itself from the established Church and its influential network. The established Church dominated chaplaincy from the onset and has been continuously influential. For example, the 1952 Prison Act still requires that each prison in England and Wales has an Anglican chaplain. The NHS anticipated meeting the spiritual needs of patients and staff and spoke of the need to appoint chaplains (Orchard, 2000). This brought in chaplains mainly from other Christian denominations. This development also had a wider impact on chaplaincy services supported by other social, religious and political factors such as equality and diversity policies, Human

Rights legislations, pluralism, initiatives taken by New Labour and the decline in numbers of churchgoers. These factors helped in initiating the concept of multi-faith chaplaincy, a potential big leap from Christian chaplaincy.

Chaplaincy departments in the NHS Trusts are located in a range of areas in organisational structures within hospitals, depending upon the size of the department and the management model of the hospital. Common locations include clinical directorates or divisions of Nursing and Allied Health Professionals, Hotel Services and Human Resources (Cobb, 2005). The Health and Social Care Act 2012 made changes to the structure of the NHS though it has not affected the position of chaplaincy departments. New 2015 chaplaincy guidelines also suggested, under best practice, to have the location of chaplaincy departments alongside allied health professionals or similar clinical groupings. New arrangements for the appointment of healthcare chaplains came into place from January 2012 with the appointment of healthcare chaplaincy advisers drawn from the different religions and faiths in England. These advisers are recommended to Trusts who seek assistance in the complex process of appointing chaplains to acute and mental health hospitals. Chief executives may wish to consider these new arrangements, and the importance of providing equitable access to chaplaincy for faith communities in order to support the spiritual wellbeing of patients and staff, when commissioning services.

Development of Multi-Faith Chaplaincy

The changing demography of Britain in the 20th century led to the formation of interfaith groups to foster friendship, trust, tolerance, understanding and co-operation among members of the faith communities. Concord (Leeds Interfaith Fellowship) is one of the oldest interfaith groups in the UK, which started in 1946. Many other interfaith groups existed at local levels depending upon funding for the purpose of community cohesion. The Interfaith Network for the UK, based in London, came into existence in 1987 and since then, it has worked as an umbrella body for other interfaith groups and forums across the UK. Its aim is to advance public knowledge and mutual understanding of the teachings, traditions and practices of the different faith communities in Britain, including awareness both of their distinctive features and their common ground, and to promote good relations between faith communities. These steps, at a national and local level, laid the foundations for government initiatives with ready-made expert knowledge of nine major world faiths (Baha'i, Buddhism, Christianity, Hinduism, Islam, Jainism, Judaism, Sikhism and Zoroastrianism) considered for service delivery. The first decade of the twenty-first century became the focus for the development of multi-faith chaplaincy with the political initiative and drive of New Labour.

NHS Chaplaincy Guidelines 2003

The New Labour government initiated certain steps to emphasise the role of religion and faith in society, believing that they play a crucial role in community cohesion, and to provide equality in health care provisions. This led to the convening of a multi-faith conference to address the agenda brought in by New Labour in 1998. The Secretary of State for Health attended this conference, thus making it high profile. It was clear from the start that a more inclusive and representative chaplaincy was at the heart of the government agenda. As a result, a Multi-Faith Joint National Working Party, representing the major world faith communities and NHS Chaplaincy organisations, emerged following the meeting in London. This established the beginning of the work towards the production of the NHS chaplaincy guidelines published in 2003: 'Meeting the religious and spiritual needs of patients and staff'. The work of the Multi-Faith Joint National Working Party ceased with it and the Multi Faith Group for Healthcare Chaplaincy (MFGHC) was launched on 23 June 2003. The purpose of the group was to develop multi-faith working, particularly to co-ordinate those activities required to ensure minority faith communities had the training and opportunity to become involved in chaplaincy work.

It became clear from the government's initiative that multi-faith chaplaincy was the focus, and the Anglican Church backed this evolution. It showed the government's commitment to social inclusion and chaplaincy bodies were keen to harness political support for the security and development of chaplaincy as a whole.

Writing the foreword for NHS Chaplaincy (2003), the Chief Nurse of England described the essence of the document as follows:

> *The cornerstone of the modern NHS is the ability to respond sensitively to the diverse nature of the communities it serves; all services, including spiritual ones, should be delivered appropriately to service users and NHS staff. One of the key aims of this guidance is to enable chaplaincy services to meet the needs of today's multi-cultural and spiritually diverse society.*

From this, it appears that the long tradition of a Christian domination of chaplaincy was giving way to a broader and more inclusive stage of development. This report also seems to place chaplaincy within the NHS, moving away from churches by 'allowing local management maximum scope to develop an appropriate multi-faith chaplaincy service for its Trust by making locally informed judgements about facilitation of chaplaincy delivery'. It offers guidance about providing spiritual care that is equal, just, humane and respectful. The guidelines also made a distinction between religion and spirituality:

> *Spiritual needs may not always be expressed within a religious framework. It is important to be aware that all human beings are spiritual beings who have spiritual needs at different times of their lives. Although spiritual care is not necessarily religious care, religious care, at its best, should always be spiritual.*

There is no doubt that the guidance engineered a new framework for chaplaincy by giving it its own identity and by locating it in health services, away from the dominance of any single creed or theology.

It has done justice by turning the attention of chaplains to minority faiths and by giving a clear definition to spirituality. The document ensured that 'these services develop to their full potential and maximise their utility for all' as mentioned in its introduction.

MFGHC did not have sufficient funding to establish its own independence, another factor contributing to the hindrance of the development of multi-faith chaplaincy. The governance of the group was under the influence of the group's chief officer who was concurrently the Chief Executive of the Hospitals Chaplaincies Council (HCC). The Chief Executive post was for an undefined period whereas the chair of the MFGHC changed every two years. As a result, the facilitation of the group by the HCC inevitably related more to the politics of chaplaincy, which had an upper hand.

> *The inception of the Multi-Faith Group can in this light be seen as an attempt to retain authority for chaplaincy through faith leadership, and re-assert the model of chaplain involvement via patronage. There is ample evidence that the English Multi-Faith Group has built to a significant degree on Anglican foundations - and this inevitably gives a certain shape to what is being constructed. (Swift, 2006).*

Swift further added that the HCC characterised its role in the creation of the group as one of facilitation and assistance, and living out of its social mandate as the Established Church. The research undertaken by Beckford and Gilliat (1996) further supported Swift's views, when they suggested that so long as the HCC underpinned the Multi-Faith

Group, it was likely that the progress of the group to develop an independent agenda would be severely curtailed.

The 2003 chaplaincy guidelines seemed to be comprehensive and representative guidelines, with multi-faith chaplaincy at its heart. In practice, they had a limited impact, as such a venture required committed policy, planning and protected funding, none of which existed. In reality, they proved to be incompatible with the nature of small faith communities due to their rigid interpretation by practitioners. The framework specified a formula for calculation of total chaplaincy/spiritual care provision in '*Annex 1*: Every 35 beds = one unit of chaplaincy-spiritual care'. This numerical criterion has been strictly applied by those in a position of recruiting staff, despite the guidelines stating that it represents guidance as opposed to a definitive statement. This particularly affected those smaller faith communities, mainly originating from the Indian subcontinent, who could not produce that figure in each Trust, and may not be able to meet this criterion even in the near future. This, in effect, has a negative impact on recruitment from BAME non-Christian communities, defeating the purpose and essence of the document in spite of it being an excellent document with political backing.

Sheikh and others conducted their research after the publication of the 2003 report, which was published in 2004. In their article headed 'The Myth of Multi-faith Chaplaincy', they revealed their findings based on the survey of 72 health care providers that the number of posts held by chaplains of faiths other than Christians were limited, with the exception of Muslim chaplaincy. They also found that the majority of chaplaincy and worship spaces seemed to be overwhelmingly Christian. The Church of England report (2010) also confirmed the findings of Sheikh and others. The situation has not changed a great deal since then. This view is supported by the fact that there were only two registered male Sikh chaplains, one in acute health and one in mental health (UKBHC register of accredited chaplains 2019). Another source suggests nine based on headcounts (NHS Digital, 2018). The official NHS data on chaplaincy workforce are rather unsatisfactory based on headcounts rather than specifying full or part-time.

This group (MFGHC) later changed its name to Healthcare Chaplaincy Faith and Belief Group (HCFBG) with the aim of promoting and supporting religious, spiritual and pastoral care in NHS England. The Network for Pastoral, Spiritual & Religious Care in Health (NPSRCH) replaced the HCFBC in 2017, with similar aims to facilitate a common understanding of, and support for, chaplaincy amongst faith and belief communities, chaplaincy bodies and other providers of religious, spiritual and pastoral care. The group also claims to lend its support in capacity building for faith and belief communities through education, training and authorisation for their chaplains and volunteers.

NHS Chaplaincy Guidelines: Promoting excellence in pastoral, spiritual & religious care (2015)

The new *NHS Chaplaincy Guidelines: Promoting excellence in pastoral, spiritual & religious care* (2015) replace those published in

2003. These claim to provide a comprehensive description of good practice in chaplaincy care for the NHS in England. The guidelines recognise the development of chaplaincy in a range of specialities, including newly recognised communities, community chaplaincy, General Practice and in areas such as Paediatrics and Palliative care and chaplaincy staffing. Overall, they attempted to cover many areas such as raising awareness, importance of research and innovation, not only for improved practices, but also as a basis for commissioners to understand the benefits of spiritual care. The guidelines put much more emphasis on auditing needs and collecting data, which is good practice within any professional service.

The executive summary of the 2015 guidelines concludes that 'the document responds to changes in the NHS, society and the widening understanding of spiritual, religious and pastoral care'. It further suggests that 'in the light of the 2010 Equality Act, new guidance is provided for the care of patients and service users whatever their religion or belief' (p. 5). The introduction states towards the end of paragraph 4: 'but critically the experiences of patients and carers is enhanced by ensuring either religious or non-religious pastoral support is available' (p. 7). This suggestion seems to be mainly directed towards those with no faith. The guidelines also introduce the concept of appointing generic chaplains:

Allocating 3.75 hours per week of chaplaincy care for every 35 patients not identified with a particular faith or belief system. Posts relevant to this population are to be open to any

appropriately qualified chaplain of any recognised religion or
belief community that can effectively carry out the role. (p. 16).

The suggestion of appointing generic chaplains from other faiths is a step forward but is unlikely to happen in practice considering the numerical criterion of patients belonging to no faith as compared to minority faiths. This will make it hard to achieve the process of recruiting chaplains from minority faiths. It has been accepted that there is hardly any harmony between the recommendations and operational systems so far. Most recruiting managers have a rigid mindset on holding to the numerical criterion in terms of recruiting staff. Secondly, generic chaplains are most likely to serve patients with no faith and the majority of them presumably being from Christian background and belonging. The author wonders if there is any data to support or prove that this has been put in practice since 2015.

The guidelines (2015) speak of the provision of high-quality care for all. They state that 'Chaplains are an essential resource for achieving the ambition to provide high quality care for all and promote the protected characteristics of both religion and belief' (p. 7). This appears to be a good approach if they can raise awareness and promote services for the protected characteristics of both religion and belief.

The guidelines further suggest:

Where requests for support relate to a particular religion or
belief the chaplaincy service should be able to access

appropriate support for the patient or service user and, when this cannot be matched, other chaplaincy support should be offered (7ᵗʰ bullet point p.9).

This suggests a good chaplaincy practice. The only visible statement made in the guidelines on minority faiths is:

The benefits of pooling resources within a locality and region are significant. Where smaller religion or belief communities would struggle to gain resources for chaplaincy in a given area, links with neighbouring regions - and the use of remote support - could enable isolated patients and service-users to be supported and valued. (p. 23)

This appears to be a good and practical solution for small and scattered communities. However, it is extremely hard to achieve in practice, especially in an environment of austerity.

The opening lines of the executive summary state: 'Local NHS trusts are responsible for determining, delivering and funding religious and spiritual care in a way that meets the needs of their patients, carers and staff' (2015, p. 5). This implies that local funding is provided for the local community as a whole, not only for assimilated religions. It is a general trend to consider that this funding is only for assimilated religions and their fringe services. There is an expectation to seek special funding to appoint staff from smaller faith communities rather than mainstreaming them. This is a discriminatory practice, potentially depriving people of their rights.

It must be embarrassing for the Trusts who claim their services are person-centred and value diversity.

The guidelines have a full page on volunteers in chaplaincy covering the role of volunteers, their relationship with chaplains and necessary requisites in selection, training, supervision and ongoing development. It further adds to how best practice for quality pastoral, spiritual and religious care provided by volunteers is achieved. (2015 p. 13). The guidelines add that: 'Many religion or belief groups, which are numerically small in the catchment area of a provider may also have volunteers serving in chaplaincy to provide advice and support for these communities. In some cases the latter may be referred to as "Honorary Chaplains" if their NHS training and status in their local belief or religious community matches the criteria for paid chaplaincy staff' (2015, p. 13). This page has given all sorts of necessary information for and around volunteers except progression into paid jobs particularly in the case of minority faiths.

The strength of the 2015 guidelines lies in the suggestions made in 'Chaplaincy Staffing' where some suggestions applicable to minority faiths are made. The opening line states that chaplaincy services should have adequate resources to carry out the work an employer requires. It further suggests that wherever possible, patients should have access to a chaplain of their own religion or belief to ensure appropriate pastoral, spiritual or religious care. It also touched upon an important area of data collection about the religion or beliefs of patients, which according to the guidelines, is both limited and frequently inaccurate. The guidelines state:

> In order to fulfil the Public Sector Equality Duty health care organisations should make every effort to request and record information about the religion or belief of service users and patients. Audits to verify the accuracy of this data, check users' awareness that chaplaincy is available to them, and monitor the quality of experience and any agreed religious, spiritual or pastoral outcomes. This will enhance an organisation's ability to demonstrate that it is meeting the Equality Duty (2015 p. 14).

It is important to collect data and it has an enormous effect not only on staff appointments but also on spiritual assessment. There is hardly any mention of whose responsibility it is.

The NHS England Chaplaincy Guidelines 2015: Equality Analysis

The NHS England Chaplaincy Guidelines 2015: Equality Analysis is a review document, first published on 6th March 2015, ensuring the compliance of the new guidelines with the Equality Act 2010 and the Public Sector Equality Duty. It is also to confirm that due regard is given in advancing equality for people belonging to certain protected characteristics, including religion and belief. The review document was developed by engaging with key stakeholders and using census data, the British Social Attitudes survey 2013, and research on religious and non-religious identification. The document has a review summary and recommendations for the guidance of future consultation.

The smaller faith communities are covered by the term 'multi-faith'. The Equality Analysis review document agrees with the guidelines when it relates 'the guidelines set out a framework for the provision of multi-faith and belief spiritual and pastoral support that is expected to have a positive impact on the wellbeing and recovery for people with either religious or non-religious beliefs using NHS services' (2015 p.14).

The Equality Analysis made good suggestions:

No data has been provided on numbers of chaplains by religion or belief. This data should be collected and made available in the revised guidelines as part of the review. This will ensure that the needs of patients by religion or faith are aligned to the available workforce. (p.15)

The review summary of analysis also suggests: 'Taking steps to meet the needs of people from protected groups where these are different from the needs of other people' (2015 p. 22).

In the recommendation as part of the Equality Analysis review, 'the role of the chaplaincy service in arranging for and providing interpreters and communication support for people who have little or no English is made clearer' (2015, p. 23). It may be good practice for certain disabilities and for out-of-area minority faith populations where there may be a single or occasional patient from minority faiths. In general circumstances, it seems unfair for patients and their families, especially those at the point of serious diagnosis and near death, when people who need to express complex emotional experiences have to use an interpreter. It restricts the flow and they are not always able to express body language. It undermines the quality of chaplaincy services.

Finally, the review is aware of the concerns raised about the words 'chaplaincy' and 'chaplain' by many faiths other than Christianity and lately by the British Humanist Association (p. 24). These two words are inherently Christian and do not seem to comfortably fit into the present nature of British society. There is also another word, 'pastoral', frequently used in the chaplaincy field. The words 'spiritual' and 'spirituality' can often be interpreted in different ways and many patients fail to grasp the real meaning, even when interpreted in their own spoken language. Therefore, spiritual and religious care may be better especially for the '*dharmic*' (faiths founded in the Indian sub-continent) communities.

Review Process

The NHS Chaplaincy guidelines published in 2015 had a commitment to review the guidelines. NHS employers circulated a national survey between July and September 2018 that asked respondents questions on the impact of the guidelines in terms of best practice, inclusiveness and alignment with organisational strategic and operational thinking. It was subsequently followed by two review workshops held in London (15th November 2018) and the other in Leeds (10th December 2018).

The speakers were invited to analyse sections of the guidelines with the purpose of making revised guidelines more inclusive and in line with the equality analysis, to make the guidelines more patient/service user and staff focussed, and to educate on how to use the future guidelines as a strategic tool that helps to support the 10-year NHS plan. An additional workshop on minority faiths was also organised in London on 20th February 2019 to hear the experience and views of volunteers belonging to minority faiths. The most sensible suggestion was that instead of using the formulas set out in the guidelines, efforts should be focussed on following a multi-faith, team-centred model of chaplaincy, and going beyond numbers and representation. As a result, the 'Healthcare Chaplaincy Review Recommendations' were prepared by the NHS Employers in 2019.

Healthcare Chaplaincy Guidelines Review Recommendations (March 2019)

Three years after the publication of the 2015 guidelines, NHS employers were commissioned to work with partners and stakeholders including NHS chaplains and managers to review the impact of the guidelines. They were also tasked with suggesting ways of revising the guidelines in order to help to improve support for the hospital community in the NHS. The main purpose was to help to review the existing guidelines and address whether the best practice outlined in the guidelines was up to date and fit for purpose; to understand and address how organisations have integrated growing equality considerations within healthcare chaplaincy and to identify where more work needs to be undertaken to address inequalities of provision; to share and to learn about best practice in the field of healthcare chaplaincy that could be considered for inclusion in the proposed revised guidelines and to develop recommendations to support a revision/rewrite/refresh of the future guidelines (2019, p. 3). The review process definitely had a wider consultation.

The review highlighted the need to undertake further work to engage chaplains of all backgrounds as well as other key stakeholders in the system who can play a crucial role in (a) integrating future guidelines into their work; (b) supporting the delivery of chaplaincy within the NHS; (c) influencing the chaplaincy profession; and (d) looking at ways of integrating the impact of chaplaincy services within the governance processes of the NHS – including the inspection processes of the Care Quality Commission (CQC) (Review, p. 4). The process of the review has also highlighted the lack of consensus on the language and terminology and a wide divergence of views on even some of the most fundamental terms involving the chaplaincy guidelines (Ibid, p.4). Key themes reflect a convergence around the language used in the guidelines and other barriers such as defining some terminology and accommodating minority faiths and belief/non-belief groups within these definitions to its effective implementation (ibid pp. 4-5).

The key finding from the survey is that the word 'chaplaincy' being rooted in religion may be preventing non-religious patients from accessing the chaplaincy services. There is also a strong view that the term 'chaplaincy' being associated with the Christian religion is deterring minority faiths from accessing chaplaincy services. It is felt that the language of the guidelines puts emphasis on religiosity even though the guidelines mentioned that the term chaplaincy is used for convenience.

The review survey suggested that the guidelines are unclear as to whose responsibility it is to record and audit patients' religious, pastoral and belief information. The ambiguity of ownership could affect the pursuit of accurate data on patients' faith and beliefs. There was also a feeling that where accurate data is obtained, the smooth transfer of this information to chaplaincy services, even on the patient's request, could arguably be prevented or hindered by the Data Protection Act and other related regulations (ibid pp. 5-6).

The survey data disclosed that a large number of respondents had limited knowledge of the content and implementation strategy of the Chaplaincy Guidelines. The survey also had a similar response on the question of how confident respondents were that their organisations had integrated key findings from the equality analysis document. They were clearly not confident on whether there existed an action plan or strategy to support mainstreaming of the guidelines. For the details and percentage of responses see p. 6 of the review.

The above-mentioned points heavily influence minority faiths, therefore they are discussed in detail. The majority of responses on the remaining contents of the guidelines as mentioned in the survey are concerned with developing the best practices in chaplaincy services.

Recommendations of the Review

There are specific recommendations provided for each section of the existing guidelines. In addition, there are general recommendations addressing key equality considerations such as integration of equality analysis within future revised healthcare chaplaincy guidelines, mainstreaming healthcare chaplaincy guidelines within existing NHS enablers and promoting the importance of service improvement, staff and patient voice within the healthcare chaplaincy guidelines and finally, recommendations of a 'Long-term Plan' for system leaders. The general recommendations followed a bottom to top approach.

Specific Recommendations

These are read with the lens of belonging to minority faiths. The author has added comments where it seems necessary and has left out some sections as they are concerned with chaplaincy as a profession or general chaplaincy services. Sections b, c, g, h, i, j, k, l and m seem to be well covered.

1. Introduction section of the 2015 guidelines

Section a) This specifies that a clearer and broader understanding of the term 'chaplaincy' and the role of chaplains is required. It recommends changing the title 'chaplaincy' due to its strong religious connotation, closely associated with Christianity in an attempt to make the service accessible to the wider community. This should be mindful to retain the name of the profession and also needs to address the breadth of what chaplaincy engages in, such as cultural care and existential care. This recommendation is close to the hearts of minority faiths as discussed in the chapter under Sikh chaplaincy.

Section d) The recommendations are much needed on chaplaincy endorsement as there is a need for NHS organisations to have in place clear and proactive procedures and processes around endorsing chaplains through their respective faith communities, also defining subjective terms like 'good standing'.

Section f) This section is much more relevant to minority faiths and belief/non-belief communities. There are terms and terminology which are either alien or vague for minority faiths. The terms chaplain, chaplaincy and pastoral care are alien to non-Christian communities, also 'spiritual care' (not the word as much as its vagueness and uncertainty in interpreting the term) and 'generic' need clarification. Consideration of 'person-centred' as opposed to religion focussed is good to follow, but there are *dharmic* traditions, whose caring needs revolve around religion and culture, and spirituality is an inbuilt part of their *dharam.* Religion is not to be used as a tool to promote religion, though religious essence and culture are the main means for caring for human emotions in *dharmic* traditions. There is a concern about the use of 'generic' in chaplaincy services. This section has made some good points on how chaplaincy becomes understood as a service for people of all faiths and beliefs (2019, p.10).

Section i) This is related to chaplaincy and equality and covers many diversities including religion and belief.

Section k) This focuses on out-of-area and general provision for people of minority faiths and belief/non-belief groups, recommending that future guidelines encourage organisations to have clear procedures in place that outline how they proactively plan and manage service provision to help support people of minority faiiths and belief /non-belief groups.

2. Patient and Service User care, equality, safety and compassion

This covered many areas applicable to general chaplaincy services though three of them are particularly relevant to minority faiths e.g. (e) spirituality and pastoral care, (f) out of area minority faith/non-religious faith provision, and (i) equality and inequalities (2019 pp. 13-14). The author argues that the future guidelines have to be conscious that the provision should go beyond volunteers for maintaining equality and quality, and every city should make provisions to appoint at least one qualified chaplain from each minority faith community on proportionate hours if not full-time, preferably discarding the numerical criterion of 35 beds from the chaplaincy funding.

3. Staff and Organisational Healthcare Support: informed, competent and critical

Sections a) on role definition and b) on chaplaincy department and definitions are relevant to minority faiths. It is important to involve someone with professional and practical experience from a minority background to participate and contribute. Definitions always influence the outcomes.

4. Key Components for an Effective Chaplaincy Service

The points discussed are covered in other places.

5. Volunteers in chaplaincy

Volunteers mainly deliver chaplaincy services to minority faiths at present in many NHS Trusts. Training and diversity as mentioned in this section are good and relevant. It is important and also timely to discuss how to promote volunteers from minority faiths to enter the profession and for those keen to own it, to encourage, support and give opportunities to professionalise them. This is much more important not only for enhancing the chaplaincy service, but also for preparing resources and getting the opportunities to become professional in order to have an informed discussion at policy levels.

6. Chaplaincy Staffing (Acute Care, Mental Health, General Practice, Specialist Palliative Care, Specialist Paediatric Care, Community Care

These areas and 24/7 chaplaincy provision demand competent services and time to learn and develop in these areas. There is a limit to what volunteers from minority faiths can contribute especially when they are not given opportunities to develop. Careful consideration is needed for minority faiths as there is a comparatively growing number of old people in these communities and some of them have complex needs.

The rest of the review is for general chaplaincy practices, also covering different organisations connected with chaplaincy services.

The review definitely picked up some unresolved issues along with others that need further improvement and made recommendations to enhance the services in compliance with the Equality Act 2010. The outcome depends on the future guidelines and their implementation in practice. The first two guidelines failed to improve the situation for minority faiths because of operational inefficiency to comply with the recommendations of the guidelines.

Fit for the Twenty-First Century? Inclusion and Equality Report

Fit for the Twenty-First Century?, a report produced by the Network for Pastoral, Spiritual and Religious Care in Health (NPSRCH) in 2020, aims to promote and support high quality, person-centred pastoral, spiritual and religious (PSR) care services across the NHS in England that are easily applicable in other healthcare settings. This is the first document outside the guidelines to ensure the development of services that meet the need of an increasingly diverse society with a particular focus on communities with belief or no belief and minority faith communities.

This report has picked up the root cause of appointing staff from the under-represented groups by NHS managers in their recommendation: 'staffing ratios in PSR teams should be brought in line with NHS England 2015 Guidelines and an appropriate level of funding provided to advance equality of opportunity for under-represented groups' (2020, p. 11). It has to be seen whether this will be applied to all deprived groups or just to groups of belief and no beliefs, being predominantly Christian.

The 2015 Chaplaincy Guidelines and the Equality Analysis Review followed by the Healthcare Chaplaincy Review Recommendations (2019) and the NPSRCH report (2020) have provided enough information to NHS England to revise, rewrite or refresh future guidelines which are fair, patient-centred and inclusive with a view to having long-term influence.

Chaplaincy in Sikhism

Suffering from illness or disease is a common human experience which makes individuals dependent on others. Individuals, communities and faith groups respond in a variety of ways in order to care for and support ailing individuals or groups. The Sikh faith has emphasised the caring of the sick, wounded, poor and vulnerable since its origin in the late 15th century. This core value of looking after the sick and needy was practiced by the Sikh *gurus* and became an accepted Sikh tradition. They took initiatives, introduced new projects to care for the sick and vulnerable, and encouraged their followers to participate. Sikh volunteers (*sevadars*) gave them pastoral care by being present, listening, giving patients support and fulfilling their physical and spiritual needs.

Contributions of Sikh *gurus:* The second Sikh *guru,* Angad Dev (1539-1552) was famous as a healer of incurable diseases. He outlined the daily routine for Sikhs and instructed them on how to carry it out (*GGS,* pp.305-306), giving Sikhs a disciplined way to help improve their health and spirituality introducing preventive care. He also encouraged physical recreation aimed at maintaining good health and a healthy lifestyle (Singh and Singh, 1989). *Guru* Amar Das (1552-1574), the third Sikh *guru*, created a remedy centre by growing medicinal plants to give herbal treatment to the ill and suffering. They were cared for under his supervision and were fed from the common community kitchen. The fifth *Guru* Arjun Dev (1581-1606), opened an asylum for lepers at Tarn Taran (Punjab), treating and caring for people suffering with leprosy

(Singh and Singh 1989) and those severely affected by infectious diseases. The seventh *Guru* Har Rai (1644-1661) took a great deal of interest in healthcare. He had a good knowledge of herbs (Singh, 2010), and opened a hospital and dispensary at Kiratpur (Punjab) where medicines and treatment were given free of charge. The eighth *Guru* Har Krishan (1661-1664) was known as the healer of the sick. He devoted his life to looking after the sick and the poor. The *Guru* kept himself busy at Delhi (the capital city of India) healing people suffering from a smallpox epidemic at risk to his own life (Khokhar, 2002; Singh 2010). During the period of the tenth *Guru* Gobind Singh (1666-1708), an incident took place. *Bhai* Kainahya, a devout Sikh, was on duty to give first aid and drinking water to the wounded in the battle between Mughal forces and Sikhs. Some Sikh soldiers complained to the *Guru* that he was nursing and giving water to the enemy soldiers. As a result, he was brought before *Guru* Gobind Singh and was charged for helping the enemy. In response to the charges, he explained to the *Guru* that he saw no "Mughals or Sikhs there, but saw the Guru's face everywhere" (Singh, 1985, pp.99-100). He further added that the *Guru* was fighting the enemy and he was destroying the roots of enmity, thus introducing the concepts similar to those of the Red Cross. The *Guru* was pleased with him and blessed him for his true spirit of service to humanity not to discriminate between friend and foe when treating the ill or wounded, giving water to the thirsty and food to the hungry.

Caring in the Sikh community: Caring for the sick thus became a firm Sikh tradition. Many *gurdwaras* (Sikh places of worship) in

India have hospitals and dispensaries attached to them, giving free medical care to those who are in need and cannot afford it. There are many specialist hospitals attached to *gurdwaras* for infectious and chronic diseases, run by donations mainly from the Sikhs. Volunteers (*sevadars*) who listen to the patients and provide religious care to in-patients visit charitable specialist hospitals run by *gurdwaras*. At home, traditionally, families or relatives take care of the physical and spiritual needs of the sick, old and vulnerable. Family play a dominant role and the ultimate onus of caring falls on the family, with the decisions made by the family for patient care. The situation in the West and India has different pathways.

The structure of healthcare in India is different from that of the UK. Healthcare is not a nationalised service in India. There are hospitals funded by the government, private hospitals run by individuals or groups of doctors, and free hospitals run by religious bodies and charitable trusts. Modern healthcare chaplaincy as it has developed and is understood and structured in Britain, does not yet exist in the Punjab (India) where Sikhs come from.

Sikhism, health and illness

Sikhs came to Britain from India mainly in the 1960s and from East Africa in the 1970s. The structure of healthcare in India and East Africa is different from that of the UK. They were not acquainted with the NHS, and its facilities were new to them. When they were seriously ill or dying, they wanted the *gurdwara granthi or bhai* (priest) to pray for them. The NHS did not have any such in-house facility and hospitals in the earlier days met their demands through *gurdwara granthi* (priest) or religious leaders, depending on their availability. The *granthis* had no experience of providing chaplaincy services like ordained priests and ministers' in Christianity, and their job description did not include pastoral duties and hospital visits. Sikh patients had to pay for their services when they came to pray in the hospitals. The main problems were that it was difficult to get hold of them and there were, and still are, language barriers, as many *granthis* are not fluent in English to properly engage with hospital staff and do not have sufficient knowledge of hospital bureaucracy. They had no concept of chaplaincy services and were not acquainted with hospital protocols and procedures. There are still families who ask for a *granthi* from a particular *gurdwara* to perform *Ardas* (supplication). This was happening partly from their own tradition of asking a *granthi* to pray, and partly through the lack of awareness of this service in hospitals, which did not exist until recently.

Chaplaincy, being a Christian oriented word, is difficult to grasp and understand by Sikhs. They associate this service with Christian patients, and do not think it is for everyone in the hospital. This does not imply that they are unaware of spiritual care and its significance. A positive development for the Sikh community that came out of the Multi Faith Group for Healthcare Chaplaincy was the setting up of the UK Sikh Healthcare Chaplaincy Group (SHCG) in 2005. It is a registered charity and its mission statement is: 'To provide services to both the Sikh community and to chaplaincy departments across the NHS and within hospices'. Its services include guidance on patient-related care, patient advocacy, training and authorisation. The group became effective mainly in raising chaplaincy awareness in the Sikh community through media and national prayer days, recruiting, training and authorisation of volunteers. There remains a need for professionalisation and for the group to become an active voice for advancing Sikh chaplaincy. At present, Sikh volunteers are the main source of service delivery and they work in isolation, with hardly any supervision or resources.

The words chaplaincy and chaplain are generally understood to have a Christian connection being related to Christian churches and their ordained priests. The 2015 guidelines used the term spirituality as a blanket coverage for spiritual, pastoral and religious care and also gave this profession a neutral term, departing from the domination of any particular religion and empowering the NHS to make its own decision. There is no appropriate word or term in Panjabi which can capture the essence of the terms 'chaplain' and 'chaplaincy', though the Sikh Healthcare Chaplaincy Group (SHCG) suggested using *'rogi asara'* (supporting the sick or supporter of the sick). It is good term for a support worker but not necessarily for chaplains, chaplaincy visitors and volunteers. This term is only applicable to a patient, ignores the rest of the hospital community, and is unable to capture the full extent of a chaplain's work. Therefore, it is suggested using 'Sikh *ruhani carer*' (Sikh spiritual carer or caregiver) as it makes the distinction between the *granthi* and the chaplain, and it encompasses the hospital community and covers much of the chaplain's work. The Sikh volunteers can be called 'Sikh ruhani *niskam sevak'*. Chaplaincy can be interpreted as '*Dharmic* and *Atmic dekhbhal or Dharmic and adhyatmic dekhbhal'*. Sikh patients also struggle to grasp the meaning of pastoral care. It can be termed as compassionate care (*Rehamdil Dekh bhal*). Most Panjabi terms used in this book are given in Appendix 1.

Conclusion

Sikh volunteers are the main source of delivering chaplaincy services at present. There is a need to appoint qualified Sikh chaplains and to promote those volunteers interested and committed to this profession. They should be encouraged to participate in research projects in order to create resources and the NHS should allocate funding to appoint chaplains from minority faiths. In the absence of that extra funding, recruitment managers have the responsibility to serve the whole community, and not only majority communities. The NHS allocate funding to the Trust to care for their local community. The accepted numerical criterion should not be applied to these posts as long as the applicants are qualified. This will give minority faiths the opportunity to enter and develop further within the profession through training, learning and supervision. It has become necessary with the changing nature of British society to consider an alternative neutral term for chaplain, chaplaincy and pastoral which could easily be accepted and adopted by the majority. Other terms such as 'multi-faith' and 'generic' need to have standard definitions leaving little capacity for varying interpretations and understandings.

References

Autton, N. (1966). *The Hospital Ministry*. London: Church information Office.

Beckford, J.A. and Gilliat-Ray, S. (1996). *The Church of England and other faiths in a multi faith society*. Warwick 1996.

Church of England (1951). *Health Care Chaplaincy and the Church of England: A review of the work of the Hospital Chaplaincies Council*. London 2010. Report CA 1003, 1951.

Cobb, M. (2005). *The hospital chaplain's handbook: a guide for good practice*. Norwich: Canterbury Press.

Guru Granth Sahib (n.d.). Amritsar: *Shiromani Gurdwara Prabandhak* Committee.

Khokhar, K. S. (2002). *Essays on Sikh values*. USA Chester: Khokhar Publishers.

NHS Chaplaincy (2003*). Meeting the religious and spiritual needs of patients and staff: Guidance for managers and those involved in the provision of chaplaincy/spiritual care.* London: Department of Health.

NHS Chaplaincy Guidelines (2015). *Promoting excellence in pastoral, spiritual & religious care* prepared by Chris Swift in consultation with the Chaplaincy Leaders Forum (CLF) and Health Inequalities Team. London: NHS England.

NHS Employers (2019). Healthcare Chaplaincy review Recommendations. v. 4. March 2019 pp. 19.

Orchard, H. (2000). *Hospital chaplaincy: modern, dependable?* Sheffield: Sheffield Academic Press.

Savage, D. (2019). *Non-Religious pastoral care*. London: Routledge.

Sheikh, A, Gatrad, A.R., Rashid, A, Sheikh, U., Panesar, S. S. and Shafi, S. (2004). The myth of multi faith chaplaincy: A national survey of hospital chaplaincy departments in England and Wales. *Diversity in Health and social Care* 1: 2 (2004), pp. 93-98.

Singh, H. (1985). *The heritage of Sikhs*. New Delhi: Manohar Publications.

Singh, S. (2010). *The Sikhs in history*. Amritsar: Singh Brothers.

Singh, T. & Singh, G. (1989). *A short history of the Sikhs*. Patiala: Publication Bureau.

Swift, C. (2006). The political awakening of contemporary chaplaincy. *Journal of Health Care Chaplaincy* 7: 1 (2006), pp. 57-62.

Swift, C. (2009). *Hospital chaplaincy in the twenty-first century*. Surrey: Ashgate.

Swift, C. (2014). *Hospital chaplaincy in the twenty-first century: The crisis of spiritual care on the NHS*. 2nd ed. Surrey: Ashgate.

Todd, A. (2011). Responding to diversity: Chaplaincy in a multi-faith context. In: Threlfall-Holmes, M. and Newitt, M. (2011) *Being a chaplain*. London: SPCK.

Wilson, M. (1971). *The hospital - A place of truth*. Birmingham: University of Birmingham.

Websites

Association of Hospice and Palliative Care Chaplains (2003). *Competences, standards, and code of conduct*. [online] Available at: http://www.ahpcc.co.uk/employment/chaplaincy-standards/ [Accessed 31 July 2018].

Changing Horizons (2018). *Idi Amin's Expulsions of Asians*. [online] Available at: https://www.changing-horizons.com/the-expulsion-of-the-asians/ [Accessed 23 June 2018].

Gov.uk (1952). *Prison Act*. [online] Available at: http://www .legislation.gov.uk/ukpga/Geo6and1Eliz2/15-16/52/contents [Accessed 24 June 2018].

Gov.uk (2012). *Health and Social Care Act 2012*. [online] Available at: http://www.legislation.gov.uk/ukpga/2012/7/contents/enacted [Accessed 19 Mar. 2018].

Interfaith (2018) *Interfaith Network*. [online] Available at: https://www.interfaith.org.uk/ [Accessed 24 June 2018].

NHS England (2015) *NHS England Chaplaincy Guidelines 2015 Promoting Excellence in Pastoral, Spiritual and Religious Care: Equality Analysis.* [online] Available at: https://www.england .nhs.uk/wp-content/uploads/2015/03/nhs-chaplaincy-guidelines-2015.pdf [Accessed 31 July 2018].

Network for Pastoral, Spiritual and Religious care in Health (2020) *Fit for the twenty-first century?* [online] Available at: http://dharmic web.com/network-health.org/documents/NPSPCH_report_web.pdf [Accessed 16 Mar. 2020].

UKBHC (2018) *UKBHC register of accredited chaplains.* [online] Available at: https://www.ukbhc.org.uk/for-the-public/the-register/ [Accessed 16 July 2018].

UK SHCG (2018) *Sikh Chaplaincy.* [online] Available at: www.sikhchaplaincy.org.uk/. [Accessed 31 July 2018].

Chapter 5

Role of a healthcare chaplain – skills and competencies

Introduction

This chapter outlines who a chaplain is, as well as the values, roles and responsibilities of a chaplain. It also draws attention to the knowledge, experience, skills and competencies that underpin the chaplain's role, drawing particular attention to the shared skills and competencies needed to deliver religious, spiritual and pastoral care to become a competent chaplain to work in an environment of multi-faith chaplaincy, serving diversities of faith and no faith. It also covers what and how Sikh chaplains and volunteers can contribute to the development of spiritual care in NHS hospitals and hospices. It further describes the chaplain's role as faith advisor for patients, families, hospital staff and the NHS. It gives information on ward etiquettes and hospital management, information governance and multi-disciplinary care.

Chaplains and their values

A chaplain is a healthcare professional who works as part of a team based in a chaplaincy department in hospitals or within a healthcare setting, such as in hospices, to provide or facilitate spiritual, religious and pastoral care to patients, staff, family and carers. Chaplains also work in the community and provide services according to the identified needs of the service users. It is person-centred holistic care, given in an ethical way that respects people's diversity, values and beliefs, whilst maintaining their privacy, dignity and confidentiality. Chaplains contribute to holistic care by working with multidisciplinary teams.

Joan Ashton suggests chaplaincy is a work of dedication and compassion to fulfil the needs of individuals. Chaplains offer spiritual care to patients of all faiths and none and the hospital community. Chaplains enter into the life of patients by their willingness to share deep feelings, fear and spiritual pain (Ashton, 2011). Ashton in her definition makes three points very clear; that their ministry is to those of all faiths and none; it is person-centred care that is offered; and that chaplains enter the service user's space with his or her consent to alleviate their spiritual pain.

Values: Chaplains value that spiritual well-being and pastoral care are important in promoting health and healing as an integral part of holistic care. It is important to make clear the meaning of spirituality as used within this context: faiths and beliefs are an essential part of spirituality, including the beliefs and values of those with no faith. It has become a blanket term for pastoral, spiritual and religious care according to the 2015 national guidelines for chaplaincy.

The role of the hospital chaplain

There are a number of sources which describe the role of a chaplain. Since the advent of the NHS in 1948, the primary role of a chaplain has been widely accepted as meeting the pastoral, spiritual and religious needs of the hospital community. The role of the chaplain depends largely upon the type of healthcare organisation, the nature of its services, the aims of the chaplaincy department and the overall direction of the NHS Trust. Chaplains work in different capacities and grades, which determine their role. Other influential factors shaping a chaplain's role and practice are the chaplain's own knowledge, skills, beliefs and faith tradition. Chaplains have managerial roles, responsibility for ensuring corporate governance and human resource policies, delivering a cost-effective service, meeting the overall aims of the Trust, appointing and managing the chaplaincy team, managing the department's strategy and service development, and liaising with local and faith communities to ensure their engagement and participation in the life of the hospital and the chaplaincy department.

Mark Cobb explains:

The basic role of the chaplain is to collaborate with other health professionals in the provision of holistic care focussed on the whole person and not only the person's physical health. It includes social, emotional and spiritual health and overall well-being of a person. This is an ethical and skilled practice that challenges the alienation and isolation of illness, affirms humanity and nurtures hope. (2005, p.14)

Cobb, in his definition, draws attention to person-centred holistic care in which the chaplain plays a significant role. He also suggests that the role of a chaplain is ethical and requires skilled practices.

In practice, the role of the chaplain can be summarised in the following generic key tasks:

- The key role of hospital chaplain is the task of accompanying people through times of transition (Newitt, 2010). It means offering hope of transformation, facilitating a journey of exploration or helping to find nurturing and rejuvenation. Newitt further adds, 'Within healthcare, the chaplain's context is that of change – supporting people as they are restored to health, adapt to impaired physical function, or come to terms with their own or a loved one's mortality' (Threlfall-Holmes and Newitt, 2011, p.105). Chaplains provide spiritual, pastoral, and religious care to the hospital community (patients, their families and carers, visitors and staff) and not only to patients.

- Chaplains meet religious needs, when requested, by planning and conducting religious ceremonies, life-cycle rites and rituals. The request comes mainly from the patient and sometimes from the family or other carers. There is an added advantage of appointing Sikh chaplains. They can provide religious care and conduct religious rites and rituals, as Sikhism does not have a standard form of priesthood. The purpose of healthcare chaplaincy in hospitals and hospices is to give spiritual care according to the patient's needs, thus contributing to holistic care. Manzano, Swift, Closs and Briggs (2015) found in their recent research the perception that chaplains may persuade patients to join a religious group, and chaplaincy volunteers experience this on a daily basis. They also perceive chaplaincy as a representation of the power of religious institutions: their experiences of such organisations translate into a fear of being judged. Chaplains need to be cautious of this.

- Chaplains provide support and care for the end of life and to the bereaved family. Most people end their lives in hospital, and their families or carers need support at those critical moments to face the death of their loved ones, and to deal with its consequences, such as planning the funeral (Cobb, 2005). Chaplains conduct funerals as and when requested as a part of the service offering. Sikh patients and families need special care at this time and the presence of a Sikh chaplain is essential to give them good care and full support. Chaplains plan and conduct worship and prayers and manage memorial events.

- Chaplains respond to referrals within the given timescale as set by the Trust or hospice.

- Chaplains act as faith advisors on faith perspectives concerning issues that arise from time to time in healthcare, such as abortion, IVF, organ donation and blood transfusion. The chaplain serves as a resource for those addressing the complex ethical issues in which they are involved.

- Chaplains participate in case conferences regarding patients and/or any areas of concern. There is a particular need for Sikh chaplains/volunteers to participate in this area as some Sikh patients lack confidence and have communication problems. It will help and enable them to make informed decisions.

- Chaplains contribute to service development that is responsive to the needs of patients by being sensitive to healthcare changes. Chaplains also contribute to service reviews, clinical audit and problem solving. This is an area where Sikh volunteers can make invaluable contributions.

- Chaplains also participate in training programmes, learning opportunities and research activities for their own professional development. Working in teaching hospitals brings with it the responsibility to ensure that there is an engagement with the continuing development of healthcare and its provision. It is one of the criteria to satisfy the requirements of the UK Board of Healthcare chaplaincy and the NHS Knowledge and Skills Framework (Simpson, Collin and Okeke, 2014). The chaplaincy team is therefore committed to the training and development programmes of the Trust and engages in research. 'Research has not always been the remit of the chaplain. However, evidence-based practice within the NHS means that chaplaincy must engage with the research agenda' (Simpson, Collin & Okeke, 2014). Self-development is particularly in the interest of Sikh chaplains and volunteers.

It is in their own interest to grow in the profession, taking advantage of chaplaincy courses and any ongoing training. Research is much needed to create resources, and there is a lot of scope for research within Sikh chaplaincy.

- Chaplains have a role in recruitment, training, mentoring and supervision of volunteers and students on placement. Some chaplains have the responsibility of coordinating outside use of religious resources in hospitals and hospices. Sikh volunteers can be quite helpful in coordinating outside resources for healthcare organisations.

- Chaplains have a role of being a link between the hospital and the faith community, faith leaders and the chaplaincy department. Sikh chaplains/volunteers can lend support to strengthen the bonds between their own faith community and hospital/hospice. It will help in raising awareness, building confidence and breaking barriers.

- Chaplains carry out some other specific responsibilities, such as making notes on patients, and recording information following hospital guidance after the visit. Other chaplains and healthcare professionals access these notes for follow-up or for emergency visits. They need to strictly follow the policy of confidentiality and information governance. The Data Protection Act 1998 (DPA) dictates how to maintain the records and their scope. The General Data Protection Regulations (GDPR) introduced in 2018 represent a significant change for organisations, including the NHS and hospices, which hold and process personal data. This has affected volunteers and honorary chaplains of minority faith communities including Sikhs, as they do not have access to patient records in the NHS. By denying this role to them, their contributions may go unrecognised. Hospices have much better arrangements where volunteers have access to notes and record their visits, with details of their interactions. It becomes much more important for those faith communities where the service relies upon volunteers. In fact, it helps in auditing the needs of the patients belonging to that faith community. Need identification is the very basis for structuring an effective service.

- Chaplains should be able to maintain the health, safety and security of themselves and others.

These are the general key tasks of a chaplain. However, chaplains also carry out some other specific responsibilities:

- Chaplains have a role of advocating on behalf of staff and patients. There are chaplains who support staff and are often involved in staff advocacy in certain services. The NHS is an organisation constantly undergoing change. Staff are not immune from the pressure that builds from working in such an environment. Chaplains support staff when they find themselves under pressure or facing disciplinary measures. On a routine basis, a chaplain provides formal and informal support, debriefs and reflects learning sessions following critical incidents.

- Chaplains have a role in myth-busting. There is a perception that a hospice is a place where people go to die. It is only a myth, as many go home with distressing symptoms alleviated (Blake, 2011). Some patients and hospital staff associate the presence of a chaplain with impending death. Some patients fear proselytisation when seeing a chaplain. Sikhs perceive a chaplain and chaplaincy as only for Christians, which of course is not true. In theory, it is for all communities.

- Sikh chaplain/volunteers can help and support the patients belonging to other minority faiths who share the similar culture and language. They can be helpful in working with other faith and belief communities, as respecting other faiths and beliefs is one of the main Sikh values.

- Chaplains play a significant role in collecting and building resources. All chaplains contribute to this process. They collect religious scriptures and prayer books. They collect books and journals on spiritual care, religious artefacts, prayer cards and cards for festivals of all faiths and occasions.

- Chaplains/volunteers from minority faiths, including Sikhism, not only perform chaplaincy duties, but also need to develop resources. They need to raise awareness in their own faith community in the manner most effective for them and to meet community expectations. There is much more to be done as

Sikh chaplaincy is not integrated within the chaplaincy provision and there is a desperate need for resources.

Ward etiquettes and hospital management

Chaplains need to have knowledge of hospital/hospice protocols and ward conventions, and the ability to equip themselves with some practicalities.

The NHS is a large hierarchical organisation. It helps a chaplain to know the ward etiquettes and to be acquainted with hospital management. Hospital departments, clinical areas and wards may have their own rules, hierarchy, procedures and routines. Chaplains often work in areas or spaces shared by other people, and in many cases, on other professionals' territory. It is essential for a chaplain/volunteer to respect, observe and follow the working practices of others in order to work with them harmoniously.

Clinical Areas: The primary task of chaplains is to work in clinical areas. They spend most of their time visiting wards. A new chaplain needs to be familiar with the basic rules and protocols of clinical areas to avoid any potential conflict. Clinical areas may differ in practices and hierarchy. Chaplains should be knowledgeable of major aspects such as ward etiquette, infection control, spiritual care assessment and multidisciplinary care, which they may have to address in a clinical setting, in addition to their own responsibility of spiritual, pastoral and religious care.

Ward etiquette: The traditional places in hospitals where patients are collectively cared for are wards. Wards differ in layout (standard wards have a combination of bays with four to six beds or single occupancy beds). Chaplains usually work on many wards. Wards have certain conventions, policies and protocols in order to ensure an efficient, safe and orderly environment for patients, their visitors and staff. It is essential for chaplains to know, understand and be sensitive to what is expected of them in terms of their behaviour and practice on a ward or clinical area. There may be generic conventions or a special ethos created by influential staff or a particular ethos of individual clinical areas. Ward etiquette is an accepted social behaviour on a ward that is about courtesy, good communication, respecting hierarchy and safe practice (Cobb, 2005). Ward etiquette is important for any chaplain to observe. The most important factor that relates to etiquette is hierarchy. Hierarchy establishes the level and scope of authority that individuals can exercise and identifies who is responsible for what. A senior nurse usually manages a ward, is responsible for all aspects of nursing and who, with nursing staff, co-ordinates the health and social care needs of patients. The senior nurse is often responsible for the many decisions about the day-to-day operation of a ward and can be a key member of staff to liaise with for a chaplain. It is a courtesy to introduce yourself and make your arrival on a ward known at the nurses' station. This will make staff aware of the presence of a chaplain/volunteer on the ward. It is also a good opportunity to make contact with nursing staff and to find out what is happening on the ward. For example, the doctors may be doing a ward round, or a patient might not be in bed, or may be undergoing a procedure or test. Otherwise, the chaplain could easily miss important information regarding the patient. If the chaplain has come to the ward in response to a referral or a follow-up of a specific patient or carer, then these cases should be discussed with the relevant nurse prior to seeing the patient. When a chaplain is carrying out a general ward round, it is an opportunity to find out from nurses if anyone has expressed the wish for contact with a chaplain. It also gives an opportunity to explore any risks and to assess the situation in order to take adequate precautions before making contact with patients, for example, wearing personal protective equipment. In particular, if the chaplain intends to administer any rituals, it is good practice to discuss things with the relevant health professional involved with the patient.

Ward visits: It is courteous for a chaplain to introduce him/herself to the patient, giving their name, what they do and the purpose of their visit. It is also helpful to the patient to explain how the service can be accessed. It is important to ask the patient if he/she is willing to talk to the chaplain and obtain their consent for future visits. Many Sikh patients do not know what a chaplain does. Those who have some vague idea equate a chaplain with a *gurdwara's gyani* (priest). It is a good practice to tell patients, families and carers what exactly a chaplain does in order to make them aware of this service.

Wards are busy places where a number of activities take place, such as mealtimes, visiting hours, and ward rounds by doctors and personal carers. Chaplains, like other healthcare professionals, go to visit patients. If any other healthcare professional is seeing the patient, the chaplain must not interrupt unless there is a pressing need for this. Similarly, other healthcare professionals without the same pressing need must not interrupt chaplains. When the curtains are drawn around the patient's bed, the chaplain should not enter in order to respect the privacy and personal space of the patient, unless expressed permission is sought from the patient, carer or nurse. It is also inappropriate to seek out patients in bathrooms and toilets. There are times when the patient is taken off the ward for diagnostic investigations, assessments, therapy and surgery. These are planned activities but may not always happen at scheduled times. It is good practice to leave a note of your visit for the patient when he/she is not in the bed. Chaplains should liaise with the relevant nurse or other staff if they want to see the patient at a particular time. A patient might want to see a chaplain alone or in the presence of family. It is therefore important for a chaplain to be sensitive to the patient's wishes and circumstances, including the right to decline chaplaincy contact and visits. Never insist or follow a patient around to talk. Be courteous to patients and let them know chaplains are there whenever they need them.

Infection control: Infection control is a priority in any healthcare organisation. There are all sorts of patients in hospitals and hospices. There is every possibility that patients can get an infection through different routes. Chaplains should be aware of infection control and must comply and adhere to its procedures.

Hand washing: Healthcare practitioners, including chaplains, can be a route for hospital-acquired infections for patients. Hands are frequently identified as the route of transmission in outbreaks of infection (Wilson, 2006), making it necessary for chaplains to wash their hands regularly to ensure effective hand hygiene. This requires chaplains to observe and strictly follow high standards of hand hygiene in clinical areas, whether it is a hospital or a hospice. It is difficult to predict or control what happens during an encounter with a patient. It could be direct contact with skin, food or any other equipment. The chaplain may have to touch or hold the patient's hand during bedside prayer, may have to hold a glass if the patient asks for water, or may have to move equipment to make space for him/herself. The best practice to follow is always wash your hands before and after contact with a patient, after using the toilet, and after cleaning up any spillage. Hospices are particularly keen to observe the handwashing policy strictly, and there are monitoring procedures in place to check the observance. The hand cleaning gel is available in all wards, normally attached to a wall near the entrance or placed over the sink, making it easily accessible. Chaplains must wash hands thoroughly using soap by rubbing palms, fingers, thumbs, and then drying with paper towels, decontaminating to a level sufficient for safe practice.

Chaplains must be bare below the elbow when working in clinical areas. The top or shirt should have short sleeves above the elbows to reduce the build-up of transient organisms on sleeves. The nails are to be kept short and clean without varnish (clear or coloured) or nail polish in order to avoid any possibility of infection. Wearing artificial nails is not allowed, as they discourage vigorous hand washing (Larson, 2001). It is important to cover any cuts and abrasions with a waterproof dressing before washing the hands.

The chaplains have to be careful not to wear watches and wrist jewellery such as bangles while visiting the ward. The need to remove the *kara* (steel bangle) by a Sikh chaplain or volunteer should be discussed with the manager. It is also important to remove jewellery (rings with stones or ridges) or any other hand and wrist jewellery. It is essential to wear shoes that are easy to wipe clean and which cover the feet properly.

Protective clothing: Chaplains must follow the procedures and instructions about infection control operating in a clinical area that is applicable to the general ward or for an individual infectious patient. Gloves, aprons and masks are used to reduce the transmission of microorganisms to patients and to protect staff from contamination by exposure to a patient's bodily fluids, secretions and excretions. The protective clothing must be discarded in a clinical waste bin immediately after the visit, and hands washed. The decision to use the protective clothing is made on risk assessment by the nursing staff or members of the infection control team. If a chaplain is not sure what to do or has any doubt, they should ask at the nursing station. Volunteers working in a hospital are not allowed to see infectious patients for their own safety. Chaplains must take special precautions when dealing with infectious patients, in terms of taking them for group prayers. It is always good to have this approved by a healthcare professional.

Similarly, if a written prayer is given to a patient, it should be a paper copy so that it can be discarded after use, especially for patients who are isolated for different reasons.

Information governance

Chaplains and volunteers are in a unique position to access all sorts of information regarding patients, their families and carers, staff and others involved. Maintaining confidentiality is key and most important for anyone working in a hospital, hospice or any other healthcare setting.

Confidentiality: It is crucial and ethical binding for any chaplain or volunteer to maintain confidentiality. A Sikh chaplain and volunteer has to be much more careful due to the nature of the numerically small community, where they know each other through social relationships and congregation. The chaplains and volunteers are not supposed to reveal the identity of any patient in the community or any other information regarding the patient and his/her family. Chaplains should never disclose confidential information over the telephone unless they are certain that they are speaking to the intended person. It is important to remember not to take confidential information home. If there is a need to dispose of any paper containing confidential information, the best way is to shred it or place it in a confidential waste bin. Make sure that confidential information is sent in a sealed or tamper proof envelope, marking it confidential if required. No personal identifiable data should be sent by email or through social media. Never give anyone's personal details outside the hospital or hospice and do not talk about or discuss any confidential information in public spaces. It should be ensured that drawers and filing cabinets are locked and that no confidential information is left on the table before leaving the room and computers are shut down when not used.

Chaplains in healthcare share with other professionals a commitment to promote wellbeing and to care for the ill and injured. Chaplains are committed to establishing how spiritual, pastoral and religious care can help patients in their most difficult times. In order to do this, they share common intellectual and practical interests and practices, making chaplaincy a distinctive discipline. Any discipline requires focusing on the development of particular skills and knowledge.

Skills and competencies

Chaplains in healthcare focus on spiritual care. It is essential for any discipline to concentrate on the development of particular skills and knowledge in order to develop and promote good practices to comply with the set standards.

- Chaplains need specialist skills to acquire a wide range of information and knowledge of medical related work and terminology. Chaplaincy can also benefit from a basic understanding of relevant aspects of the clinical sciences, including an understanding of common medical terminology, major disease processes, diagnostic investigations, common types of therapies and patient management.

- It helps them to have experience of their own religion/faith and an open-minded approach to religious variations and other faiths in order to function harmoniously and effectively.

- It is important for chaplains to have effective communication skills in order to converse with individuals and groups. Good conversation makes a huge impact on patients and service development. Chaplains from the minority faiths need to have the language skills of their own scripture and the community they serve. The ability of reading, writing and speaking the language helps them to connect with the community, as well as to understand their culture and traditions to make sense of their stories. It is also necessary for chaplains from minority faiths to have good communication skills in English.

Shared skills and competencies

There are some shared skills and competencies for pastoral and spiritual carers which are mentioned here rather than repeating them in other chapters. These are active listening, listening to patients' stories and interacting with them, being present, reflecting skills and reflective practice. It is helpful to possess spiritual, religious and cultural competencies in the present environment.

Ward visits

Chaplains spend much of their time routinely visiting patients on the wards, knowing their well-being and listening to their anxieties and concerns. Ward visits are essential for religious, spiritual and pastoral care. These visits are the very basis of spiritual care requiring specific skills to operate effectively.

Active listening: This is the most powerful tool in gaining the trust of the patient. Listening has a specific purpose for chaplains. It helps them to go deeper into the patient's private space, accompanied by compassion. It is a powerful skill to gain trust and form a relationship with the patient by showing empathy and unconditional positive regard. It helps them to make sense of what patients are saying by capturing their own words to discern their needs. This requires attentive listening, listening to what and how they feel. Lartey rightly suggests: 'It is much more complex than the "just listening" of everyday conversation, listening openly and permitting the other person to be what they are, freely, without controlling, coercing or censoring what they say' (2003, p.90). Lartey further adds: 'The essential features of active listening are: look and be interested, inquire with open questions, stay alive to the speaker, test your understanding by checking, empathize and neutralize your feelings' (Lartey, 2003, p.91). Brayne and Fenwick suggest some good rules of listening that can help one to open up communication. Their suggestions are to be respectful, be honest and try to understand the patients' body language. While listening to patients, it is important for chaplains to concentrate on patients, putting his/her own thoughts aside, and to stay calm (2008, p.13). They further add how to converse with patients, and for that they suggest using open questions (how, when, where, who, what and why), direct and indirect questions, leading questions (If you become really ill, would you like me to sit with you?) and using short sentences (2008, p.14). Kidd suggests:

Effective listening and responding entail absorbing what the speaker says and then offering it back in order to bring the dialogue to a deeper level. Such transformative listening involves attending to the entirety of the speaker's message, hearing the speaker's words, and discerning the emotions behind them (2014, p. 92).

Skilled active listeners not only listen to the words, but also pay attention to body language, non-verbal cues and gestures. Highlen and Hill (1984) suggested that nonverbal behaviour regulates conversations, communicates emotions, modifies verbal messages, provides important messages about the relationship, gives insights into self-perceptions and provides clues when clients are not saying what they are thinking. The face and body are extremely communicative.

Listening is a core skill in any form of care (Pattison, 1989). No one can be trained to listen, what one can learn is how to listen in a way that will help the patient best. The patients find it hard to express very deep and painful emotions when they are emotional and have language problems. Give the patient time and prompt sympathetically. The patient may take some time to sort their thoughts out and then put them into words. This requires patience and perseverance, especially in the case of patients with little English, and from minority cultures. It is important to concentrate on the patient's problems and concerns rather than judging them by their first impression, appearance and communication skills.

Chaplains should avoid taking control and should instead play the role of a facilitator. It is important for a pastor/chaplain to create a caring and warm atmosphere to enable the patient to explore his/her feelings. Some patients find it hard to open up. Their silence should not be an indication that they do not want to talk. Sometimes there is a need for prompting. The art of being with the patient when he or she is not actually saying anything is a difficult one to cultivate (Egan, 1998). As chaplains/volunteers, we should ask ourselves what we are doing, why we are doing it, and how effective it will be for both the patient and the care provider. As care providers, we need to be open minded, honest, committed, non-judgemental and unbiased. Skilled pastors allow enough time to finish the encounter, especially when the patient is pouring out his or her emotions. They should avoid any distractions.

Recent research conducted by Manzano, Swift, Closs and Briggs (2015) has revealed the advantages of an active listening intervention for hospital patients. In particular, they shared a common belief that when people are listened to, it directly reduces their anxiety levels. A listener with no agenda, no judgement, or disapproval is an important attribute of this intervention. This is a listening technique that is patient-driven and non-directive. Giving patients enough time becomes much more important, especially in the present environment of time constraints in the NHS. Under the circumstances, healthcare professionals have little or no time to provide a more individualized form of care. Nurses do not always have time to spend listening to patients, and patients do not always share things with relatives or families, as perhaps they do not want to upset them with certain illness-related issues. Manzano, Swift, Closs and Briggs also mentioned the factors that could hinder patient engagement with active listening. These were associated with patients' perceptions of chaplaincy services and patients' individual characteristics. Hospitalisation is a time of fear and vulnerability for the individual who may well have to face their own mortality for the first time. (2015, p. 211).

Being present: Being present is a skill which is difficult to acquire or learn. To be present does not only mean to be there physically, but also mentally and emotionally, with empathy and sensitivity. Hoppe (2006) advises that active listening is really a state of mind requiring us to choose to focus on the moment, being present and attentive while disregarding any of our anxieties of the day. Being present and not only in presence is a much-required skill. Some encounters may be viewed as mundane and unnecessary, such as when the patient chooses to talk about their personal stories or everyday things such as the weather, television or sport. In fact, this can be the way of opening the door for the chaplain. This is an opportunity for a chaplain to build a relationship with the patient in an informal setting. The author remembers: "Seeing one woman over 100 years old who told me her life story and her favourite dishes with ingredients". It may sound like an irrelevant conversation but for a chaplain, it is a step forward to hold the hand of a patient and walk together in the dark alleys. Being present in pastoral care is psychologically supportive for patients in distress. 'In this role, it is no longer acceptable for the chaplain to simply "be present" with the patient or family member without some sense of how the patient might benefit from that presence' (Handzo, 2014, p. 29).

Reflecting skill: This is an extension of good listening skills. This needs to develop the ability to reflect on words and emotions and to clarify that you have understood the speaker correctly. However good you think your listening skills are, the only person who can tell you if you have understood correctly or not is the speaker. Therefore, it is a way to ensure that the speaker and the listener are in harmony. Kidd suggests: 'Reflecting is the bedrock prerequisite skill for effective listening and responding. Reflecting is distinctive from other types of listening because it focuses on the emotional content of the patient's words' (2014, p.95). This reflection will help in identifying the way in which chaplains may have shaped an encounter. Chaplains need to be conscious of the fact that reflecting back does not work in every situation, such as bereavement or acute and life-limiting illness.

Reflective practice: This is a useful skill for self-development in dealing with complex and difficult situations (Moon, 1999). Reflective practice needs to develop critical, constructive and creative thinking (Thompson, 2015). It is the concept of learning from experience. It is an essential skill for chaplains, as they work with a multitude of people. It is about thinking and reflecting on what you do, what happened, and how you can improve yourself. In a way, it is a critical analysis of one's own performance for raising self-awareness and for improving performance. It requires a conscious effort to think systematically about events and develop a critical insight of them. It is about thinking, understanding and exploring ideas. It may be one's own thinking, but it becomes a shared activity. Appraisal interviews, occasional one-to-one sessions, reviews of particular events and feedback from service users are helpful to gain the views of others, which aid self-assessment and personal development. It is not only a process of finding how to develop but to gain strength from what one does well. It helps in developing a better understanding of others, influencing good working relationships.

Listening to stories: Patients often talk to chaplains and tell them what is on their mind. This needs the skills of compassionate care. Many pastoral care writers have observed the great relevance and significance of the use of words in pastoral care (Lartey, 2003). Deeks (1987) begins with an examination of how storytelling and conversation can be of value in pastoral care. Pattison (1989) makes an analysis of 'conversation' as a useful way of conceptualizing and engaging in theological reflection on pastoral practice. In the story-listening role, the pastoral caregiver enables people to hear their own stories aloud, and to hear it for themselves, and thus possibly obtain a more objective view of who they are in their multi-faceted complexity.

The stories typically told by Sikh patients relate to their experience and what effect those have on individuals. Stories include family disputes, marital problems, disrespectful behaviour of siblings, attitudes of daughters-in-law, and financial impropriety by family or friends. Some patients take pride in telling stories of success and of unity in their families. In the light of stories told, it appears there exists inner conflict in the minds of patients. This creates anger and anxiety where the relations are fractured or broken. The chaplain needs to support them to resolve their contention and enable them to find personal integrity. Making sense of stories requires cultural competency and language skills. Listening to their stories enables both speaker and listener to get in touch with what may well be the core of a person's need (Lartey, 2003).

Interaction: There is a hospital protocol in the NHS on conversing with patients embedded with Western values and putting emphasis on listening. The Sikh culture has its own unique way of communication. Sometimes cultural differences make it obligatory to differ, for example, in the Sikh culture, participatory conversation, listening, and responding with empathy and understanding is expected. They should keep in mind, however, that listening needs to precede responding if pastoral communication is to be effective (Jacob, 1985). McClure speaks of the 'pastoral carer not just being a listener to stories and an interpretive guide, but a participant. This will mean engaging in a wide variety of practices involving interpreting, consciousness raising, coaching and advocating' (2012, p.14). Christian chaplains are unlikely to know many Christian patients personally, whereas Sikh volunteers happen to know most Sikh patients. This makes it hard for them when balancing relationships and professionalism. Taking a patient's consent for visiting is most important and it works in their favour. Due to the close-knit nature of the Sikh community, volunteers could bring their own problems into conversation and may dig into patient's personal information, which is considered prying. It is unethical and affects trust building. Patients would like to share their feelings and stories with someone they can trust. Trust-building in the Sikh community is a skill, as the word spreads quickly in either a negative or positive way due to the interconnected nature of the community. Maintaining patient confidentiality is necessary in hospitals (Foskett and Lyall, 1990). Sikh volunteers need to be extra careful and use their own judgement to assess the situation. Referral should be made to another colleague when unsure of the situation. It is of utmost importance for Sikh volunteers not to cross ethical boundaries.

Language: This is a medium of communication between the care receiver and the care provider. Communication in the language of the patient is important for conversing fluently and understanding their emotions, gestures and expressions. Lartey also pointed to the need to pay attention to the form of language, including the issue of dialect, intonation, choice of expression, familiarity with particular idioms as well as meaning (2003, pp.73-74). The listeners should have empathy and self-awareness (Rogers, 1951). He also suggested the need to examine one's own practice concerning language. Empathy is the ability to enter into the feelings of others (Egan, 1998) and this word occurs frequently in spiritual and pastoral care. Sikh chaplains/volunteers need to possess language proficiency in Panjabi and English in order to converse with all the stakeholders.

Culture and cultural competency, ethics and cultural sensitivity, spiritual and religious competency

Culture: Culture is the shared values, beliefs and rituals by which a community lives and which it abides by. It plays a dominant role in one's life. Culture, as defined by Henley and Schott 'is a shared set of values, assumptions, perceptions and conventions, based on a shared history and language, which enable members of a group or community to function together' (1999, p.2). Sikh culture is different from Panjabi culture, though many Sikhs still practice Panjabi culture, which is a fusion of Hindu and Muslim culture. Sikhs need to make a distinction between the two. Culture influences the many values of human life. Society often accepts them and behaves accordingly.

> *Understanding patients as persons is fundamental to respecting their equal values and worth, but understanding persons in terms of their beliefs, values, and behaviours enables specific care to be delivered that is relevant to and congruent with the individual's worldview* (Cobb, 2005, p. 87).

The delivery of such service depends on the individual's capability and on organisational capacity to be responsive to difference and diversity and this requires cultural competency.

Cultural competency: 'Cultural competency is the ability to interact successfully with people from various ethnic and/or cultural groups. As healthcare providers, we must gather information from the patient and/or family that could be useful in the plan of care' (Gutierrez, 2014, p.407). It is the ability to understand, communicate with and effectively interact with people across cultures. It is about our will and actions to build understanding between people, to be respectful and open to different cultural perspectives, strengthen cultural security and work towards equality of opportunity. Underlying cultural competence are the principles of trust, respect for diversity, equity, fairness, and social justice (Make It Our Business, 2017).

Culture is not static, it changes in response to new situations and emerging values from time to time. Consequently, cultural competence is not static, and our level of cultural competence changes in response to new situations, experiences and relationships. It is important at three levels. At an individual level, it includes the knowledge, skills, values, attitudes and behaviours of individuals. At service level, it includes management and operational frameworks and practices, expectations, including policies, procedures, vision statements and community voices. At the broader system level, it covers how services relate to and respect the rest of the community, agencies, elders, and local community protocols (Make It Our Business, 2017).

Culture plays a leading role in the way people perceive illness and hold their beliefs in respect to health and healing. Healthcare also has its own culture of a set of common learned values and beliefs that are manifested in behaviour, social interaction and the manifestation of experience. The skill of responding to the patient whose culture is different from that of the chaplain is a challenge that requires cultural competency.

Ethics and cultural sensitivity: Chaplains and volunteers spend most time in public spaces with patients of all ages, backgrounds and cultural and religious traditions. Touch and posture have strong connections with culture and ethics. Touch is a basic human gesture and physical contact is an integral part of healthcare. Christians make use of touch in the anointing sacrament. It is a 'means of comfort and healing' (Sayre-Adams and Wright, 2001, p.3). Touch conveys reassurance, care, and concern, and it can be a valuable expression of a supportive or therapeutic relationship (Cobb, 2005). Touch is a powerful nonverbal signal, and one that is often perceived as being deeply meaningful (Hayes, 2000, p.469). It is conditioned by social and cultural norms. However, the use of touch to and by strangers in the Sikh culture is unacceptable. From the author's research, it appears that some Sikh patients are willing to discuss the circumstances of touching in favour of its therapeutic and psychological benefits. Patients also realise that female Sikh chaplains/volunteer visitors might feel intimidated holding hands or putting their hand on a stranger's head, especially of the opposite sex, when praying or blessing. The author argues, to start with, it should only be done in exceptional circumstances, and not as the norm or as a rule. Care providers have to make decisions with which they can live with and feel comfortable. If prayer has to be performed by holding hands, the consent of the patient, and if possible, the presence of a family member, is desirable. Touch is not value-free, and it can convey powerful signals. Therefore, touch may be perceived as threatening or manipulative (Cobb, 2005, p.159). There is also an emphasis on posture. Some chaplains sit on their knees to be at parallel to the patient's face and lean a little forward to maintain eye contact with the patient to indicate their presence. The chaplains have to be mindful that this may not be applicable for all cultures, including the Sikh culture. It is essential to know, especially for generic chaplains who come from a Christian background, to be sensitive to this. The main thing is to be respectful, genuine, and to have a caring mindset with a calm and relaxed presence, sitting squarely and facing the patient. It is also important that Sikh chaplains and volunteers dress modestly as dictated by their religion.

Spiritual and religious competency: Spirituality lies at the heart of many patients' core values and beliefs. It is necessary for chaplains to have an understanding of the word 'spirituality' and its coverage. The 2015 guidelines make spirituality an umbrella term covering faiths, beliefs and pastoral care. Different faith and belief communities define religion and spirituality differently. Definitions of spiritual and religious competence often refer to the need to be aware and attentive to the religious and spiritual needs and orientations of patients. In order to understand their religious needs, it is important to have knowledge of the world's religions, as well as an understanding of the religious terms and vocabulary commonly used by those religions. This will help chaplains to understand and build a rapport with the patient, and to make referrals if necessary. This understanding will also help in assessing patients' needs and plan for services. Spiritual sensitivity is essential because of the huge coverage of what patients' beliefs are and a person-centred approach to patient care.

Being culturally, spiritually and religiously competent is about not only respecting and appreciating the spiritual, religious and cultural contexts of patients' lives, but also about understanding the way healthcare is delivered, whilst responding to the needs of a diverse population. It needs staff from diverse communities with bilingual skills and bicultural understanding. It helps in enhancing the quality of service by understanding the patients' needs. Caring for a patient with cultural, spiritual and religious competency will raise patients' satisfaction if the healthcare is provided in the language they speak, or understood in a manner compatible with their cultural, spiritual, and religious beliefs. It becomes necessary in the case of Sikh elders and new arrivals in this country who cannot speak fluent English. It helps to understand and be responsive to different languages, attitudes, values, family norms, traditions, body language and verbal clues.

Multidisciplinary care

The principal aim of the multidisciplinary teams is to deliver care effectively and consistently, bringing together a range of disciplines necessary to meet the needs of patients. Teams usually cover various specialities and expertise including physiotherapy, occupational therapy, CT scans, and social work. Teamwork is considered to be of great benefit to healthcare in terms of improving the quality and coherence of the care provided, resulting in enhanced patient and user satisfaction. Chaplains work with other healthcare departments, advising them on the religious and spiritual needs of patients. One of the major gaps highlighted by this research was lack of attention to meals, personal care, hygiene and private spaces for those minority faiths which are not yet accommodated adequately in the NHS.

Hospital meals: Food is obviously a human necessity. All patients need and deserve food that they find appetising, healthy and acceptable. The hospital menus normally have a wide range of choices so that every patient can find something to eat and enjoy. Sikhs are both vegetarian and non-vegetarians. Some Sikhs eat fish and eggs. Some non-vegetarian Sikhs eat meat but do not eat beef and pork respecting Hindu and Muslim traditions. The vegetarian Sikhs are mainly lacto-vegetarians. Staff have to be careful not to serve religiously prohibited meat to all patients for example, halal or kosher meat to Sikh patients. They eat *jhatka,* the bird or animal killed in one stroke. Menus should be presented to patients as Indian menu, vegetarian menu and *halal* menu. There is a tendency to present '*Halal* menu' to all Asians, which upsets not only Sikhs but many Indian patients belonging to other religions and denominations. It is important that vegetarian and non-vegetarian food should have separate serving spoons. Strict vegetarians will not eat food cooked in utensils used for cooking meat or exposed to prohibited food, and vegetarian food is not to be kept or stored in close proximity with non-vegetarian meals (Greenwood, 2010). Sometimes serving staff are not sensitive enough for the needs of patients. It is important to serve soft food that is easy to chew and swallow to elderly patients. It is also necessary to use ingredients in cooking and preparing menus keeping in mind the 'hot and cold effects' of food. Suitable meals and how these are prepared, preserved and presented give patients fulfilment and satisfaction helping their recovery. Sikhs are prohibited to have alcoholic drinks though some Sikhs do not adhere to this religious dictate. Before offering them drinks particularly near the end of life, it is better to check with the patient before serving. Food is a common issue for Sikh patients in many hospitals. Therefore, it is important that the Sikh chaplains/volunteers liaise with the catering department to explain the needs of Sikh patients and continuously monitor the situation.

Private space, personal hygiene and gender issues: There are also issues around modesty, hygiene, gender and private space for families when death occurs. These are mentioned where applicable in other chapters. Sikh chaplains/volunteers need to get involved with the relevant department to resolve them.

Conclusion

Chaplains need to be skilled to deliver spiritual, pastoral and religious care to patients. The most important skill is active listening to discern the needs of the patients, picking on key words said by them to be used to give the patient hope, comfort, and to uplift their spirit. The second skill is presence, which can be active or passive. The active presence is required to do things requested by patients or listening to what exactly a patient wants the chaplain to do for him or her. Some patients ask existential questions about suffering and the purpose of life near death. There is also passive or silent presence. The chaplain sits with the patient silently, sometimes holding the patient's hand, accompanying a patient's journey without saying a word. Visiting particularly non-religious patients broadens one's views by observing how patients explore themselves imaginatively and constructively, independently and without any boundaries or barriers. These patients are looking for hope or trying to find a solution. It is important for a chaplain to possess the skills to enable patients to retain and maintain hope that helps patients to carry on. The above-mentioned skills and competencies support chaplains in gaining the trust of patients to become a friend in their most difficult journey showing that they have an understanding of their needs. Appropriate language and interaction skills leave lasting effects.

References

Ashton, J. (2011). Rotherham NHS Foundation Trust In: Threlfall-Holmes, M. and Newitt, M. (2011) *Being a chaplain*. London: SPCK.

Blake, L. (2011). The Rowans Hospice In: Threlfall-Holmes, M. and Newitt, M. (2011) *Being a chaplain*. London: SPCK.

Brayne, S. and Fenwick, P. (2008). *Nearing the end of life: A guide for relatives and friends of the dying.* Sue Brayne and Dr Peter Fenwick in association with the Clinical Neuroscience Division, University of Southampton. Text c 2008 Sue Brayne work Ltd.

Cobb, M. (2005). *The hospital chaplain's handbook: a guide for good practice.* Norwich: Canterbury Press.

Deeks, D. (1987). *Pastoral theology: an inquiry.* London, Epworth.

Department of Health and Social Security (1978). *Directives on healing organisations* issued on 13 July 1978. London, DHSS.

Egan, G. (1998). *The skilled helper: A problem management approach to helping.* 6th ed. USA: Brooks/Cole Publishing Company.

Foskett, J. and Lyall, D. (1990). *Helping the helpers: supervision and pastoral care.* London, SPCK.

Greenwood, D. (2010). *Ethical dilemmas in hospital chaplaincy.* Unpublished MA thesis, University of Huddersfield.

Gutierrez, N. (2014). In: Roberts, S. B. (ed.) *Professional spiritual and pastoral care: A practical clergy and chaplain's handbook.* Woodstock: Skylight Paths.

Handzo, G. (2014). The process of spiritual/pastoral care: A general theory for providing spiritual/pastoral care using palliative care as a paradigm. In: Roberts, S. B. (ed.) *Professional spiritual and pastoral care: A practical clergy and chaplain's handbook*. Woodstock: Skylight Path.

Hayes, N. (2000). *Foundations of psychology*. 3rd ed. London, Thomson Learning.

Henley, A and Schott, J. (1999). *Culture, religion and patient care in a multi-ethnic society: a handbook for professionals*. London: Age Concern.

Highlen, P.S. and Hill, C.E. (1984). Factors affecting client change in Counselling. In: S.D. Brown, W. Lent (eds.) *Handbook of counselling psychology* (pp. 334-396). New York: Wiley. Quoted in Egan's book p.70).

Jacob, M. (1985). *Swift to hear: facilitating skills in listening and responding*. London, SPCK.

Kidd, R. A. (2014). Foundational listening and responding skills. In: Roberts, S. B. (ed.) (2014) *Professional spiritual and pastoral care: A practical clergy and chaplain's handbook,* pp 92-103. Woodstock, VT: Skylight Path.

Larson E. L. (2001). Hygiene of skin: when is clean too clean? *Emerg. Infect. Dis.* 7 (2), pp. 225-9) cited by Wilson chapter 7, *Infection control in clinical practice*.

Lartey, E. Y. (2003). *In Living color: an intercultural approach to pastoral care and counselling*. London, Jessica Kingsley Publishers.

Manzano, A., Swift, C., Closs, S. Jose and Briggs, M. (2015). Active listening by hospital chaplaincy volunteers: Benefits, challenges and good practice. *Health and Social Care Chaplaincy.* Vol. 3, issue 2, 2015.

McClure, B. J. (2012) cited in: Egan, K. (2014). Pastoral care today: widening the horizon. In: Flanagan, B. and Thornton, S. eds. *The Bloomsbury guide to pastoral care.* London, Bloomsbury.

Moon, J. (1999). *Reflection in learning and professional development: Theory and Practice.* London: Kegan Paul.

Newitt, M. (2010). The role and skills of a hospital chaplain: Reflections based on a case study. Practical Theology 3/2, pp. 163-77.

Pattison, S. (1989). Some straws for the bricks: A basic introduction to theological reflection. *Contact: The Interdisciplinary Journal of Pastoral Care* 99, pp.2-9.

Rogers, C. R. (1951). *Client-centred therapy.* London, Constable.

Sayre-Adams, J. and Wright, S.G. (2001). *The Theory and Practice of Therapeutic Touch.* 2nd ed. London, Harcourt Publishers.

Simpson, J., Collin, M. and Okeke, C. (2014). What do chaplains do now? The continuous process of adaption. *Health and Social Care Chaplaincy,* Vol. 2.2. 2014.

Thompson, N. (2015). *People skills.* 4th ed. London: Palgrave.

Threlfall-Holmes, M. and Newitt, M. (eds.) (2011). *Being a chaplain*. London: SPCK (Society for promoting Christian knowledge).

Wilson, J. (2006). *Infection control in clinical practice*. Balliere Tindal.

Websites

Gov.uk (2018). *Data protection act*. [online] Available at: https://www.gov.uk/government/collections/data-protection-act-2018. [Accessed 18 April 2019].

Hoppe, M. H. (2006). *Active listening: Improve your ability to listen and lead* [Internet], Greensboro, NC: Center for Creative Leadership. Available at: https:// tomynelokiky.tk › business-management-and-leadership> mic… [Accessed 20 Oct. 2019].

Hoppe, M. H. (2006). *Active listening: Improve your ability to listen and lead* [e book]. Greensboro, NC: Center for Creative Leadership.

IT Governance (2018). GDPR Overview. Available online: https://www.itgovernance.co.uk/data-protection-dpa-and-eu-data-protection-regulation [Accessed 18 April 2019].

Make It Our Business (2017). *What does it mean to be culturally competent*? [online] Available at: http://www.makeitourbusiness.ca/blog/what-does-it-mean-be-culturally-competent [Accessed 18 April 2019]

Chapter 6

Spiritual and pastoral care

Introduction

This chapter explains spiritual and pastoral care, and their meaning and importance in holistic care. Spiritual care also explains the components of spirituality, for example, soul, spirit, spiritual care and its application. It also precisely explains how spiritual needs are assessed, care plans are prepared and interventions are made, and their effect on patient experience. Pastoral care is the very basis of spiritual care: this chapter will explore what pastoral care means, its origin and expansion, and how it differs from spiritual and religious care. It also covers how Sikhism impacts spiritual and pastoral care.

Spiritual care

Spiritual care has become high on the agenda of the NHS in order to ensure holistic care to all patients, irrespective of their faith, beliefs and culture. It recognises and affirms the increasing engagement of spirituality within healthcare which has been taking place over recent years and is based on the Care Quality Commission's expectations of 'putting people first', Standards for Healthcare Chaplaincy Services (UKBHC, 2009) and National Chaplaincy Guidelines (2015). It has been recognised and supported by the World Health Organisation's definition: 'Health is not just the absence of disease; it is a state of physical, psychological, social and spiritual well-being' (World Health Organisation, 1948), followed by the HSG 92/2, the Patient's Charter (1991) and the Equality Act 2010. The concept of spiritual care is ancient, though it received prominence in NHS chaplaincy with the changing nature and culture of British society. The main influential factors for this change are the increased faith and beliefs diversity, the emergence of the post-modern era and the New Age movement, the rapid decline of the number of churchgoers, scientific and technological progress, stress on human rights and personal choices, the Patient's Charter and other government initiatives, and global migration. Above all, it was down to the changing attitude of the population as a whole who retreated from Christian observance that seemed to need something to fill the void. (Billings, 2016).

What is spirituality?

Spirituality is a multidimensional part of human experience that can fulfil one's life. Many seek spirituality through religion, or through a personal relationship with the Divine. Many have the urge to connect with the transcendent, referring to God or a supreme power, or a value system and cosmic consciousness (a higher form of consciousness than that possessed by the ordinary man). Many pursue this by connecting with nature, other activities of their interest, or through a set of values and principles by which one lives one's life. Others may find it in poetry, music, art and artistic pursuits, meditation, yoga or any other activity that gives them a sense of self-fulfilment. Some may seek it in their social network and relations, including family and friends, to live and connect with the community. Spirituality gives meaning and purpose to life. It is a source of hope, comfort, consolation, support and fulfilment. Robinson et al. suggest: 'Spirituality is about the practice and outworking of the spirit and the ways in which it is developed, with its different aspects and relationships connected, sustained, and understood' (2013, p. 23). Spirituality is the specific way in which individuals and communities respond to the experience of spirit. Swinton argues: 'Spirituality is the outward expression of the inner workings of the human spirit.' (2001, p. 20). He further adds that it is a personal and social process that refers to the ideas, concepts, attitudes and behaviours that derive from a person's or a community's interpretation of their inner experiences of the spirit. McSherry's (2006) research findings suggest:

> That healthcare professionals and some patients perceive spirituality as something that influences the physical, psychological and social aspects of our being in an integrated manner. Spirituality is an invisible force that brings unity and harmony to self, others and the larger universe. The spiritual dimension is a mysterious and transcendent force that assists the individual in finding meaning, purpose and fulfilment. It is a force that transcends the rational and intellectual capabilities of our human state, uniting us with the whole of creation, both at a material and supernatural level (2006, p. 85).

Spirituality is the nurturing element of the spirit. Swinton gives the essence of this. 'The human spirit is the essential life-force that undergirds, motivates and vitalizes human existence. Spirituality is the specific way in which individuals and communities respond to the experience of the spirit' (2001, p.14). He further adds that this distinction is quite subtle, but very important. Anderson is of the opinion that: 'Spirituality is to be seen as more than a religious aspect of the self. The spiritual core of the self is what makes religion possible' (2003, p. 68).

Spirituality nurtures the human spirit and its extent is beyond any boundary. Its nature and scope make it a part of holistic care, tending to human needs (emotional, physical and mental wellbeing) and making it person-centred. The concept of holistic care is to recognise the importance of considering the physical, psychological/emotional, social, cultural and spiritual aspects of need and care (Dossey and Dossey, 1998; Stoter, 1995). Some patients may define their problems as spiritual rather than religious. By spiritual, they generally mean a transcendent relationship between the person and the higher being – 'a quality that goes beyond a specific religious affiliation' (Peterson & Nelson, 1987). The Department of Health described spirituality as:

a subjective experience that exists both within and outside traditional religious systems. Spirituality relates to the way in which people understand and live their lives in view of their core beliefs and values and their perception of ultimate meaning. Spirituality includes the need to find satisfactory answers to ultimate questions about the meaning of life, illness and death. Spirituality can be seen as comprising elements of meaning, purpose, and connection to a higher power or something greater than self (DoH, 2010, p.18).

Spirituality has further been defined as: 'The aspect of humanity that refers to the way individuals seek and express meaning and purpose and the way they experience their connectedness to the moment, to self, to others, to nature and to the significant or sacred' (The National Consensus Project for Quality of Palliative Care, 2013). Therefore, spirituality is deeply personal and unique to every patient who expresses it in their own way, within or without religion. In other words, it has been said in these definitions that spirituality is personal, it exists in every human being and it can be found through religion, personal beliefs and artistic pursuits and activities.

Spirituality in Sikhism

A Sikh focus group of seven Sikh participants was organised in 2019 to seek their views on how to define spirituality as it means to Sikhs. Five participants gave their views:

Participant 1: "It is a personal experience that cannot be separated from religion."

Participant 2: "Spirituality is very personal. It is an act of faith to believe that there is a greater purpose to be realised through meditation and reflection."

Participant 3: "Spirituality in Sikhism is entwined with religion and expressed through the acts of faith as *naam simran* and *Samadhi.*"

Participant 4: "The focus of *Sikhi* is the sense of connection to something bigger than ourselves – the one-ness of everything."

Participant 5: "It is a personal belief to lead one's life. Most Sikhs draw those beliefs from their religion."

This makes spirituality entwined with religion and the Sikhs express through the acts of faith. It is a sense of connection to something higher than us. It is a subjective experience, expressed in one's own way by the act(s) of faith to nurture soul and spirit. Therefore, spirituality as defined based on the focus group:

> *It is a subjective experience expressed through one's beliefs to nurture the soul and follow pursuits to energise the spirit to find meaning, purpose and fulfilment in life with the ultimate aim of working towards spiritual growth to reach a higher goal.*

The close and impartial study of the *GGS* suggests that Sikhism has an integrated approach, whereas spirituality and religion are entwined through the prescribed way of Sikh life; giving humans a purpose of life, a value system, ways and means to develop truthful living, and ways to maintain consciousness. Humans are created to care for God's creation – humans, nature and environment. God is a source of support, hope, motivation and *nadar* (grace), turning the impossible to possible for the believers. There are secular suggestions as well as contemplative suggestions given in the *GGS*.

Many secular activities and pursuits are mentioned in Sikhism, such as voluntary service (*seva*), truthful earning and living, and contentment and peace acquired by good deeds, such as sharing with those in need and by enjoying the basic human needs. At the same time there are religious rituals such as '*kirtan*', (melodious singing of hymns) which nurtures not only the human mind and soul but also uplifts one's spirit, and contemplative means such as *samadhi:* meditating upon the name of God to improve concentration and find tranquillity. Truthful living, services towards humanitarian causes, working towards motivation, and personal growth are the basis of spirituality. The *GGS* also mentions the five stages of spiritual development: duty, knowledge, humility, efforts and grace. It clearly suggests that Sikhs express their spirituality through their religious beliefs and values. Good deeds nurture the soul and human pursuits, such as art, music and other hobbies uplift the spirit. Therefore, spirituality has two strands: the soul (invisible) and the spirit (visible) through body language, signs and symptoms.

The ultimate aim of every Sikh is to develop truthful living. Truthful living is the only means in Sikhism to move towards spiritual growth to attain a higher goal. It does not matter what one's personal beliefs are, every human being exists with a spiritual centre within his or her being in search of truth. The *GGS* includes the writings of saints from other religions that simply reflected the truth and reality of life. Spirituality is beyond any boundary, it is variable, and not static. Spirituality is a universal concept, and those who are spiritual believe that attaining spiritual growth is the ultimate aim of every human being, indicating that they also believe it is an essential human need. Spirituality is about attitudes, values, practices and motivations that influence one's thinking, behaviour and approach towards life, community and humanity. It gives meaning and purpose to human life. Sikhism also differs on how it defines religiosity or being religious. A religious person in Sikhism is one who reads, listens and puts *Gurus'* teachings into practice. Praying in a congregation is beneficial and recommended in Sikhism. If, for any reason, a person cannot attend *gurdwara,* that does not mean he or she becomes a person of no faith. Religious teachings and cultural values shape Sikh beliefs and behaviour. The Western concept of spirituality includes meditation, mindfulness, yoga and other such activities; these are the part of the Eastern religious behaviour.

Spirituality is an integrated part of the Sikh religion. This is one of the reasons that many find it hard to define and why many patients do not always understand its meaning. It may widen its scope further for Sikhs living in the West, influenced by contemporary thoughts, if they adopt secular values. The author is of the opinion that the human body is made up of physical (visible), spirit (visible - high or low from body language) and soul (invisible). Spirituality energises the spirit and nurtures the soul by the medium of spiritual care. The energising factors include many activities to lift the human spirit, religious or secular, which makes spiritual care person-centred. It also cares for the soul and is related to virtues that involve humans choosing actions, beliefs and paths to become a good human being. Chaplains and chaplaincy are about caring for humans and what is distressing them. It is not about proselytisation or imposing one's own views. Religions are a framework or guidance for becoming good human beings and spirituality is whatever it means to individuals to lift and energise one's spirit and soul.

Why is spirituality important?

The essence of humankind is soul and spirit. It is important to nurture the soul and spirit in order to be holistically healthy.

> *Spiritual development is an innate evolutionary capacity of all of humanity, a movement towards wholeness, an integral part of our existence. Just as our physical bodies naturally grow and develop, the capacity for spiritual growth is as normal and intrinsic to biological human life.* (Grof and Grof, 1990 pp.1, 34)

It is also important for better health outcomes. It prepares humans to cope with their adverse circumstances. For Sikhs, spirituality and religion are almost synonymous. Some Sikhs who do not attend *gurdwara* regularly and do not pray routinely even though they follow Sikh religious values call themselves spiritual and not religious, to follow the Western definition of spirituality. Spirituality is a personal way of life and individuals explore and choose beliefs and values that give them meaning and purpose, fulfilment, happiness, self-satisfaction, support, and strength in coping with adverse situations. These values and beliefs can be adapted from other sources, not necessarily religious ones. Spirituality helps in recovery and its importance becomes intense when a person is ill, bereaved, dislocated, facing adverse circumstances or feels incapable to do something he or she wants to do or achieve. Spirituality is also helpful when one suffers with soul pain or spiritual distress. Sikh patients often express this as '*mera dil nahin lagda*; *mera dil kam vich nahi lagda*'. This means that they do not feel normal and lack motivation, and they do not feel like doing anything. There is nothing wrong with them physically, but they are suffering from spiritual distress. Most chaplains find that talking to patients with compassion and empathy gives them support, hope and fulfilment by helping to heal their soul pain and to alleviate spiritual distress. This raises the question of what soul pain and spiritual distress are.

Soul pain: It can be identified in a number of ways and from the words and vocabulary used by patients, for example, distress, anguish, suffering, confused (*duvida* in Hindi and Panjabi). When there are physical, emotional and social symptoms, which are the source of the patient's suffering, it is important to nurture the soul. Kearney explained: 'Soul pain is the experience of an individual who has become disconnected and alienated from the deepest and most fundamental aspects of himself or herself' (2007, p.45). He further adds that there may be an all-pervading sense of emptiness, hopelessness and meaninglessness. Thomas Moore says: 'When the soul is neglected, it does not go away, it appears symptomatically in obsession, addiction, violence and loss of meaning…the root problem is that we have lost our wisdom about

174

the soul, even our interest in it' (1992, p. xi). Sikhism heals it with devotional music, chanting religious hymns, meditation and supplication. Listening to someone with compassion and empathy helps enormously, and this is proven from the body language of the patients.

Spiritual distress: Spiritual distress and spiritual crisis as described by Hay (1989) and Smucker (1996) occur when individuals are unable to find meaning, hope, love, peace, comfort, strength or connections in life, or when they experience a conflict that occurs between what they believe and what is actually happening in their lives. It is also experienced when life is not going smoothly in spite of one's best efforts. This spiritual distress could have a detrimental effect on an individual's physical or mental health. Similarly, serious and terminal illnesses can trigger spiritual distress in patients and family members. Sikhs believe in making efforts and doing their duty, whether they get rewards or not. Accepting the Will of God (*hukam*) works for religious-minded patients.

Soul, spirit and spiritual care

There are terms that occur frequently when exploring spiritual care, such as soul and spirit. It is important to explain them so as to have a clear understanding.

Soul: Soul in Sikhism is known as '*Atma*' or '*Ruh*', often personified in feminine form in the *GGS*. It has a theological essence, as it is considered a part of the Supreme power 'God' and therefore is immortal and invisible. Since the soul is a Divine spark in the human body, it is associated with guiding the person to do noble deeds. This view supports Cobb when he says: 'soul denotes something essential, noble and sincere; it is a word of some gravity and much historical significance' (2001, p.25). Soul sustains life and keeps the person going through breath. It is the equivalent of 'life', breath, which keeps humans alive. Charles Gerkin (1984) also suggests that the term 'soul' is a theological term, and it is the gift of God bestowed upon the individual with the breath of life. It is something humans can ponder on, which cannot be visualised and is beyond the comprehension of modern science. Kearney says: 'For many the word "soul" may have religious connotations and be understood as some "vague and ethereal phantasm"' (2007, p.41). While emphasizing that soul defies definition, Hillman (1979) states there are nonetheless certain things that can be said about it. First, to speak of soul is to speak of depth, for soul refers to 'the deepening of events into experience'. Soul brings with it a sense of significance, that is, a subjective experience of meaning, which is an altogether different thing from the rational mind's preoccupation with extracting meaning from experience. He further adds that soul is indeed connected to depth, to death, to the imagination, and that it brings with it a sense of meaning. Soul is the living connection between the surface and the unfathomable and meaning-rich depths of who we are (Kearney, 2007).

Soul is connected to death is also similar to what Sikhs believe in. When a person dies, the soul departs from the human body. 'Atma' looks for a new home where it can grow further, getting rid of the previous life's negativity. This process continues until it becomes pure and is ready for liberation in order to merge with '*Parmatma*' (Supreme *Atma*-God), linked with the Sikh belief in the doctrine of transmigration. According to this, death is regarded as a gradual transition from the human state to another state according to one's actions, deeds and conduct (*karma*) in this world, indicating the continuity of life beyond death. Therefore, the soul is not only the breath giver but also is a medium of connection between human beings and God (*GGS*, p. 661). All human beings, good or bad, believers or non-believers, have a soul, and how they nurture it depends upon the individual's beliefs, actions and behaviour.

Spirit: Spirit is a human energy, a life force motivating us to do things. The word 'spirit' is described within contextual situations. McSherry writes:

> *The word 'spirit' relates to the unique spirit of an individual that is their life force, the essence and energy of their being. It is this force that develops in an individual the ability to transcend the natural laws and orders of this life, allowing access to a mysterious transcendent dimension. The 'spirit' derives and motivates individuals to find meaning and purpose, allowing expression in all aspects and experiences of life, especially in times of crisis and need.* (2006, p.45)

Stoll (1989) describes a person's spirit as the image of God that is present within every person, making them a thinking, feeling, moral, creative being able to relate meaningfully to God (as defined by the person, self and others). In the views of Dickinson (1975), spirit is the animating but intangible principle that gives liveliness to the physical organism as well as the literal breath of life. These definitions make no distinction between soul and spirit. Sikhism, however, makes a clear distinction between soul and spirit. Spirit is energy and life force in Sikhism. This is depicted from these words when a Sikh says *'chardi kala'* (high spirit). Every human being possesses spirit, though its degree may vary in each individual. In Sikhism it is also applied to mean a *'jot'* (illuminating light or flame) given by God to a selected few such as the Sikh *gurus* (Singh, 1964; Firth, 1999, p.162). Anderson's views are that:

> *Spirit is used frequently in contrast to the soul and is never used as a practical synonym for soul. Where soul means 'life', spirit means 'vigorous life' or an inspired life; in particular God will give his own spirit to a chosen person, and even be asked to bestow it upon one* (2003, p.31)

Sikhism clearly suggests that soul and spirit are not identical, and Anderson's view aligns with the Sikh view.

Spiritual care: Spiritual care means nurturing the spirit, an important part of human life, which helps humans to feel energised and spirited. Spiritual care is a part of holistic care. Holistic, according to Robinson et al, means 'cognitive (to do ideas about the world), affective (to do with emotions), somatic (to do with 'body language', including tactile communication) and interpersonal'

(2003, p.31). This can give some insight to the aspects of a patient's life and how these affect each other. This is not static and changeable from time to time. It is also about sources of hope, comfort and support. It involves compassion, presence, listening and the encouragement of realistic hope (O'Connor, 1986) and might not involve any discussion of God or religion. It is about recognizing and responding to the 'multifaceted expressions of spirituality found in patients and their families' (Derrickson, 1996). Govier (1999) has summarised the concepts of spiritual care as the 'five Rs of spirituality': Reason, Reflection, Religion, Relationships and Restoration. People with special training in this area, for example, a chaplain, ideally perform it. They are trained in how to nurture the human spirit when someone is feeling low or is faced with chronic or life-threatening illness.

Many professional bodies and academics have defined spiritual care and it is not within the scope of this book to relate and discuss all. It is important to give some ideas to help readers to clarify this concept. NHS Education Scotland defines:

> *Spiritual care is that care which recognises and responds to the needs of the human spirit when faced with trauma, ill health or sadness and can include the need for meaning, for self-worth, to express oneself, for faith support, perhaps for rites or prayer or sacrament, or simply for a sensitive listener. Spiritual care begins with encouraging human contact in compassionate relationships, and moves in whatever direction need requires* (NHS Education Scotland, 2009).

Spiritual care nurtures the needs of the human spirit in adverse circumstances to find the meaning and purpose of life through religious pursuits, beliefs or secular approaches, such as being present, or active listening with compassion and empathy. The most important is being person-centred and making no assumptions about personal conviction or life orientation. 'Spiritual care is not necessarily religious. Religious care, at its best, should always be spiritual.' (Scotland Chaplaincy and Healthcare, 2002). These parts of the guidelines make a distinction between religious and spiritual care, making it explicit that religious care at its best should always be spiritual. This second part 'religious care, at its best, should always be spiritual' is applicable to Sikhism due to its *dharmic* nature.

Spiritual care is enabling patients to speak honestly about how they feel their illness has impacted them physically, mentally and emotionally. It is up to patients what they want to share with chaplains. Chaplains are privileged to be with patients, spending time with them and giving them the feeling that they are not alone. Spiritual care should be impartial and available to all faith communities and those with no faith, taking into consideration the wide range of beliefs, lifestyles and cultures. This requires openness, sensitivity, integrity, compassion and the capacity to make and maintain attentive, helping, supportive and caring relationships (Scottish Guidelines, 2002). It is person-centred, fair, collaborative, accountable and empowering. It is important in the present environment of cost-effectiveness to have documentation of patients' religious affiliation and beliefs. This can be helpful in auditing and assessing needs in order to provide person-centred care and to prepare a systematic care plan.

The overt emphasis on this term may also be a beginning of the departure from the dominance of a particular religion and church in the NHS, giving it the autonomy to make its own decisions. It became central to the attention of the 2015 national guidelines on chaplaincy, which made spiritual care a recommended term that the NHS uses when it refers to the aspects of healthcare that involve spiritual, pastoral and religious dimensions. It is not only a term of convenience but also a neutral term to avoid association with any particular faith community or practice and therefore should be acceptable to healthcare professionals and multi-disciplinary teams and the widest number of people. The author argues that religion should be treated on a par with spirituality and not a component of spirituality, making it religious and spiritual care to maintain and retain the essence of the profession and also to be suitable for all *dharmic* traditions.

Spiritual screening, history and assessment

Spiritual assessment is a broad category covering spiritual screening, spiritual history and spiritual assessment. There is a view that these are distinct in form and function (Massey, Fitchett and Roberts, 2004). A spiritual assessment differs significantly from a screen and a history. It is important to explain them and their differences.

Spiritual screening: Spiritual screening is a precise discussion with patients on their faith or beliefs affiliation by asking simple, rudimentary, and static questions. The clerk at the admission performs the basic spiritual screening so that patients can appear on the hospital list. Chaplains and volunteers get a list of patients to visit. These lists are not always comprehensive in their coverage as some patients are missing from the list and therefore cannot access chaplaincy services. It is important to mention that screening cannot be a replacement of spiritual history.

Spiritual history: Spiritual history is the first step for spiritual assessment and a structured way of taking detailed information. A spiritual history focuses less on what a person believes and more on how the person's faith and/or beliefs function to help them cope positively with their illness crisis. In the case of minority faiths where religion is a way of life, it also covers diet, hygiene, modesty and cultural needs such as touch, body posture and eye contact. It further adds whether they can communicate in English, or any other concerns they anticipate facing during their hospital stay. It is the process of gathering information regarding their needs affecting the patient's medical and holistic care. It will also help to update their medical chart by adding this information and circulating it to the relevant healthcare professionals. It does not always stay static and can alter during the patient's single hospitalisation or progression of a disease. Fitchett and Risk (2009) suggest chaplaincy departments are constantly seeking the perfect one or two questions that will generate an appropriate chaplaincy referral. The author argues that referrals are not only the motive of chaplains;

first it is the initial contact when chaplain and patient talk face to face and get to know each other; secondly it is the first step for auditing patients' needs and knowing exactly what the patient wants or expects from healthcare professionals during their hospital stay; and thirdly it is an opportunity for a chaplain to build a relationship of trust with the patient. Those taking the history must keep in mind the five criteria (must be brief, easy to remember, obtain appropriate information, patient-centred and validated as a credible) suggested by Koenig (2007).

Spiritual Assessment: Spiritual assessment has become the centre of attention with the recommendation of making 'spiritual care' an umbrella term encompassing religious care in its fold and person-centred care for those who do not espouse to any faith in the 2015 chaplaincy guidelines. Spiritual assessment gathers detailed information on a patients' spiritual needs. It is an in-depth look at the patient's spiritual makeup with the goal of identifying potential areas of spiritual concern and determining an appropriate treatment plan (Anandarajah and Hight, 2001). Studies suggest that there is a positive correlation between a patient's spirituality and religious commitment and health outcomes leading to the importance of spiritual needs assessment. The strength of this approach is that it has flexibility for an open-ended exploration of the patient's needs and concerns and serves as a natural follow up for further discussion of other support mechanisms. There are a number of 'spiritual assessment tools' used by healthcare professionals for assessing the needs of patients. These four, HOPE, FICA, FACT and SPIRIT happen to get mentioned frequently and their details and applications are given in appendix 2. HOPE includes effects on medical care and end-of-life issues and therefore is more likely to be used in hospices. FACT is easy to remember and simple to use, asking direct questions may be easy for Sikh patients to understand as compared to the questions asking for sources of hope, comfort and peace in some of the tools. Hodge says:

When it comes to assessing spiritual need there is no set 'norm' against which to measure so that action can be planned. The assessment of spiritual (and religious) needs can be seen as a developing relationship in which the key essence of need may be expressed (2011).

The key questions are to ascertain spiritual needs and how those are met, and the outcome of intervention in terms of patient experience.

Those assessing spiritual needs should remain patient-centred, non-judgemental and unbiased, especially when the beliefs of the assessor and the assessed differs. It is important to build and create a trusting environment where the patient can discuss his/her spiritual concerns. The assessor should choose an appropriate time for getting more in-depth information and may open the door for further discussion. Chaplains should have an active listening skill where they can, and pay attention not only to words, but also to body language. They should also be skilful in interpreting verbal and non-verbal cues from patients, which can help in making an effective care plan.

Assessment helps to set a care plan and a goal within a realistic period that is mutually acceptable to both the patient and the healthcare professional. Spiritual care can be delivered more effectively if it is integrated into the work of professional care teams and delivered collectively, as opposed to a chaplain's work in isolation, especially in the case of 24/7 care. It becomes more important for minority faiths and patients with no faith where the service is mainly given by volunteers. Hospices work differently. Present care environments also demand the effectiveness of spiritual intervention. In the case of Sikh patients, feedback from the patients is crucial. When a Sikh patient is asked "how are you feeling today?" they normally give feedback from the previous visit(s). 'Thank you' cards are another source, even though it is not a common practice within the Sikh community. The occasional ones that were received mentioned the usefulness and effectiveness of the service. When a chaplain visits the patient, it is normal to ask, "would you like to see me again?" If the answer is "yes", it is an indication that the patient must have found the encounter beneficial, but sometimes they say "no", which should not be misconstrued as a comment on the negativity of the given service. Chaplains often get feedback from patients of the volunteer's encounter. These useful cues contribute to evaluation. Setting goals and criteria against which spiritual care can be measured is complicated, particularly in the hospital environment, due to patients' short stay, shortage of staff, lack of continuous care and time constraints. Hospices are in a much better situation. They provide holistic care in an integrated manner and follow this up by working in the community.

The basic information on spiritual care is explored here to broaden the knowledge of Sikh chaplains and volunteers and to offer the systematic approach to administer it. There are rich resources available based on Abrahamic traditions for in depth study for those interested, in order to expand their knowledge further. Research is desperately needed in relation to Sikhism. Many elderly Sikh patients do not understand what spirituality actually means and, in some cases, they do not even grasp this term in their own language because of confused views on spirituality in healthcare.

Conclusion

The 2015 National Guidelines embedded spirituality into the discourse of healthcare chaplaincy in an attempt to make chaplaincy responsive to the diverse needs of the present nature of British society. The logic given behind this decision was that it is a representative concept for faith and belief traditions and is a neutral term without bias towards any faith, belief or those activities that nurture the human soul and energise human spirit. Spirituality is not as complex and confusing a subject as many have portrayed. It is its understanding within the profession and lay people that is creating confusion. The spiritual care model has been operational in hospices. It is important to bear in mind that these two organisations (NHS and hospices) differ in management, operations, capacity, turnover of patients and ethos, though both fit within the notion of individualised and holistic care. Hospices and care homes are predominantly Christian, backed by their policies, until recently having a little knowledge of other minority faiths and communities. It is suggested that the word religion should be retained, making it 'religious and spiritual' as spiritual is generally associated with a person of no faith, thus avoiding any confusion for the general masses.

Pastoral Care

Introduction

Care and caring are ancient concepts that existed and developed alongside the development of human civilization. They are secular words describing actions that are inherent in human nature and are therefore an intrinsic part of human behaviour irrespective of their faiths, beliefs and culture. Human beings have looked after and helped each other from time immemorial. They cared and are still caring for each other in their times of need and when in distress. The concept of care was termed differently in different languages according to culture, religion and beliefs. Religions also promote goodness in human behaviour and shape their interpretation according to their own theology: for example, 'pastoral' by Christianity, 'seva' by Sikhism, and recently, non-religious pastoral care has developed for humanists and those who have no religion (Savage, 2019). It is belief based. With scientific and medical advances, its coverage has expanded across various disciplines:

for example, theology, psychology and counselling. In the recent national guidelines of chaplaincy, pastoral care has been covered as a subset of spiritual care. The essence remains the same: 'care and help given in the times of need, distress and illness'. What we do and how we do it depends upon our religion/belief and culture. In public spaces, it is obligatory to observe the organisational rules and boundaries.

What is pastoral care?

It is necessary to clarify what pastoral care is and how it differs from religious and spiritual care. It is distinct from religious and spiritual care, though it touches their boundaries in a different way. Religious and spiritual care are connected with the performance of rituals and rites, whether those are religious or non-religious, whereas pastoral care is concerned with general human wellbeing and their needs, particularly emotional needs, by listening to their fears and anxieties. It is about making sense of their concerns of living and finding meaning and purpose. It is about giving unconditional love, making one feel valued and included, treated with empathy as opposed to sympathy. Pastoral care is to explore what is on the mind of the patient by talking and listening attentively. It is an ability of how we relate, connect and make relationships of trust with people, which comes with a person's own qualities, learning, reflection and experience. The very basis of a good relationship is acceptance, encouragement and affirmation. It is not a relationship of power but of understanding, companionship, and friendship to support and energise in darkness and blind alleys. Pastoral care aims to help patients in their recovery and well-being by making them feel valued and giving them a sense of self-worth by appreciation and praise for their good qualities. It is important to listen to what a patient is saying, even though it sounds unnecessary and may not be related to his or her health at that moment, but deep down there may be a hidden concern. The skilled chaplain helps them to find a meaning and solution in it. The author remembers an encounter where a patient told her his whole life story. When he finished, she said that he was brave to persevere all those painful experiences and through his inner strength he had made such a successful life. His face glowed, he thanked her for listening, and he felt relieved of the stress he was holding all those years. Patients open up when you pay attention to them, show your respect and look interested in what they are relating. Body posture, dress, and manner of the pastoral carer also play a significant part in how a patient assesses the carers, in order to trust and share their concern with them.

Pastoral care relates to patients' holistic care in hospitals, hospices and other healthcare organisations, where it becomes an activity of caring for someone as a whole person, being mindful of his or her needs and addressing those by a wide range of actions, depending upon the situation. Pastoral care helps recovery and wellbeing by comforting and giving support required by sufferers, and points to the basic human need of dependency on each other (Wright, 1982). McNeill (1977) confirms Wright's comment on this basic human need in the statement that the concept of care existed before the Christian era. Derek Blows confirmed this in his foreword to the book written by Wesley Carr (1985) 'Brief Encounters'. He writes: 'Pastoral care in every age has drawn from contemporary secular knowledge to inform its understanding of man and his various needs and of the ways in which these needs might be met'.

The word pastoral has its origin in the Christian tradition, based on the story of 'shepherd and flocks'. It is considered a Christian concept and is heavily influenced by Christian theology. The term here is used for convenience, and not necessarily for its links with Christianity. The concepts of 'compassionate and pastoral care' are both adopted, developed, and named in Holy Scriptures: compassionate care in the *Guru Granth Sahib* (the Holy Scripture of Sikhs) and pastoral care in the Judeo-Christian Scriptures (Old and New Testaments). The source of both is God's love in Christianity and compassion in Sikhism. Pastoral care is the Christian commitment to the statement 'God is love', implying that love is the strongest force in the world (Wright, 1982, p.4). The Sikh belief that human beings are created to care for God's creation (humans and nature) on this earth binds itself with divine love, compassion, kindness, caring, and sharing with others, not only with Sikhs, but with the whole of humanity. This is clear from a hymn: 'Be kind to all beings - this is more meritorious than bathing at the sixty-eight sacred shrines of pilgrimage and the giving of charity' (*GGS*, p.136). Examples of caring for the sick and vulnerable are found in the life stories of Sikh *gurus*. Any skilled person can provide *pastoral* care as priesthood is not necessary in Sikhism, whereas traditionally in Christianity priests, vicars and ministers care for their church congregational members and their catchment area. As mentioned earlier, it changes and develops with changing human civilization as indicated by Savage (2019).

The word pastoral is foreign for Sikhs and there is hardly any parallel term that can provide the exact expression in Panjabi. The term 'seva' covers mundane, religious and compassionate care. Caring for a patient's non-clinical needs, i.e. compassionate care (*Rehamdil dekh bhal/seva*), is the nearest approximation to pastoral care. It is used as a noun and it means giving compassionate care to someone distressed, ill, or frail in the family, to a congregational member in *gurdwaras*, to the community at large or helping to meet a particular need for humanitarian causes. It is of three types; physical (manual), mental (psychological) and financial (monetary help) as related in the GGS. It has a wider coverage depending on the situation and needs of the individual and community. Compassionate care and concerns for those who are suffering, sick or infirm form an intrinsic part of the Sikh traditions (Rait, 2010, 2013). It is the central dimension of our humanity. 'Pastoral care is not the preserve of any particular religion or culture. At the heart of most religious traditions lies an injunction to care, to love or to pay attention to self and others' (Lartey, 2003, p.15). There is a long history of guidance and care in, for example, the Jewish, Muslim and other Eastern Traditions (Gilliat-Ray, Ali and Pattison, 2013). Almost all religious and non-religious traditions, including Sikhism, have references to caring for human beings and humanity.

Pastoral care and its definitions

There are many pastoral care definitions given by Christian and Jewish academics, chaplains, and writers. These definitions mainly have elements of Christianity and Jewish faith with the inclusion that it should be provided by a Christian representative. These may not fit into the present environment, as the nature of community has changed from mono-faith to multi-faith, and many Christians do not adhere to their own faith any longer and have become more spiritual (no faith). Sikhism has a neutral stance, suggesting caring for all human beings, and any knowledgeable and skilled person can provide this. In the present environment, there is a need for a neutral definition, unbiased towards any religion and belief. The definition given by the NHS Education for Scotland fits the bill for this modern day and age.

> *Pastoral care is considered as a distinct and unique activity carried out in response to the needs of patients, their families and hospital staff. It is a supportive activity of caring for someone as a whole person, being mindful of his or her best interests and willing to promote those interests by a wide range of actions* (NHS Education for Scotland, 2009).

The key words 'unique' and 'supportive activity' in response to the needs of the hospital community are worthy of noting and instilling in actions. Since then, chaplaincy services are also extended beyond hospital and hospice boundaries and are provided in the community.

192

A pastoral care focus group consisting of Sikh patients gave their understanding of pastoral care. These statements suggest a mixed reaction based on the views of the participants.

> 'Pastoral care is a Western concept. It is linked to the priest in the church who is also a pastor. The care given by a pastor came to be known as pastoral care'.

> 'Pastoral care covers a sort of spiritual care within the member community, care within the home and family; cover care that is offered by one community to another'.

> 'Pastoral care is probably formed of more or less of religious duty to the person requiring the support'.

> 'It is a kind, caring, and supportive presence at critical times, with thorough understanding of culture and religion'.

> 'Pastoral care has a concern for the community, a concern for life beyond the individual, has relevance for non-Christian communities in its traditional religious meaning'.

Therefore, it summarises:

Pastoral care is a kind, caring, and supportive presence at critical times, with thorough understanding of culture and religion. It has a concern for the family and community, a concern for life beyond the individual, and has relevance for non-Christian communities in its traditional religious meaning.

Compassionate care therefore consists of caring and supportive activity and actions carried out in the family for family members, in the *gurdwaras* for the congregation and in the healthcare settings for patients, their families and staff responsive to their needs within the confines of their religion, belief and culture. Pastoral care is different from spiritual and religious care, even though it draws its resources from religion/belief and culture.

Pastoral provision

Religious, spiritual, and cultural values influence pastoral care. It is definitely so for the patients belonging to those faiths which affect their way of life. Service providers should be aware of this in order to provide an effective service. Carey and Davoren (2008) gave a detailed description of pastoral provision, which includes physical resources and skills based on a sensitive approach. They further added prayers, scriptural reading and organising or assisting with rituals under specialist pastoral religious functions, making a distinction between religious and pastoral care. Being there/presence, listening and giving reassurance are covered by sensitive approaches. Wright (1982) suggests that it is an important service that addresses or seeks to answer the deepest needs of patients by listening to them, providing end of life care and visiting them on wards. Resources should respond to the needs of service users.

Pastoral Assessment

Pastoral carers assess patients' needs through their everyday work. Donovan suggests that:

> *The role of the clinically trained pastoral professional is to assess the degree to which the client's emotional and spiritual equilibrium has been disturbed by a particular event and to determine what interventions should be appropriate to help the client restore that equilibrium and when such intervention would be employed.* (Donovan, 2014).

Donovan also suggests three elements of the assessment process e.g. relationship and connectivity, meaning and purpose, and degree of understanding and congruence of response (2014, pp.45-56). Relationships and connectivity are important for every human being. Chaplains make an initial assessment of a patients' key relationships and their sense of connectivity. From a theological perspective and lived experiences, it proves that human beings value and benefit from good relations. When human relationships are flourishing, it gives happiness, a sense of harmony, a sense of security, and allows humans to face even the most difficult times with a sense of wellbeing. When these relationships are not working well, are fractured, or are broken, they become painful, and an overall sense of wellbeing and security can feel threatened. They not only need each other, but also the divine/transcendent or any other faith or belief they hold or practice. It is therefore important to make an accurate assessment of their connectivity, and not to rely on any assumptions. Family relationships are very important to Sikhs, and it is their main support mechanism. In desperate need, when all other means are exhausted, they rely on the support and grace of God.

Most chaplains ask patients what gives them meaning and purpose, often looking for their faith and beliefs. One should never assume how those beliefs affect their healthcare, particularly in faith communities. The author remembers seeing a patient whom she often saw in the *gurdwara.* It is normal to assume that she is religious, but while talking to her she came to know that she does not believe that religious chanting alone can improve her health. People often subscribe to many values. It is important to know which among those the patient would like to rely on during their difficult and distressing times. The values people hold may not necessarily be religious; it can be personal, professional, familial or cultural. It is important that the pastoral care providers give care that is congruent with the patient's values and beliefs and helps him or her to make decisions to cope with their clinical situation.

It is necessary to assess the patient's preferred way of communication, the language they understand and the language they prefer to speak. This helps not only patients and their families, but also the pastoral care provider, to give conversation a flow. It eases communication; they can talk without hesitation, making the pastoral encounter real and effective for them. Additionally, those serving Sikh patients must have proficiency in Panjabi, the spoken language of Sikhs. Most Sikhs over 65 have some sort of communication difficulties. According to the audit conducted by the author in a local hospital, 60% of Sikh patients (and the percentage is higher for Sikh elders over 60) have difficulty in speaking fluent English. They obviously prefer to talk in Panjabi. It is also found that some educated patients prefer to talk in Panjabi when there is an emotional situation at hand. The pastoral carer must choose a suitable time to talk to the patient and use appropriate words according to the patient's mood and situation. Resources should respond to the needs of service users.

Whose responsibility?

Pastoral care has a wider scope depending on the situation, organisation and specialities involved. Any caring person, such as a support worker, nurse, priest, chaplain, and the laity can provide pastoral care within hospitals, hospices and other healthcare organisations. Chaplains and volunteers are the main providers of pastoral care in NHS hospitals and hospices. What differentiates chaplains from other pastoral professionals, as argued by Donovan, 'is their understanding of the clinical environment and their ability to integrate seamlessly with the other members of the interdisciplinary team for the benefit of the patient and the patient's family' (2014, p.53). Volunteers do the bulk of work on wards, visiting and listening to patients. It is a feeling of support, felt psychologically, that they are not alone. When patients talk to someone they trust, it helps them to resolve their personal problems or concerns to some extent. Sometimes, it can affect patients adversely if the motive of the volunteer visitor is to dig into personal and family information to become the centre of attention in the community, or if the volunteer is physically present but not emotionally or mentally present (often referred as not in presence). On the contrary, as suggested by Kirkwood: 'A visit to a patient in hospital must be offered in deepest sincerity and with a genuine desire to provide positive pastoral care' (1995, p.6). There are suggestions about how to provide chaplaincy services to minority faiths. Carey (2008) suggests that Christian chaplains can provide traditional religious pastoral care to people of non-Christian faiths with increased training. His suggestion needs careful consideration on the grounds of acceptance, language proficiency and religious and cultural competency. This suggestion also seems impractical and shows the tendency to keep chaplaincy services with Christian chaplains being experts in the field. Jhutti-Johal (2013) concludes by raising the question of whether healthcare providers should step away from catering for religious and cultural needs that do not affect treatment outcome, and instead put the onus on individual communities to provide resources to meet the spiritual, cultural and religious needs of patients. This idea is contrary to the NHS ethos and values of holistic care and will create many practical difficulties related to community politics.

Conclusion

Pastoral care is essential and beneficial for patients: it helps in making a loving and caring relationship with patients and their families. It enables chaplains not only to build a relationship with them, but also gain their trust to become a friend or companion in the most difficult times of their life journey. It also helps to make referrals to other healthcare professionals and specialists. Above all, it makes patients feel valued, loved and cared for.

References: Spiritual Care

Anandarajah, G., & Hight, E. (2001). Spirituality and medical practice: Using the HOPE questions as a practical tool for spiritual assessment. American Family Practice, 63, pp.81-88.

Anderson, R. S. (2003). *Spiritual caregiving as secular sacrament: A political theology for professional caregivers.* London and Philadelphia: Jessica Kingsley publishers.

Billings, A. (2016). The place of chaplaincy in public life. In: Swift, C., Cobb, M., and Todd, A., eds. *A handbook of chaplaincy studies: Understanding spiritual care in public places.* London: Routledge, 2016.

Cobb, M. (2001). *The dying soul: Spiritual care at the end of life.* Buckingham: Open University Press.

Department of Health (1992) HSG (92) 2: *Meeting the spiritual needs of patients and staff.* London: HMSO.

Derrickson, B. S. (1996). The spiritual work of the dying. *Hosp. J.,* 1996; 11, pp.11-30.

Dickinson, C. (1975). The search for spiritual meaning. *American Journal of Nursing 75, 10,* pp. 1789-1793.

Dossey, B. M. and Dossey, L. (1998). Body-Mind-Spirit: Attending to holistic care. *American Journal of Nursing 98, 8,* pp.15-38.

Firth, S. (1999). Spirituality and ageing in British Hindus, Sikhs and Muslims. In: Albert, J. ed., *Spirituality and ageing.* London: Jessica and Kingsley.

Fitchett, G. and Risk, J. (2009). Screening for spiritual struggle. *Journal of Pastoral Care and Counselling, 63,* 4, pp.1-12.

Gerkin, C. V. (1984). *The living human document – Provisioning pastoral counseling, in a Hermeneutical mode.* Nashville: Abington Press.

Govier, I. M. (1999b) *Spirituality in Nursing Care.* Unpublished MSc thesis. SIHE, University of Wales.

Grof, C. and Grof, S. (1990). *The stormy search for the self.* New York: Tarcher/Penguin.

Guru Granth Sahib (n.d.). Amritsar: *Shiromani Gurdwara Prabandhak* Committee.

Hay, M. W. (1989) Principles in building spiritual assessment tools. *Am J Hosp. Care* 1989, 6, pp. 25- 31.

Hillman, J. (1979). *The dreams and the underworld.* Harper and Row.

Hodge, D. J. (2011). "Chaplains – How Are They Known?" *UK Journal of Health Care Chaplaincy* 11(2), pp. 32–40.

Kearney, M. (2007). *Mortally wounded: Stories of soul pain, death and healing.* New Orleans, Louisiana: Spring Journal Books.

Koenig, H. G. (2007). *Spirituality in patient care: why, how, when and what.* Philadelphia & London: Templeton Foundation Press.

Massey, K., Fitchett, G., & Roberts, P. (2004) Assessment and diagnosis in spiritual care. In: Mauk, K. L., & Shmidt, N. K. eds. *Spiritual care in nursing practice.* Philadelphia, PA: Lippincott, Williams and Wilkins, pp.209-242.

McSherry, W. (2006). *Making sense of spirituality in nursing and health care practice: An interactive approach.* 2nd ed. London: Jessica Kingsley Publishers.

Moore, T. (1992) *Care of the Soul: A guide for cultivating depth and sacredness in everyday life.* New York: Harper Collins.

NHS (2015). *NHS Chaplaincy Guidelines* 2015, London: NHS England.

O'Connor, P.M. 1986). Spiritual elements of hospice care. *Hosp. J.* 1986, 2, pp. 99-108.

Peterson, E. A. and Nelson, K. (1987). How to meet your clients' spiritual needs. *Journal of Psychological Nursing.* 25, pp. 34-39.

Robinson, S., Kendrick, K. and Brown, A. (2013) *Spirituality and the practice of healthcare*. Hampshire: Palgrave Macmillan.

Scottish Executive Health Department (SEND) (2002). *Guidelines on chaplaincy and spiritual care in the NHS in Scotland* (NHS HDL (2002) Edinburgh: Scottish Executive).

Scottish Government (2009). Spiritual care and chaplaincy. Edinburgh: The Stationery Office.

Singh, T. (1964). *Sikhism: Its ideals and institutions*. Calcutta: Orient Longmans.

Smucker, C. A. (1996). Phenomenological description of the experience of spiritual distress. *Nurs Diagn,* 1996.

Stoll, R.I. (1989). The essence of spirituality. In: Carson, V.B. ed. *Spiritual dimensions of nursing practice* (4-23). Philadelphia: WB Saunders.

Stoter, D. J. (1995). *Spiritual aspects of healthcare*. London: Mosby.

Swinton, J. (2001) *Spirituality and mental health care: Rediscovering a 'forgotten' dimension*. Second impression, 2003. London: Jessica Kingsley Publishers.

Websites

Department of Health (2010). *Spiritual Care at the End of Life: a systematic review of the literature.* [online] Available at:

https://assets.publishing.service.gov.uk/government/uploads/syste
m/uploads/attachment_data/file/215798/dh_123804.pdf [Accessed
26 Nov. 2019].

Gov.uk (2015). *Equality Act 2010: guidance.* [online] Available at:
https://www.gov.uk/guidance/equality-act-2010-guidance
[Accessed 30 May 2019].

National Consensus Project (2013). *Clinical practice guidelines
2013.* [online] Available at: http:/www.nationalconsensusproject.org/
NCP [Accessed 6 May 2013].

NHS Education for Scotland: (2009). *Spiritual care matters: an
introductory resource for all NHS Scotland staff.* [online] Available at:
http://www.nes.scot.nhs.uk/documents/publications/classa/010207
nes-standards-final.pdf [Accessed 30 May 2019].

Scottish Executive Health Department (2002). *Guidelines on
chaplaincy and spiritual care in the NHS in Scotland.* [online]
Available at: https://www.sehd.scot.nhs.uk/mels/hdl2002_76. pdf.
[Accessed 17 June 2019].

UK Board of Healthcare Chaplaincy (2009). *Standards for
Healthcare Chaplaincy Services.* [online] Available at:
www.ukbhc.org.uk/publications/standards [Accessed 9 July 2019].

VHA Office of Patient Centered Care and Cultural Transformation
(2014). *Spiritual Assessment Tools Clinical Tool.* [online] Available at:
http://projects.hsl.wisc.edu/SERVICE/modules/11/M11_Spiritual_
Assessment_Tools.pdf [Accessed 23 Nov. 2019].

Wikipedia (1991). *Patient's charter.* [online] Available at: https://en.wikipedia.org/wiki/Patient%27s_Charter [Accessed 30 May 2019].

World Health Organisation (2010). *Spiritual Assessment in Healthcare Practice.* [online] Available at: https://epdf.tips/spiritual-assessment-in-healthcare-practice.html [Accessed 26 Nov. 2019].

References: Pastoral Care

Blows, Derek. In: Carr, W. (1985). *Brief encounters.* London: SPCK.

Carey, L.B. and Davaren, R. P. (2008). Inter-faith pastoral care and the role of the healthcare chaplain. *Journal of Healthcare Chaplaincy.* 11 (1), pp. 21-32.

Donovan, D. W. (2014). *Assessments* based on D. W. Donovan and Melvin D., PhD. *The pastoral assessment tool: Developing the centrepiece of the pastoral care strategic plan* (unpublished presentation).

Gilliat-Ray, S., Ali, M. M., and Pattison, S. (2013). *Understanding Muslim chaplaincy.* Surrey: Ashgate.

Guru Granth Sahib (n.d.). Amritsar, *Shromani Prabandhak* Committee (Standard version of 1430 pages in Punjabi).

Jhutti–Johal, J. et al. (2013). Understanding and coping with diversity *in healthcare. Healthcare Analysis*, Sept. 21 (3) pp.259-70.

Kirkwood, N. A. (1995). *Pastoral care in hospitals*. Alexandria (Australia) E.J. Dwyer.

Lartey, E. Y. (2003). *Living color: An intercultural approach to pastoral care and counselling*. London, Jessica Kingsley Publishers.

McNeil, J. T. (1977). *History of the care of souls*. New York: Harper & Row.

Rait, S.K. (2013). *A guide to being a Sikh chaplain*. UK, SKR.

Rait, S.K. with Bhogal, I. (2010). *Understanding Sikhism*. Ripon, Plug and Tap.

Savage, D. (2019). *Non-Religious pastoral care: a practical guide*. London: Routledge.

Wright, F. (1982). *Pastoral care for lay people*. London, SCM Press.

Website

NHS Education for Scotland (2009). *Spiritual care matters: an introductory resource for all NHS Scotland staff.* [online] Available at: http://www.nes.scot.nhs.uk/documents/publications/classa/010207nes-standards-final.pdf [Accessed 30 May 2019]

Chapter 7

Religious care and rituals

Introduction

This chapter covers the importance of religion in the Sikh way of life by detailing religious care and rituals, which form an intrinsic part of Sikh life. It explains the significance and meaning of the Sikh symbols of identity, emphasising how they should be respected and cared for in healthcare settings. It also describes religious care given to Sikhs through prayers, recorded music, and supplication, and its supportive effects. It further expands to the care of life-cycle rites and rituals such as birth, initiation, naming, marriage and death, and how these should be conducted in healthcare settings to support patients and their families. The Sikh religion influences end of life and medical decisions, and also the contents of medicines and diet habits. It also guides chaplains to give a faith perspective on matters arising from time to time in healthcare and recently on the topic of this pandemic virus.

Religion and its importance

Religion is manifested in all societies and its ubiquity demonstrates its usefulness to humanity. 'Religion is that behaviour or conduct of man which supports and sustains the total life - individual, earthly and cosmic – in all its aspects such as physical, moral, emotional, intellectual, spiritual and mystic' (Singh, 1990). In particular, religion is a response to the awareness of a transcendent reality, expressed in a framework of meanings by which people can live in a relationship to the sacred or the holy (Cobb, 2005, p. 41). Sikhs are generally religious by nature, and religion plays a prominent role in their life, during periods of happiness, sorrow and grief. Sikhism has its own distinct practices and life-cycle rites. The Sikh Scripture (*GGS*) covers all aspects of life, including coping with troubling life circumstances, especially sickness and acute illness. It gives their life meaning and purpose and has a clear focus on the practices, doctrines, narratives, experiences, ethics, social organization and material aspects of a faith tradition.

Religion often becomes the root of identity for many human beings. Religious beliefs also influence the medical decisions made by patients when seriously ill such as whether to accept blood transfusion, transplantation and donating and/or receiving organs. Religions influence end of life medical decision-making, such as the patient agreeing to go for aggressive therapy in case of terminal illness or staying on a life-support machine. The contents of certain medicines, drugs or tablets may not meet the patient's religious requirements and they need to be adjusted. This also is applicable in food contents and food served in hospitals, hospices and other healthcare organisations. Religion plays a significant role in coping with depression, suicide, substance abuse, positive emotions, social support and physical health. Koenig's research on religious coping suggests it is the use of religious beliefs or practices which reduce the emotional distress caused by loss or change (2002, p.7).

The chaplain plays an important role in hospitals, hospices and other healthcare settings. The main areas where chaplains play a considerable role are providing religious and spiritual care to the hospital community, performing rituals requested by patients and their families, and playing an advisory role for the hospital community and the NHS. They also offer a faith perspective and advice on the matters that health professionals, patients, and their families are not sure about. The main areas where chaplains play a considerable role are:

Symbols of Sikh Identity: Caring for the Five Ks

Sikh symbols of identity have meaning and special significance for initiated Sikhs. Healthcare workers need to understand their sanctity and associated sensitivities for Sikhs (Nesbit, 2007). It is essential for chaplains and caring staff to know how they should be cared for and handled. These are:

Kes (hair) Sikh men and women are not allowed to cut, shave or remove hair from any part of the body, such as head hair, beard and eyebrows. Many devout Sikhs never cut their hair, and men do not shave or trim their beards. This makes it important for healthcare staff to know how to care for their hair. After combing a patient's hair, it may be plaited for a female, and fixed up on the head in a bun for a male patient. Sikhs comb their hair twice a day to keep it clean and tidy. In case it becomes necessary for some medical treatments to remove hair, discuss this with the patient to seek his/her permission. Henley and Schott suggest: 'The prohibition on cutting and shaving hair specifically bans the use of razors and scissors. If it is essential for clinical reasons to remove body hair, it may sometimes be more acceptable to use a depilatory cream' (1999, p. 578). Most important is the sanctity of hair and not the way it should be removed. In either case, respect the wishes of the patient and ask their permission. Wishes must also be respected where permission is declined. In 2020, with the spread of Covid-19, it came to light that face masks supplied to Sikh doctors are not suitable for turbaned and initiated Sikhs, and so they may have to shave their beards to wear those masks. It is not that adequate face masks are not available, but these are little more expensive than the ordinary ones. The NHS has to be sensitive and careful where decisions affecting religious values are concerned.

Kangha: Every initiated Sikh man or woman uses this to comb the hair twice a day. After combing, they clean the *kangha* and keep it in their hair all the time (Rait, 2013). Neuberger suggested:

If for some reason it cannot be in their hair, as in the case of someone who has had an operation on the head or has had chemotherapy leading to severe hair loss then the kangha should be close by and should never be taken away by hospital staff without express instruction (2004, p.55).

A *kangha* contains a steel symbol in the middle. In case of medical treatment, such as having a head scan or operation on the head, there may be a need to remove it. Seek the patient's consent. If the patient has given permission to remove it, wrap the *kangha* in a clean paper and keep it on a clean surface or any other convenient place that is easily accessible to the patient.

Turban: All initiated and *kesadhari* Sikhs tie a turban, though some Sikhs also wear *keski* (small turban that is kept on at all times and worn underneath the normal turban) to keep their hair clean and tidy. In case these need to be removed, it is important to keep them on a clean surface or clean bag and avoid mixing with dirty clothes and shoes. When a Sikh patient is on the ward, a clean basket may be provided to keep the *keski* and turban in shape, which can be sterilised after use. In case this is not possible, it can be placed on a clean surface near the bedside. It needs to be handled with care and respect.

Kirpan (sword): The general experience of patients suggests that 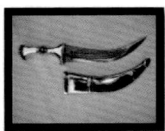 many healthcare staff do not understand the *kirpan's* significance and this has caused difficulties and confusion in healthcare settings which are beyond imagination. Some healthcare staff use expressions such as 'knife' and 'sharp dagger', which can be extremely hurtful for Sikh patients who are already in a stressful situation due to their illness. Neuberger suggests,

It is now usually a few inches long, blunt and useless. Nevertheless, hospital staff particularly tend to get upset at

seeing some kind of knife on the bedclothes, so that usually it is a good idea for the family to explain (1999, p. 43).

If a *kirpan* has to be removed completely for any reason, such as surgery, consent should be obtained from the patient. When removed it is essential to wrap it in a clean cloth and keep it on a clean surface. It is important for staff to know that it is not used as a weapon and they avoid equating it with a sharp knife or a dangerous weapon.

Kara is the circular round steel wristlet worn by Sikhs generally on 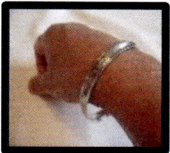 their right wrist. Neuberger states: 'It is a source of considerable distress even to non-*amritdhari* Sikhs if the *kara* is removed for an operation or for any other reason. Before any surgery, the *kara* should be covered with tape as a wedding ring is and not be removed.' She further adds:

In the very rare cases where removal is essential, such as for surgery on that part of the arm, the reasons should be carefully explained and the patient encouraged to wear it on the other wrist or keep it under the pillow or in a pocket (2004, pp. 55-56).

Kacchera: Initiated Sikhs wear this at all times, not even removing  it for a bath or shower. The changing of *kaccha* for initiated Sikhs is carried out in a particular way which must be strictly followed (Rait, 2013). It is changed in such a way that at one time, one leg of the *kacchera* is taken off, and replaced by the washed undergarments, repeating the same process for the other leg (Rait, 2013; Neuberger, 1999). It should never be completely removed. It may sound complicated, but it is essential for the initiated Sikhs.

> *This worry about modesty is even more common amongst older Sikhs, and with a dying patient, it is crucial to respect this concern and to help to keep a leg in the kaccha even when using a bedpan or having a bed bath* (Neuberger, 2004, p. 57).

This can create some difficulties if any treatment has to be done near the groin. The solution lies in talking to the patient and their families, convincing them why it is necessary to remove the *kacchera* and taking their permission to do so. The author's experience of working with Sikh patients suggest that they are adaptable and cooperate if spoken to politely, convincing them of its necessity.

There is a need for training for the caring staff as how to care for the *Five Ks* in hospitals and hospices. There is enough material available written on this subject, but still there are occasions when healthcare staff dealing with these articles often panic, not recognising the emotional impact of this on the patients.

Religious care of the life-cycle rites and rituals

Religious rituals are important for Sikhs, as these involve a familiar action and pattern of actions that work to connect an individual with their faith and larger community. Sikh life-cycle rites are dictated by their religion, and there are set ways of conducting them. Religious rituals are also significant for those whose daily life takes little account of religion and who do not attend the *gurdwara* on a regular basis. Henley and Schott suggest: 'Having a prescribed way of doing things also helps many people deal with the uncertainty and anxiety that accompany new situations, both positive and negative' (1999, p.97).

Religious communities often designate who may conduct the ritual. Any knowledgeable Sikh, preferably an initiated, can conduct Sikh rituals, though in practice, a *granthi* (designated Sikh priest) in *gurdwaras* and a Sikh chaplain in healthcare settings perform them. Whether religious or spiritual, most Sikhs adhere to their religious rites and rituals, as all life cycle rituals are bound with the *GGS* and take place in the presence of a Sikh congregation in a *gurdwara* (Sikh place of worship). Religious care can differ within the life cycles and on an individual basis, making it person-centred.

Religious rites

Every religion has its own prescribed rites and rituals with set ways as to how these should be conducted. There exist many Sikh rituals, though the rituals given here are those which are directly relevant to spiritual care in NHS hospitals and hospices. These are birth, naming, marriage and death, which a chaplain may have to perform in hospitals or hospices.

Birth: The birth of any child (boy or girl) should be accepted as a blessing and a gift from God. When a child is born, chaplains routinely visit the mother and child asking about their health and well-being. The mother may request a Sikh chaplain or volunteer to bless the baby. The chaplain should perform a bedside prayer for the wellbeing of the mother and child and for giving thanks to God for this precious gift given to them. The baby is then blessed. This blessing ceremony is normally held where the child is born (home or hospital). The word *Vaheguru* (God is wonderful) is whispered in the child's ear. It is important for a chaplain to know the practice of *gurti* (ਗੁੜਤੀ), a Panjabi cultural tradition of giving the first food, usually honey, placed on the baby's lips believing, the child becomes sweet (Rait, 2013, 62; Toole, 2006, p.24). Some use *jaggery* (lumped brown sugar) instead of honey, depending on the availability. Back in the Punjab, the midwife or a kind old woman generally administers it by dipping a cotton wick in honey or alternative to the baby, expecting him or her to grow like the person who administered it. The Sikh ritual is to dissolve sugar bubble (ਪਤਾਸਾ) in water and administer a drop with the tip of a sword (Nabha, 1962). The chaplains should be cautious of giving *amrit* (holy water) or honey to the child in hospital due to medical reasons. It should be left to the discretion of the hospital staff or family (Rait, 2013). This question is often asked by young mothers living in extending families due to the belief of their elders in this ritual. Many Sikh mothers prefer to breast-feed their baby and wish to keep curtains around while breast-feeding as they do not want to be exposed in public. It is important for the caring staff to know this.

Initiation: Some parents like to initiate their child soon after birth. A newly born baby cannot understand the purpose of undertaking of this ceremony. Secondly, most mothers stay in the hospital for a day or two after the delivery under normal circumstances, and thirdly, hospitals do not have the facilities or resources to perform such rituals. The Sikh chaplain should bless the baby and suggest to the family to organise an initiation ceremony in their own time in a *gurdwara*.

Naming: Some parents will want to name their child particularly in case of a stillbirth or death occurring in the hospital. In such cases, the onus will fall on the chaplain. Should this arise, the normal procedure of naming should be followed. The chaplain should ask the family to get the first word of the random reading of GGS from the *gurdwara*. The parents choose the name, which then can be announced by the chaplain to those present in the room (Rait, 2013) followed by *Ardas* for the baby and family in hospital.

Marriage: There can be many reasons why a person may want to marry while in hospital. For example, it makes the person they marry their next-of-kin and therefore may be entitled to financial benefits or entitlements such as a pension. It also allows someone to arrange the funeral of the dying person. Being married means that the relationship can be declared on the death certificate, otherwise, the relationship is cited as 'causing the body to be buried' (or cremated), used quite often for an unmarried partner. They do not qualify as being related to the deceased, and unless present at the death have no other way of being allowed to legally register the event, which can be very distressing for them. This becomes very impersonal and can be upsetting for some especially when the relationship is close. Getting married may also show love and loyalty in the relationship. The Sikh marriage ceremony is considered a sacred institution and an essential component of a couple's social and religious life. Sikhs also go through a civil marriage ceremony but consider it incomplete until the marriage is solemnized under the auspices of the Sikh religious order. Requests for emergency marriages in hospitals are rare at present, though the occasional situation does arise. If the situation arises, it should be organised in the *gurdwaras* providing the patient is able to attend the *gurdwara*. Where the patient is immobile, disabled or bed-ridden, civil marriage should be arranged. The marriage registrar in the hospital or hospice should perform it and a chaplain should do *Ardas* and bless the couple.

Performing a marriage ceremony in the hospital became a controversial matter in the Sikh community, and was severely criticized by the UK Sikh Healthcare Chaplaincy Group based in London, which is a lead organisation to appoint, train and validate volunteers for Sikh chaplaincy (www.sikhchaplaincy.org.uk). Apart from that, it is not possible to perform the '*Anand Karaj*' ceremony in hospitals due to lack of facilities and resources. It is also impossible if the patient is unable to sit, stand, bend and walk which is crucial for the ceremony. To keep the theological essence, there is a need to compromise by having a civil marriage by the designated hospital marriage registrar and a blessing from the Sikh priest or chaplain for a dying patient to fulfil his or her last wish. Keeping to the views of the general Sikh community, it should only be carried out in emergency and extreme circumstances. Sometimes chaplains have to make a reasonable adjustment in interpreting religious practices to suit hospital demands and their environment.

Same sex marriage: The Marriage (Same Sex Couples) Act 2013 clearly states that it will allow same sex couples to marry in civil ceremonies. It also allows same sex couples to marry in religious ceremonies, where the religious organisation has 'opted in' to conduct such ceremonies, and the minister of religion agrees. It also protects those religious organisations and their representatives who do not wish to conduct marriages of same-sex couples from successful legal challenges. The law itself has helped chaplains to resolve the situation. According to the author, it can be deduced from the law that if any same sex Sikh couple wants to have a marriage in a hospital; they can have a civil marriage by the hospital marriage registrar. The Sikh chaplain does not necessarily have to bless the couple and is not obliged to perform supplication following if he or she does not believe in it.

Death: Death is a natural cycle of life. When a person is dying or has died, it is important that the family is around to organise prayers and supplications. This is the time when the family needs support from the chaplain. The chaplain should arrange a private space containing tissues, arrangements for recorded *kirtan* and availability of drinks for the family and visiting relatives. The chaplain should be prepared to give the information asked for by the patient's family and contact with the bereavement office can be helpful. The chaplain should perform the final *Ardas,* which is essential and religiously binding for any dying or dead patient before the family leaves their loved one behind. The chaplaincy services for the minority faiths mainly depend upon volunteers and the volunteers were not allowed to work during the Coronavirus pandemic. Under the circumstances, the dying Sikhs were deprived of religious and pastoral care as many NHS Trusts do not have paid Sikh chaplains. Some Sikh volunteers offered their services through digital means.

The chaplain can help in funeral arrangements by giving the family of the deceased the information they need and contacting the family's place of worship if they request. Most *gurdwaras* are very helpful and supportive. The cremation rituals are shared with relatives, friends and congregation. Families play a central role on this occasion. The last bath is symbolic of the ritual purification of the body. It is customary for Sikhs to wash the body of the deceased before the funeral in a specific way. In order to comply with this rite, certain things are required. It may be helpful for the family if the chaplain is able to guide and support the family by giving them the list of things that are needed and support in bathing if requested by the family. The family is required to provide the under-mentioned for bathing and preparation of the body for the funeral.

List of things needed

For a female

1 bath towel
2 hand towels
1 small tub of natural yoghurt
1 small tablet of soap
1 small bottle of hair oil
1 small bottle of perfume
(spray)
2 kitchen rolls
Amrit (Holy water)

For a male

1 bath towel
1 hand towel
1 small tub of natural yoghurt
1 small tablet of soap
1 small bottle of hair oil
1 small bottle of perfume
(spray)
2 kitchen rolls
Amrit (Holy water)

Items for dressing

1 *dupatta* (head cover-scarf)
1 vest and undergarments
1 *Salwar Kameez*
(Female traditional Panjabi
dress)

Items for dressing

1 *Dastar* (turban length)
1 vest and undergarments
1 *kurta pyjama* and *parna* (a
length of plain cloth used as
loin cloth usually 2 metres long)
or shirt, suit, tie and socks
depending on family's choice).

Common for both male and female

kafan (1 white sheet – 4.75 metres)
1 each *kakars*: *kangha/kara/kirpan* and *Gatra*, *kacchera* (underpants) if initiated.
1 comb in case the person is not initiated.
(The *Guru* Nanak *Niskam Sevak Jatha*)

This is a comprehensive list and covers almost everything required for bathing. It is traditional to use yoghurt and oil to wash and moisturize the hair in the Punjab. If the family prefers, they can use shampoo and conditioner instead. The use of perfume is also not compulsory, it is a matter of family choice. Bathing normally takes place where the funeral services are booked. *Parna* as mentioned above is individual's choice and also not necessary for all Sikhs except followers of *Niskam Sevak Jatha* and other initiated Sikhs.

Funeral: *Antam sanskaar* (funeral) is an important Sikh religious rite. In the West, it is encouraged that the dying person chooses what type of funeral he/she wants, the colour of flowers, the hymn(s) to be sung and who should be invited to the funeral. Sikhs have a more or less standard funeral rite according to the dictates of Sikhism. It is a communal event and is open to any member of the Sikh community and non-Sikh relatives, friends, colleagues and acquaintances. This ceremony signifies the completion of life.

Prayers

Prayer is an essential part of Sikh life, and patients request it frequently in hospitals and hospices. In normal circumstances, religious people pray regularly as prescribed by their religion. In Sikhism, they pray in the early hours of the morning, dusk and before going to bed. Many Sikhs pray all the time. There are also specific prayers for specific events such as birth, initiation, marriage, death and illness. In healthcare settings, the chaplain is the designated person to perform prayers requested by a patient or a family member. When a family requests to pray together with the patient, it is important for the chaplain to get an understanding of the patient's spiritual life to use the appropriate wording.

Sikh patients prefer to be clean before praying and listening to *gurbani.* Personal hygiene is an essential part of the Sikh religion and Sikhs observe it strictly. Therefore, patients may ask for cleaning their body and a fresh change of clothing before praying. It is necessary that the front-line staff are aware of it in order to fulfil their needs. The body can be wiped with a clean wet cloth/towel if the patient cannot get out of bed to wash. The patients need to wash their hands for handling Scriptural texts like a *gutka* (prayer book). It also applies to staff to do the same and to handle the *gutka* with respect. It is respectful to wrap prayer books in a cloth cover and keep them in a clean place (Rait, 2005; Hollins, 2009). Privacy is also required to pray.

Types of prayers: In Sikhism, prayer can be vocal, such as supplication (*Ardas*). It can be liturgical such as *kirtan* singing or the singing of familiar hymns from *GGS* together. Chaplains or family member(s) often read or chant hymns or *Mool Mantar* with patients. *Guru* Nanak's perception and understanding of the nature of God is given in his composition known as the *Mool Mantar*, a fundamental creed that literally means the 'Root Formula' (*GGS*, p.1). This is written at the very beginning of the *GGS* reflecting the Sikh's belief in monotheism (Appendix 3). There is also extemporaneous prayer, which is more conversational in nature and spontaneous in their wording. Typically, such prayers begin with an invocation (petition/appeal) of the Divine, followed by the thoughts and feelings of the individual offering the prayer. Such prayers may include words of gratitude, request for blessings and healing, or shared concerns for loved ones.

Bedside prayer: Chaplains, at the request of patients or their families, often perform bedside prayer. It mainly happens in acute settings and in life-threatening illnesses or injuries, before and after serious operations, or when the patient is dying or dead. This can take different forms, such as plea and supplication. The prayer within the hospital context should be short, supportive and comforting. The prayer should probably last less than a minute (Koenig, 2002, p. 28) and its content should be consistent with the religious denomination of the patient.

Plea: It is a way of pleading for God's grace. It starts with the name of the person for whom it is performed followed by a plea.

The name of the person is stated and then followed by:

ਲਈ ਵਾਹਿਗੁਰੂ ਅਗੇ ਪ੍ਰਾਥਨਾ ਕਰਦੇ ਹਾਂ ਕਿ ਆਪ ਇਹਨਾ ਦੇ ਅੰਗ ਸੰਗ ਸਹਾਈ ਹੋਵੋ।

ਆਪ ਬਹੁਤ ਦਯਾਵਾਨ ਹੋ ਅਤੇ ਹਰ ਇਕ ਦੇ ਮਨ ਦੀ ਆਸ ਜਾਣਦੇ ਹੋ।

ਹੇ ਕ੍ਰਿਪਾ ਨਿਧਾਨ ਅਪਣਾ ਮੇਹਰ ਭਰਿਆ ਹਥ ਇਹਨਾਂ ਦੇ ਸਿਰ ਤੇ ਰਖਣਾ।

ਇਹਨਾ ਨੂੰ ਅਪਣਾ ਭਾਣਾ ਮੰਨਣ ਦੀ ਸਮਰਥਾ ਬਖਸਣਾ।

This means in English translation:

This prayer is for------
May God be with you
God knows everyone's wishes.
God is caring and compassionate.
He is gracious and be His grace upon you.
Give them courage to remain under your Will.

Ardas **and** **its** **significance:** Supplication (*Ardas*) is the most commonly used act of prayer in Sikhism. It means a formal prayer or humble request. It is one of the universal and frequently performed prayers in the Sikh world, even though it was not written in its entirety by the Sikh *Gurus,* and cannot be found within the pages of the Holy Scripture. The '*Ardas*' was first composed by *Guru* Gobind Singh, the tenth *guru* of Sikhs (Sikh Net). He set the first eight lines in the first section reciting the virtues of Sikh *gurus* including invocation. The second part contains several paragraphs recounting Sikh symbols, places of worship and values significant and related to *Khalsa* (initiated Sikhs). This section has been fluid, revised extensively over the time and may be changed when reciting a 'short *ardas*'. The third section saluting the divine name is regarded as unalterable and cannot be omitted. It is a devotional text that has evolved over time to encompass the feats, accomplishments, and feelings of all generations of Sikhs. Each word in the *Ardas* has been carefully chosen for its significance in

Sikh history and prayer for the well-being of humanity, not only for Sikhs. The *Sikh Rehat Maryada,* the code of Sikh conduct and conventions, has published an approved version of the entire *Ardas.*

This prayer is a plea to God for help and support. It is also an appeal to God for the welfare and prosperity of all humankind, and a means for the Sikhs to thank God for all that God has given to humanity. It is performed for an individual or for a congregation. *Ardas* is to be offered humbly, standing with folded hands, and it may be offered lying down if a patient is too ill to stand. Some patients prefer to hold the chaplain's hand or fold their hands while praying. Chaplains should not hesitate to hold the hand of a patient if this is what a patient has asked for. It is important for Sikh chaplains or volunteers to know *Ardas* by heart, as they have to perform it when a patient or family asks for it. It is quite normal to perform the short *Ardas* in a hospital situation due to the pressure on time, circumstances and the environment. The short *Ardas* ends with ten *Gurus* and the next paragraph capturing *'panj pyare',* and martyrs (Appendix 3). The chaplain afterwards adds the name of the person for whom it is conducted and its purpose. There are occasional requests by patients for congregational prayer. It is generally conducted in extreme circumstances such as when there is a serious operation, or when the medical treatment becomes ineffective. *Ardas* is considered to be most powerful and is believed to be effective if performed from the depth of one's heart with absolute faith in God. Most patients ask the chaplain to pray for them in such a futile situation in order to keep their hope alive and intact. It is human nature to seek religious support, especially at difficult times in one's life.

Most Sikhs believe in mainstream Sikhism and they believe in the *GGS* as their living *guru*. This *Ardas* is for them. There are some denominations which claim to belong to Sikhism. For such patients, prayers should be performed according to their belief.

Recitation: It is a normal practice in the Sikh community to recite *gurbani* in adverse circumstances. When a patient is seriously ill, the family may request the chaplain to do *naam simran* (reciting the name of God) by saying *Vaheguru* (wonderful God) or recite *Mool Mantar*. It is considered the most powerful *mantar,* frequently recited during Sikh prayers and by individuals seeking God's grace. Chaplains are requested to recite with the patient or with his or her family repeatedly to create a tranquil atmosphere. Sometimes the request is also for *chupaye* (hymns of protection and security) and *Japuji Sahib* (hymns for balancing and uplifting).

Recorded *Gurbani* or *kirtan* are easily available on CDs, iPod and iPhones. Many hospital chaplaincy departments normally acquire them and make arrangements to play them at the patient's bedside if requested. Some of the patients have apps on their smartphones and they may prefer to listen on their own devices at their own convenience. This can easily be organised in single occupancy rooms in hospitals without disturbing other patients. Headphones should be used by patients if the bed is in a shared area. Listening to Scriptures and *kirtan* is always soothing.

Role of the chaplain as a faith advisor

Chaplains also offer a faith perspective and advice on the matters that NHS, health professionals, patients and their families are unsure of. Sikhs also want to make sure that the decisions they make are not against their faith or beliefs.

Organ donation: Organ donation is the gift of an organ to help someone else who needs a transplant. It is generally accepted in the Sikh community that organ donation, during life or after death, and receiving organs are putative on the grounds of donation (part of *seva*), and it is a humanitarian cause. It is considered an extremely positive act, coming from the compassionate desire to benefit others. It helps someone to save his or her life or to improve the quality of life. It is an individual's choice to donate their organs when they die. This includes heart, lungs, kidneys, liver, pancreas and small bowel. Tissues such as skin, bone, heart valves and corneas can also help others. An organ may be removed or donated only after the person is declared dead. However, the patient needs to be kept alive with the aid of a machine until the organ is retrieved. Those who want to become a donor have to join the NHS Organ Donor Register to ensure that their wishes are recorded and should let their decision known to those closest to them. Hospitals do not enforce their authority on it. It is only done with the good will and acceptance of both patients and their families. The NHS has also prepared leaflets on organ donation and transplantation giving a multi-faith perspective and which are easily available from hospitals and hospices. There is also a website for further information (NHS).

Blood donation and blood transfusions are also acceptable in *Sikhism* as part of the acts of donation and altruism (*GGS*, p. 815), suggesting good deeds for the benefit of others and belief in medical treatments.

Post-mortem: Sikhism opposes mutilation of the body and therefore autopsies (dissection, post-mortem) are not permitted unless required by state law. Every effort should be made to ensure that hair is not removed from *amritdhari* and turbaned Sikhs during the investigation where these examinations are permitted, and that the person is left in a presentable condition.

Artificial life support: The Sikh belief is that birth and death are in God's hands, and therefore, artificial life support for a prolonged period is not encouraged, especially for terminally ill patients. More than anything, the wishes of the patient should be respected, ensuring that the patient and family are aware of and understand information on the procedure. When a clinical decision indicates that there is no hope of surviving the illness without extraordinary means, and no reasonable benefit to the patient, it is permissible to remove life support equipment. The natural process of death then allows the dying person to accept the Will of God.

Faith perspectives

Chaplains are often consulted by patients, their families and staff to seek advice on the faith perspectives on the concerns and matters that arise from time to time in order to make informed decisions. These may include pregnancy and childbirth, assisted reproductive technology, screening tests, abortion, contraception, the recent Coronavirus pandemic, or for any other issues concerning religion.

Pregnancy and childbirth: The beginning of life has become a contentious subject dealt with by theology, biology and law, and has serious religious implications. There are many questions and a range of answers. Biological answers are commonly accepted, and this tends to apply to the law (the law of the land dominates many decisions). The beginning of life has two sources, natural and assisted. According to the natural source, when the chromosomes of a human egg and sperm combine at fertilisation, then a genetically unique cell is created that has the potential to develop into a baby (*GGS*, p.1022). When fertilisation happens outside the womb, it can have implications on the beginning of life and the position of a soul, though fertilisation has the potential of ensoulment (Bio Edge). At this stage, religions differ in their opinion that a human life is created that should be fully respected, whereas other opinions suggest that human life develops along with certain capacities such as sentience (capable of feeling through physical senses). It has serious implications for the work of a chaplain. Sikhism accepts that life begins with conception in the womb, and there are references to this found in the *GGS* (pp. 74, 1013, 1022; Jhutti-Johal, 2011, p.22).

A human life can also be conceived by using new scientific inventions called assisted reproduction techniques (ART). It refers to several advanced techniques that aid fertilisation and involve handling eggs and embryos outside the body, mixing them with sperm and putting the embryos back into a woman's body. It also covers treatment in which only sperm are handled (i.e., intrauterine or artificial insemination). This includes IVF as well as a few of its variations, designed primarily to help infertile couples to conceive. Assisted reproduction techniques include IVF (In-Vitro Fertilisation), GIFT (Gamete Intrafallopian Transfer), Zift (Zygote Intrafallopian transfer), ICSI (Intracytoplasmic sperm insertion) and FASIAR (Follicle Aspiration, Sperm Injection and Assisted Follicular Rupture).

The family or medical staff may ask chaplains if the faith of the mother allows the use of this technology to conceive. There seem to be no explicit injunctions in the *GGS* and there is hardly any guidance given in the Sikh Code of Conduct (1950). The interested couples with fertility problems use ART to have a biological child. In this way, children are born within the confines of marriage, the process is led by the joint decision of the couple, and uses the couple's own eggs and sperm, though these are fertilised outside the body in a laboratory. Sikhism favours family life and allows treatments to make life normal. Therefore, the procedures of ART are useful for family integrity based on theological essence. Firm faith believers think this procedure evades nature. This medical treatment is for a good cause for the couples who desperately want a child. There is also a stigma within the Sikh community that a baby is 'purchased' or 'bought' by using such techniques. Chaplains need to listen to the mother's emotions and assure her that it is not a 'bought' baby. It is a gift from God. At the request of the mother, *Ardas* should be performed for the successful treatment and welfare of the mother.

Jhutti-Johal (2011) highlighted ethical concerns over the use of ART where embryos are created from a third-party donor with whom the child will not have any relation with after birth. She raises fundamental questions around the concept of marriage, family and the role of the biological parents. She further highlights the use of artificial insemination using the sperm of a donor. According to her, the insemination of a wife with the sperm of someone rather than her husband could be viewed as only 'one step removed from adultery', resulting in adultery-like stigma attached to the process. Her main concern is that since the child will not have genetic material from the father, who will care for the child, he may not be able to form strong bonds with the child. One can argue that it is unfair to claim this as adultery-like or adultery. A medical treatment cannot be associated with adultery. It is not a 'love affair' outside marriage and does not involve sexual intercourse.

Surrogacy: Surrogacy is another method of reproduction when a woman is unable to have a child because of a medical or any other reason. This happens with one's husband or partner's sperm, with the consent of the wife, in a safe and caring environment. A surrogate mother is commissioned to bear a child. The question of biological parents is linked with surrogacy, as a surrogate woman carries the embryo for a full term and gives birth to someone else's baby. The question raised for chaplains is the morality of this. Sikhism, again, has no implicit answer for this though giving a life through legal acceptance and with the agreement of both women should defy the question of immorality. In both cases of children born through surrogacy or artificial insemination from someone else's sperm rather than their husband or partner, the concerns may not be realistic. Couples desperate to have a child use this method and will try to give the child the best possible upbringing. Chaplains need to be sensitive to the feelings of those involved in this process. It can be an emotional time. The chaplain should do what is necessary for the welfare of the surrogate mother, and the family involved. In the case of surrogacy, religious care should be given to the surrogate mother, if she needs it, during her pregnancy and hospital stay. The change in 2005 to the law of the United Kingdom concerning the anonymity of the donor is another factor which might cause disruption in a family unit, especially when the child reaches the age of eighteen (HFEA). One can argue, considering the UK laws on this matter that it is a risk parents have to take.

The religious care and faith approval that chaplains must explain around pregnancy can be quite tricky, and have implications for a range of issues, such as screening tests and abortions.

Screening tests: Screening tests offered during pregnancy are either ultrasound scans, blood tests or a combination of both. Screening was first introduced to find any health problems that could affect the mother or baby, such as infectious diseases and any abnormality a baby may have. The tests can help in making choices about further tests and care or treatment during pregnancy or after the birth of a baby. This means that they can get earlier treatment or make informed decisions about their health. These tests are not harmful, though they can lead to difficult decisions to be made by the childbearer in case of any serious diagnosis. As technology advanced, it was made possible to detect the sex of a baby. There is no religious objection if it is done to find out whether or not a baby has any abnormality, but it is disapproved of to find the sex of a baby with the intention of aborting a female foetus. Sikhism strongly opposes aborting a female foetus.

Foetus aborting: Aborting a foetus is a modern form of female infanticide. Sikh *gurus* condemned female infanticide in their times and the Sikh *Rehat Maryada* (1950) consistently maintains the same stance over it. There are clear instructions in the Sikh *Rehat Maryada:* 'A Sikh should not kill his daughter nor should he maintain any relationship with a killer of a daughter' (Article xvi). In spite of these injunctions, it became common among the Sikhs to abort the female foetus, giving preference to a boy. This has increased recently with the advent of foetal sonograms and ultrasounds, which gave couples access to find out the sex of the foetus. The Panjabi culture, which is so ingrained in many Sikhs, gives preference to boys in order to carry on the family name, perform their funerals, give them financial support and provide care in their old age. Only a minority choose girls to balance their family. In order to enforce it, an edict was issued on 18 April 2001 stating that any Sikh aborting a female foetus would be excommunicated as the practice was forbidden under *Rehat Maryada*. This practice was severely condemned by Sikhs all over the world and now there are legal restrictions, not only on finding out the sex of a baby, but also on aborting the foetus (Ahmad, 2010).

Sikhs are facing new challenges with medical advances where the parents can choose the sex before conception in techniques such as Preimplantation Genetic Diagnosis (PGD). This allows the creation of embryos outside the body, and the parents can choose which embryos, based on sex alone, will be used for their implantation (Robertson, 2003; Sermon et al, 2004). Similarly, sperm sorting involves sorting out sperm samples into male and female. Obviously, the common choice in Panjabi culture is for boys, as they are considered to be assets, and the girls a burden due to dowry, education and also caring for their *izzat* (honour) (Wikipedia). Conceiving a child through varied medical advances are acceptable on the grounds of family integrity and approval for medical treatments in Sikhism but choosing an embryo on the basis of sex is discriminatory and is severely condemned.

Sikhs need to change their mindset and adhere strictly to the Sikh teachings and culture on the status of women. Sikh authorities in India took many steps to ensure experimenting with embryos, and foetus aborting is not only discouraged, but also disapproved of. It can be argued that one of the problems with scientific advances is that humans find ways to abuse them to their own advantages, more often adopting destructive ways rather than using them to the advantage of humanity.

Abortion: Human life is regarded as a gift from God and is considered to be precious in Sikh teachings. Abortion is considered to be an interference in the creative work of God, and also does not comply with accepting the Will of God. If conception has taken place, it is a sin to destroy life, and hence deliberate miscarriage or abortion is not approved of in Sikhism. It could be justified under the circumstances, if there is a valid reason judged by medical experts, such as the physical or mental well-being of a mother or a foetal abnormality. Jhutti-Johal (2011) rightly pointed out that while aborting a foetus with a disability goes against the religious teachings of *karma* and *hukam*, it also sends out the wrong message to the community that people with disabilities are not equal or valued by society. The decision of doing so needs careful attention about the financial resources, physical capacity of the parents and the ability to provide the right care for the child. Somehow, it is prevalent in the Sikh community to have an abortion in case of unintended pregnancies from extramarital affairs or a sexual relationship outside marriage, or the pregnancy of an unmarried girl to save her *izzat* (honour) in the community. Some of them are an outcome of contradictory social norms, for example, pregnancy without marriage, or aborting a female foetus due to dowry and the continuation of the family name.

Abortion can only be justified on medical grounds when the mother's life is in danger by the continuation of the pregnancy or if it is necessary for the physical and mental wellbeing of the mother. It is also asked for in situations such as rape. There is no single verdict on this subject. It is important to view the whole situation (health of the parents, financial situation and accommodation) to make any decision. One volunteer related her encounter where a woman wanted an abortion saying that they were suffering financially and could not properly feed one child. The volunteer also added that she was genuine and supported her. The chaplain may be asked for help when the pregnant woman is struggling to make a decision, either for further tests in the case of screening, or for termination or abortion. In many cases, common sense prevails and also, as a person-centred decision, the onus is on the individual and her family, though the chaplain can give them a faith perspective to make informed decisions.

Contraception: Marriage and conception are sacred acts blessed by God. Sikhs are familiar with the concept of family planning. Family planning and birth control are mentioned in the *GGS,* stressing on self-control to regulate sexual activities. Sikhs have been pursuing family planning by following the religious teaching of restraint, the middle way between self-indulgence and abstinence (Rait, 2010). There is also a prevalent cultural practice of having sex during the safe time between the periods of a woman's menstrual cycle. It is managed through natural and experimental ways for which results may not always be consistent. Modern devices of contraception (birth control implants, intra-uterine devices (coil), the morning after pill and the contraceptive pills) have no mention in the *GGS* as these were not available when it was written. Gatrad suggests that there are no injunctions in Sikhism against the use of contraceptives within a married relationship and no insistence on abstinence in the *Guru Granth Sahib* (2005, p. 354). Sikhs should be able to use these modern devices to fulfil their physical desires in line with the *GGS* and plan their family, especially in a Western environment where many Sikh women are holding professional jobs and acquiring a high professional status. It is also important for women in developing countries to have as many children they can feed and give them a good quality of life according to their means. Conservative and religious Sikhs may consider the use of contraceptives as interfering with nature, taking charge of God's role to decide when a new life should begin. It is best to use a common-sense approach to family planning according to one's circumstances. It may become necessary, in the case of upbringing of existing children or ill health of the partner, where medical advice needs to take priority. This offers flexibility for a personal choice between modern techniques or self-restraint.

Contraception and sex education have been controversial topics, especially on the basis that they promote youngsters to do 'wrong' things, become promiscuous (immoral) or may encourage them to indulge in sexual activities. Occasionally, chaplains tending to younger patients face such issues. Sikhs have cultural differences in the society they live in. The Sikh faith does not allow sex before or outside marriage. This makes the question of contraception invalid for youngsters. At the same time, these youngsters are born and brought up in this country, influenced by indigenous culture. The onus falls on the parents to make their children aware of religious beliefs if they feel strongly. Sikhism does not allow pre-marital sex or adultery.

Conclusion

In conclusion, human life is a cycle of birth and death. Life cycle rites of Sikhs are closely linked with the Sikh religion and there are religious rites, rituals, prayers, blessings and asking for God's grace through prayers and supplication (*Ardas*). Sikh chaplains and volunteers working in hospitals and other healthcare institutions are expected to perform prayers and blessings for patients, their families and carers. Reference has been made to the religious rituals undertaken by chaplains and volunteers. On many occasions, hospital staff also need religious support to cope with difficult situations and their own emotional wellbeing. Staff also approach chaplains seeking their views, pertinent to their faiths, on issues that arise from time to time. There are certain ethical principles which are intrinsic to Sikh beliefs and practices, hugely affecting the Sikh way of life. Some issues do not seem to have the approval of the Sikh faith and others may have no mention in Sikh Scriptures. Chaplains must use their common sense and find a way to resolve situations whilst maintaining the theological essence. This creates a difficult situation for Sikh chaplains and volunteers. Lack of relevant literature, resources and support systems hardly help to ease the situation. In recent times, the Coronavirus pandemic has brought disaster on humanity and many areas of human functioning. It is important to observe any measure which can provide human safety. Health care workers belonging to BAME communities are working compassionately and tirelessly with dedication to save others' lives, with and without adequate PPE supply even when it became a recognised fact that Black and Asian communities are more susceptible to this virus. Sikh male healthcare workers are disappointed not to get suitable face masks to fit their beard.

References

Ahmad, N. (2010). Female feticide in India. *Issues Law Med* 2010. Summer, 26 (1), pp. 13-29.

Cobb, M. (2005). *The hospital chaplain's handbook: a guide for good practice*. Norwich: Canterbury Press.

Gatrad, A. R., Jhutti-Johal, J., Gill, P. S. and Sheikh, A. (2005). Sikh birth customs. *Archives of diseases in childhood*, 90: 560-3.

Guru Granth Sahib. (n.d.). Amritsar: *Shiromani Gurdwara Prabandhak Committee*. (Standard version of 1430 pages in Panjabi).

Henley, A and Schott, J. (1999). *Culture, religion and patient care in a multi-ethnic society: a handbook for professionals*. London: Age Concern.

Hollins, S. (2009). *Religion, culture and healthcare: a practical handbook for use in healthcare environments.* 2nd ed. Abington, Radcliffe Publishing.

Jhutti-Johal, J. (2011). *Sikhism today.* London: Continuum International Publishing Group.

Koenig, H. G. (2002). *Spirituality in patient care: why, how, when, and what.* Philadelphia & London: Templeton Foundation Press.

Nabha, K. S. (1962.) *Gurmat Martand.* Amritsar: *Shromani Prabandhak* Committee.

Nesbitt, E. (2007). Sikhism. In: Morgan, P. and Lawton, C. (eds.) *Ethical issues in six religious traditions.* 2nd ed. Edinburgh, University of Edinburgh Press.

Neuberger, J. (1987). *Caring for dying people of different faiths.* London: Austen Cornish Publishers in association with the Lisa Sainsbury Foundation.

Neuberger, J. (1999). *Dying well: A guide to enabling a good death.* Cheshire: Hochland & Hochland Ltd.

Neuberger, J. (2004). *Caring for dying people of different faiths.* 3rd ed. Abingdon: Radcliffe Medical Press.

Rait, S. K. (2005). *Sikh women in England: Their religious and cultural beliefs and social practices.* London, Trentham Books.

Rait, S. K. (2013). *A guide to being a Sikh chaplain*. Great Britain: SKR.

Rait, S.K. with Bhogal, I. S. (2010). *Understanding of Sikhism*. Ripon: Plug and Tap.

Robertson, J.A. (2003). Extending preimplantation genetic diagnosis: ethical issues in new uses of preimplantation genetic diagnosis'. *Human Reproduction*, 18 (3), pp. 465-71.

Sermon, K. A., Van, S. and Liebaers, I. (2004). Preimplantation genetic diagnosis. *The Lancet*, 363 (9421), pp. 1633-41.

Shiromani Gurdwara Prabandhak Committee (1950). *The Rehat Maryada* (The Sikh Code of conduct). Amritsar, Punjab, India.

Singh, R. ed. (2012). *Hukamname*: *Adesh Sandesh...Sri Akal Takht Sahib* (collection of edicts, orders and messages issued from Sri Akal takht Sahib). Amritsar: Singh Brothers.

Singh, T. (1990). Perception of Truth in teachings of *Guru* Nanak Dev edited by Taran Singh. Patiala: Punjabi University Department of *Sri Guru Granth Sahib* Studies.

Toole, M. M. (2006). *Handbook for chaplains*: *comfort my people*. New York: Paulist Press.

Websites

Gov.uk (2014). *Marriage (Same Sex Couples) Act: A factsheet. - gov.uk* [online] Available at: https://assets.publishing.service.gov .uk/government/uploads/system/uploads/attachment_data/file/270 230/140107_M_SSC__Act_factsheet_.pdf [Accessed 30 March 2018].

Gov.uk (2013). Marriage (Same Sex Couples) Act 2013. [online] Available at: http://www.legislation.gov.uk/ukpga/2013/30/contents/ enacted [Accessed 23 Mar. 2018].

HFEA (2018) *Donation law.* [online] Available at: https://www.hfea.gov.uk/donation/donors/#:~:text=Donation%20la w,for%20your%20name%20and%20address. [Accessed 30 Mar. 2018]

Jhutti-Johal, J. (2014) *Female foeticide.* [online] Available at: https://savinghumans.wordpress.com/tag/female-foeticide/ [Accessed 30 Mar. 2018].

Mishra, S. (n.d.) *Assisted Reproduction Techniques*. [online] Available at: www.academia.edu/17172331/Artificial_Reproductive_ Techniques [Accessed 20 Sept. 2019].

NHS (2019). *A Sikh perspective on organ donation.* [online] Available at: https://www.organdonation.nhs.uk/helping-you-to-decide/your-faith-and-beliefs/sikhism/ [Accessed 20 Sept. 2019].

Neaves, W. (2017). *The status of the human embryo in various religions.* [online] Available at: https://dev.biologists.org/content/144/14/2541 [Accessed 20 Sept. 2019].

SikhNet (2013). History *of Sikh Ardas.* [online] Available at: https://www.sikhnet.com/news/history-sikh-ardas [Accessed 26 July 2019]

Wikipedia (2020) *Female infanticide in India.* [online] Available at: https://en.wikipedia.org/wiki/Female_infanticide_in_India>. [Accessed 30 Mar. 2018].

Bibliography

Cole, W.O. and Sambhi, P. S. (1978). *The Sikhs*: *Their religious beliefs and practices.* London: Routledge & Kegan Paul.

Gulshan, G. S. (2005). *Darpan Sikh Rehat Maryada* (Panjabi). Essex: *Khalsa Pracharik Jatha* (U.K).

Singh, G. (2009). *The Sikh faith*: *a universal message.* Amritsar: Singh Brothers.

Chapter 8

End of life care

Introduction

This chapter relates to end of life care, and its importance in human life. It includes how to break the sad news of serious or life-threatening illnesses to the patient and family, their reaction to the news, and includes stages of human reactions towards dying. It explains future planning for any seriously ill or dying patient, such as taking care of the legal aspects of finance and healthcare matters. It further explains the role of the family, the needs of the dying and the role of a hospice. It explores the end of life experience, being there at the end, physical changes of the dying person covering how the dying patient and family is cared in their final moments. It defines euthanasia, explains the pros and cons of it and Sikh views on euthanasia and good death.

Death and dying

Sikhs believe death is the ultimate phase of human life. All human beings experience it later or sooner. Religious people believe death is in God's hands and is beyond human control. Death is an immensely personal experience, influenced by every individual's belief system, personal history and the surrounding culture. 'Religious and cultural rituals invest death with meaning from religious, psychological and social perspectives' (Firth, 2000, p.338). 'Their dying process will happen in its own time and in its own way' (Brayne and Fenwick, 2008, p.6). Sanders suggests:

> *A common belief is that death can have a power of its own, and will steal upon a person, catching everyone unawares. Countless documented accounts contradict this idea. Instead, the theme that surfaces is that many times, depending upon the physical condition of the patient and the circumstances of the death, humans can have the ability to actually choose the time in which they will pass from this earthly life* (2007, p.66).

She further adds in choosing the time and conditions of departure, the dying may be illustrating an assertive power, a final exercise of free will.

Death and dying have become a hot subject in western society, which acknowledges and promotes individual choices. The whole idea behind this is to encourage people to talk openly and freely about death, the choices to make regarding how one wants to die, how the dead body is to be disposed of, and how dear ones left behind grieve. There was a time when most people died at home, and this was a societal norm, even in the West. It has changed with shifting family patterns, women in employment, technological advancement, increased stress on independent living and the importance given to personal choices. There is nothing right or wrong in what people practice. Faith, belief, culture, and the environment in which one grows up generally influence these matters. The Sikh religion prescribes death and dying rituals leaving little capacity for personal choices. Sikhism has clear guidance on death and dying and Sikhs generally adhere to them.

Sikhism advocates for and promotes family life. Many families still live together under one roof in the Sikh community, and elderly parents generally live with their sons. It becomes their duty to look after their parents. Living in the family and looking after elderly parents are both a religious injunction and cultural tradition. Until recently, Sikh families were hesitant in sending elderly parents to care homes. The community members frowned upon it. For family members, it was an act of embarrassment. The sons were criticised for not performing their duty towards their elderly parents. Most Sikhs still prefer to die at home, surrounded by their families and friends. It is partly because they do not like the hospital environment and partly due to the cultural and language barriers. Some are not happy with hospital meals and personal hygiene and others do not want to be isolated from the family. Most hospitals and hospices do not have adequate religious care for the dying Sikhs and Sikhs prefer to die at home as they can get the care they want. Most families try to fulfil the wishes of the dying and strive hard to give the best possible care. Home is a place where people feel comfortable despite the loving and caring atmosphere and good facilities in many hospices. Family members including children become familiar with death when it happens in the house surrounded by sons, daughters and grandchildren. They all experience death and talk about it.

Many people in the West now die in hospitals, hospices and care homes, including some Sikhs. Sometimes families are not around and there are occasions when people die alone, without the presence of family members and relatives. Some people die in the hospital in the hope of prolonging their lives by availing of medical treatments and others need palliative care and medication for unbearable pain. It is the opinion of many patients, especially the elderly, that chemotherapy is painful and a horrible experience. In some cases, it only extends life for a few months. Some patients often wonder if it is necessary to put an old and frail person in that situation. The only valid answer to this question seems to be that of the medical ethics of prolonging life and doing their best medically.

Breaking the sad news to the patients

Buckman defines bad news as 'any news that drastically and negatively alters the patient's view of her or his future' (1994, p.11). He further adds that it depends on what the patient already knows or suspects about the future. It becomes necessary for a doctor or consultant to tell the patient when diagnosed with a terminal or life-threatening illness. Patients are always anxious to know their diagnosis and it is a part of professional duty. In the UK, law demands that a patient has a right to know his or her diagnosis. Buckman suggests: 'Doing this task well enhances your own satisfaction in your professional life' (1994, p. 6). Breaking news to a patient needs the special skills of good communication. It is the duty of a consultant or a senior doctor to break the news but in practice, a senior experienced nurse in NHS hospitals generally does it. The disclosing to patients after a diagnosis of malignancy is always difficult. Some physicians favour telling the relatives of the patient but do not disclose the facts to the patient in order to avoid an emotional outburst. Shirley Firth states that Hindu and Sikh doctors may also be in a dilemma because sometimes the patient or relative collapses emotionally on being told that an illness is terminal. She quotes the wordings of a doctor within the context of Hindu and Sikh patients: 'The majority of patients don't want to know - the relatives may have an inner idea, but they don't want to know. They may cry or become hysterical' (2000, p.30). In most Sikh families, it is preferred that this type of information should not be given directly to the patient, especially in the case of diagnosis of cancer. The doctors have to be careful when disclosing a diagnosis of terminal illness within Asian communities. It has been observed that while visiting Sikh patients, just the word cancer is synonymous of death, and it shocks and frightens them. They think that the person might then make no effort at recovery, and lose the will to fight, which when possessed might give him/her a little longer to live. The family normally choose a family member with whom the doctor should communicate with just to protect the patient. There may be a need, in some rare instances, where a head of the household should know of the shortness of his or her expected life in order to bring their affairs in order. A healthier, stronger individual can cope with it better if the news is broken in a manner that there is hope with new treatments. It is also easier for the family to discuss such matters in times of relative good health to arrange for financial security for the children and others while the head of the household is still functioning.

Some doctors are sensitive to their patient's needs and quite successfully present the patient with the awareness of a serious illness without taking hope away from him or her. If a doctor can speak freely with his or her patients about the diagnosis of malignancy without equating it necessarily with impending death, he or she will do the patient a great service. They should at the same time leave the door open for hope, namely new drugs, treatments and new research. The person disclosing the news should choose their wording carefully. It must be sensitive and skilful. The main purpose achieved by maintaining hope is encouraging patients not to give up. At the same time, those responsible to disclose the news should be careful not to give false hope which is unethical during a worrying time for the patient and the family.

Shirley Firth is of the opinion that:

> Lack of communication between Asians and medical staff may cause great frustration, especially in hospital. If they are kept in the dark about the prognosis and miss actually being present at the point of death. Sometimes it is felt that lack of sensitivity on the part of doctors and nurses borders on racism, particularly when assumptions are made about the patient's or relative's capacity to understand what is going on, because of real or perceived language difficulties (2000, p.31).

It is important to consider the manner and time of telling the truth, taking into consideration the individual's circumstances and capacity to take it. It is only fair if professionals can involve the family and work as a team.

Reaction of the patient to the news

The patients may react in many different ways. Neuberger suggests: 'One of the most common reactions is denial. "It is not true". "It cannot be me". "I want a second opinion". After denial comes anger and acceptance' (1999, p.106). It is normal for any human being to react to any news of a terminal illness. Kubler-Ross relates different stages of human feelings when a patient gets to know of the time-limiting illness. She describes the first stage of denial and isolation, the second stage of anger, rage, envy and resentment, the third stage that of bargaining, the fourth stage that of depression and the fifth stage is finally of acceptance (1973, pp. 34-121). Buckman (1988) related that this was unequivocally important and new work, though there have been many difficulties in applying several parts of this framework to the practical care of patients facing death. He presented the 'Three-stage Model' (Beginning-Middle-End). These stages explain human reactions based on the initial stage of illness, the middle is the chronic stage of 'being ill' and the final is the stage of acceptance (1994, pp 28-30).

Stages of reactions for Sikh patients: There is no concrete research conducted on the stages of reactions for Sikh patients.

The stages stated here are based on the author's observation of visiting Sikh patients in hospitals and hospice. These are the first stage of shock and numbness, the second stage of disbelief and denial, the third stage of dismay and depression, the fourth stage of bargaining and the fifth and final stage of acceptance or struggling to accept.

It is a common experience of Sikh patients to get shocked and numb when they first become aware of their terminal illness. The author has seen 'tears in the eyes of many' and some just become stern with the shock. It is natural and often expressed by saying: "I can't believe it"; "it cannot happen to me"; "I have been healthy"; and "there were no symptoms previously of it". Once they get over the shock, the feelings of disbelief appear and they often say: "I have never done anything wrong"; "I never think badly of anyone". Then occurs the sense of denial saying "it is not true"; "the diagnosis may not be right"; "need to have a second opinion".

For most people, denial works successfully and is not so much a phase an individual passes through as an inner shield that he or she slips behind from time to time when in need of respite from the stresses of his or her situation. (Kearney, 2007, p.68).

Once their illness is confirmed, all those feelings of shock, disbelief and denial are overtaken, mainly by dismay, envy and resentment. Sikh patients often do not get angry but feel dismayed and blame others for what has happened to them. At this stage they often say "God is not fair with me"; "the doctor has not looked after me properly"; "I have been complaining for a long time but nobody took me to the doctor" and "I have not done anything wrong in this life, it must be my previous *karmas*". They become resentful and envious of others who are enjoying their life in spite of their old age or someone coping well even after serious illness. When physicians have given up, they lose heart and many feel low and depressed. It is an outcome of loss when it becomes difficult for a patient to deny his or her illness.

Bargaining is very common in Sikh patients. They generally become very polite and compromising by this time. They begin to bargain with God to fulfil their plea in exchange of a reward or a promise. The promises made by patients are generally to dedicate their life to the *gurdwara*, doing all kinds of *seva* (voluntary selfless service), donating organs, donating money to charity, doing different types of prayers and visiting and donating to some historic *gurdwaras* in exchange for getting better, having some extended time, followed by the wish of a comfortable and peaceful end. Most bargains made with God are generally kept a secret from family and friends though sometimes these are shared with chaplains. Most Sikh patients keep their promise, especially if they believe God has become gracious and favoured their wish. Buckman (1994) thinks that bargaining is not a stage, but an individual coping strategy.

Once bargaining fails and physicians have given up, the patient may make a recovery, and this has actually happened in rare circumstances as Sikh patients have shared their experiences with me. It is therefore important that physicians should talk to a patient in a way of keeping hope alive. For those who are not so lucky to make a comeback, and other defensive strategies seem exhausted, it is the time when the end seems obvious. It is common among Sikh patients to go through it as a reaction to something beyond human control such as 'rab da bhanna' (God's Will) and for others, the alternative is to accept it. It is the difficult time of internal tension to reach the final decision of acceptance, the real reality of the situation. Not everyone accepts it. Some struggle until the end, others accept it as God's Will. Death is a final stage for Sikhs, still some fear to face it in spite of their religious beliefs of accepting the 'Hukam' (order) and remaining under God's Will. Fear of dying is universal (Becker, 1973). In practice, there are exceptional individuals who are so comfortable and well balanced in their lives that they can face the end of life with perfect equanimity. Human feeling does not work in any sequence or consistency. Some Sikh patients blame others until the very last. They cannot accept their end. On the contrary, many patients maintain hope even after knowing the reality of the situation. It is also dependent on how the physicians, chaplains and family treat them. At this time, encouragement and reassurance are not meaningful. It is a time when too much interference from visitors who try to cheer them up hinders the emotional preparation of dying. It is also important to assure the person that he or she is loved, cared for and valued. It is comforting for the patients to know that they are not forgotten when nothing else can be done for them.

It is necessary to point out that this type of depression is necessary and beneficial if the patient is to die in a state of acceptance and peace. This is the time when the patient may just ask for a prayer, when he or she begins to occupy him/herself with things ahead rather than behind. Undoubtedly, it is a difficult time for any patient. The Sikh chaplain at this stage can help the patient by listening or holding their hand in silence, as most patients do not want any conversation.

Many spouses feel that they suffer as much as the patient does. It is undoubtedly a hard and painful journey for them. It is not only the patient who goes through preparatory grief, but also the main carer. Some of them cannot even shed any tears at the time of a patient's departure, indicating the effect of their preparatory grief. Sikhs normally listen to *kirtan* or special hymns of peace (*Sukhmani Sahib*) which create tranquillity and give comfort to patients. There is a silent presence of loved ones waiting to hear lasting words from the departing soul. This is the time when the presence of the chaplain is necessary to support not only the patient, but also the family, to provide religious care, performing *Ardas* or any other preferred prayer and to answer any questions raised by the family.

This area of spiritual care needs further in-depth and structured research to establish the Sikh stages of human reaction on firm ground in order to compare and contrast them with already established patterns. For example, Buckman (1994) thinks guilt is a common reaction to dying, though it seems less common in Sikh patients, only in rare instances in this study.

Preparing for the future

There are certain documents that are necessary for everyone to make life easier after a loved one passes away. It is essential when someone becomes seriously ill or is diagnosed with a life-threatening illness to have certain documents in place, such as Lasting Powers of Attorney, Advance Healthcare Directives, and wills.

Lasting Powers of Attorney: A Lasting Power of Attorney is a legal document which appoints the person(s) of your choice to sign and make decisions on your behalf, should you lose your 'mental capacity' or the ability to make decisions for yourself. There are two types of Lasting Power of Attorney; one is to make financial decisions and the other for healthcare decisions. It is an important document to have as your spouse or child do not automatically have the rights to act on your behalf. If you have assets in your sole name and lose mental capacity, no one else is able to deal with them. In that case, an order of the court may be required which can be costly and take longer. Even then, the person appointed to act on your behalf may not be of your choice.

Advance Directives: Some elderly people are good at making it known to the family that they do not want to receive any life-extending treatment, including resuscitation. It is important and useful to make an advance decision or a living will. A person specifies what actions should be taken for their health, including refusing a specific type of treatment if they are no longer able to make decisions for themselves in this legal document. If there is an advance directive in place, the healthcare professionals follow the individual's instructions and act accordingly. The medical staff should ensure that it is clearly stated in the 'End of Life Care Plan' and is written or copied in the person's medical notes. This will help other staff in case the patient is moved from one location to another. This document also gives legal protection to professional health workers for withholding the treatment and helps the patients to die with dignity and according to their will.

Making a will: Making a will is essential to ensure that your property (the estate) goes where you would like it to go. Your estate does not necessarily pass to your spouse under the intestacy rules (the body of law that determines who is entitled to the property from the estate under the rules of inheritance). The advantage of having a will is to ensure that your property goes to the person(s) you want it to. It allows you to control the distribution of your assets, appoint guardians for your children, avoid disputes and save inheritance tax and nursing home fees. It is possible to change the will with any changing circumstances. Most professionally drawn wills are reviewed every five years.

It is normal in many Sikh families to leave it to the family to decide, which could create conflicts and family disputes. Some may end up in court cases due to the lack of legal documents. Younger Sikhs often like to take care of these documents, knowing their importance, whereas the older generation tend to stick to the traditional behaviour. Sikhs now live globally, and they need to adopt and accept indigenous traditions and get legal documents relevant to their life situations. It helps everyone: the patient, family and healthcare professionals.

Family: Family should be involved from the beginning as they play an important role in giving meaningful care to the terminally ill patient. It also helps them to prepare themselves to make the journey along with the patient. It is a general practice to tell the husband or wife of the seriousness of the illness, and the decision is left to them of how they disclose or share the information with the patient and the rest of the family.

> *The few people who have experienced the crisis of impending death have found that communication is only difficult the first time and becomes simpler with gained experience. Instead of increasing alienation and isolation, the couple find themselves communicating in more meaningful and deeper senses and may find a closeness and understanding that only suffering can bring* (Kubler-Ross, 1973, p.143).

It helps if there is accommodation for patients' family members in such treatment units. Hospices have these arrangements in place, whereas some new hospital units are trying to make accommodation available. The social worker or chaplain should be available to relatives, with sufficient time for each one of them, and physicians and nurses should be frequent visitors in such rooms in order to be accessible for listening to any concerns of the family and answering their questions.

Needs of the dying person

The dying person needs not only pain control, but also spiritual support and loving care. Brayne and Fenwick point out:

> *Of course, the dying need appropriate physical pain control. But they also have what might be termed soul needs - to feel heard, cared-for, connected and emotionally safe. They want to be understood and accepted like anyone else.* (2008, p. 9).

People react in different ways. Those who are well looked after by their families and feel loved and valued often have a peaceful death. They tend to thank those who cared for them. Those who are frightened to die still cling to hope of a miracle and often they struggle until the end. Sometimes they express their feelings in an aggressive way. People can be frightened, confused, and unable to express what they are feeling or what they want to say. Some struggle to die and they are desperate to die. There are varied and mixed experiences of dying Sikhs. Some Sikhs accept death as a normal process, without any worries or hesitation. They like to listen to prayers and ask for religious stories. They seem to have a peaceful death because of their religious beliefs and love and care given by their families. Some Sikh men and women have a story to tell. Some of them feel proud of their own achievements and are happy to share success stories of their children. Others generally have a story of how badly and unfairly their own family, and sometimes the extended family, had treated them. Some tell of joint family living and how the daughters-in-law behave. Some Sikh men talk about family conflicts. Some talk about the financial advantages and property taken by their brothers and relatives in the Punjab. This relieves them of the burden they have been holding for years. Normally, within days, they die and leave all the sufferings behind. It is good that they could relate to someone in the hospital and hospice whom they could not only trust but also feel have empathy and understanding. This indicates that they review their life and experiences and try to get rid of the painful memories so that they can die in a calm and dignified manner. Dying people try to resolve unfinished issues from the past in the way they choose.

Death was seen as a sign of failure in an advanced medical system focusing on cures and the preservation of human life. Within the process:

> *It had become depersonalized, desacralized and a terminal clinical event. It was this type of grim experience, both of the dying and those who witnessed their deaths that provided a major impetus for the development of the modern hospice movement which has attempted to reaffirm a spiritual aspect of dying and death.* (Cobb, 2001, pp. 48-49)

Role of the hospice

Hospices support people throughout their journey of care and improve their quality of life. They support patients with life-threatening, serious and incurable illnesses such as cancer, chronic pulmonary disease, respiratory, heart, lung and kidney disease, multiple sclerosis, motor neurone disease, dementia, Parkinson's and other neurological problems. There is a general perception that a hospice is a place where people come to die. Hospices support people over an extended period, not just at the end of life. Many patients feel better and return home. Hospices do prescribe certain medications and treatments that can result in better symptom management and prolonging a better quality of life, though they concentrate on making patients comfortable by treating their symptoms, such as pain control. The palliative care given in a hospice primarily aims at improving the quality of life and making the patient comfortable, whereas hospital palliative care mainly aims at prolonging life if they possibly can. Hospices prepare patients at the end for good dying by providing patient-centred holistic care covering physical, mental, social, emotional and spiritual care. A GP, hospital doctor or district nurse can refer the patients to the local hospice.

Some patients come to stay in the hospice where doctors and nurses can manage their pain and other symptoms. Hospices offer many of their services in the community in people's homes. Many people prefer to stay at home. Community nurses and chaplains visit them at their home. Services are not only given to patients, but also their families, relatives and friends are supported in their distressing time. Hospices also run day service and drop-in facilities, and support groups for the bereaved. There is no referral needed to use drop-in facilities. Hospice services are available to the local community irrespective of their belief, religion, or culture. This service is free for all. Most hospices are charities and depend heavily on the generous donations given by the community members. The NHS also provides some funding. Sikhs generally are not aware of hospice services due to the lack of outreach activities on the part of hospices and the capacity to meet the cultural and religious needs of non-Christian communities. Until recently, these services were predominantly Christian and still heavily managed and used by Christians.

Near Death Experience

Basford (1990) and Fenwick (1995) suggest that Near Death Experiences (NDE) come from a clinically dead (i.e. without a heartbeat) person who has had the sensation of leaving their body and, characteristically, floating into a tunnel towards a perceived physical source. In the Panjabi culture, including Sikhs, people do talk about their end of life experiences while they are alive and alert. The Sikh community in the Punjab believes that when a dying person speaks of the visits by, and conversation with, dead relatives, friends and religious figures who say they have come to take him or her with them, it is an indication that death is around the corner. One Sikh woman relating her husband's NDE said that he recounted when he was alive that he saw a broad, long tunnel. It became narrow and small as he was close to his death. In contrast, religious people who have end of life experiences in the Sikh community describe them as uplifting. They appear to help the person to let go of the physical world and to overcome the fear of death. They often mention that the *Guru* had come to take them away. Some Sikhs are calm, relaxed and without pain. They thank their family members for looking after them. Some Sikhs become quiet and do not want to talk. It is a common Sikh rather Panjabi practice to ask the dying person if he or she wants to say something, as lasting words mean a lot for the Sikh families. According to Brayne and Fenwick: 'our research suggests that end-of-life visions and dreams hold profound meaning for the dying and help them to come to terms with their dying process' (2008, p.19).

It is difficult to give a complete and accurate picture of how many people have such experiences as suggested, and what goes on in the mind during the sleep of a dying person. None of the patients in the author's chaplaincy experience of nearly ten years has talked about their near-death experiences. Many patients she encountered were found in their deep sleep or they were too tired to talk near the end of life, except one, who said: "save me from death." Something must have scared her: it is difficult to say whether it was a hallucination, or she had a bad dream. Sikhs' NDE suggest uplifting, scary and heaven-like transcendent exposure. For some it is a taboo subject to talk about. It is important to note that one must not confuse between two different events: nearing death awareness and Near Death Experience. Moody (2005) was able to identify nine basic elements that occur in NDEs.

Being there at the end

It is very comforting for the dying person to have the presence of someone giving the assurance that he or she is valued and loved. It is a unique experience to accompany someone to the point of death; for some it may not be easy and for others it is comforting to see the dying person calm, relaxed and prepared to let go of this physical world. It is best to sit at the bedside gently holding their hand. 'Gentle touch can provide comfort for the dying, and help communication on a deeper level. Even when a person is unconscious or semi-conscious' (Brayne and Fenwick, 2008, p. 25). Those present must know that hearing may be present until the end. It is important to talk in such a way that they can hear, even if they appear to be unconscious or restless. Sikh families want to be around the dying person, not only for love and respect, but also as a religious duty. There are four main purposes for this – the first is that they feel it is their duty to be present. Second, if the family is not there, the mind of the dying person may be distracted, wondering about the reason for their absence and may end up going through the transmigration process. Third is to administer the holy water to the dying person. Fourth is to organise *kirtan* or prayer. Sikhs play recorded *kirtan* or *gurbani* with dim light to create a calm and soothing atmosphere. It helps the dying person to concentrate on listening to *gurbani* in order to stop his or her mind wandering somewhere else. It is a Sikh belief that if a dying person keeps the Divine in their thoughts in the final moments of one's life, they shall be liberated (*GGS*, p.526).

It is normal in Sikh families to gather around the bedside of the dying person to pay their last respects. There is a need for private space with tea, biscuits, water and tissues to be arranged to talk to the family and give them privacy. This will also help in maintaining the protocol of two people visiting the patient at a time and others having a place to sit. The presence of the chaplain at this critical time is necessary to answer any questions and to offer help and support needed by the family. It can also help the normal running of the ward without any interruption (Rait, 2013).

What happens physically when someone is dying?

There are certain physical signs that indicate the person is preparing for dying. The author's experience of visiting patients suggest that the dying person may doze off or sleep often and in brief intervals. This increases gradually to extend into hours of sleep. Nearer the end, they may increasingly drift in and out of consciousness. Some cancer patients said that they had no pain and felt peaceful. The dying person loses weight due to reduced appetite. The person does not have any desire to eat or drink. Some feel cold in their limbs. Some struggle with their breathing near death. Some struggle to die and feel agitated and restless. When the person is dying, their breathing pattern changes from deep to normal. Sometimes the person will give several outward pants as the heart and lungs stop. Others may give a long, drawn-out breath followed quite a few seconds later by what seems like another intake of breath. This may be repeated for several minutes, which can be alarming for those who are not ready for it. However, this is only the lungs expelling air. Some die in a calm manner, whereas some struggle until the end, having hell-like experiences, screaming and fighting to die. No patient seems to experience all these signs, but these are the general indicators. Some patients begin to show their gratitude to those looking after them if they are alert until the end. Some express a desire to see someone: a family member, friend or a relative. The main desire of Sikhs, no matter how detached they are, is to have their family members around. Many symptoms in Sikh patients are similar to what is given via the Dying Matters website.

When death happens, it leaves its marks. A Sikh woman relating her experience suggested her husband had a deep breath that alerted her. She sat near her husband's bed and held his hand, and then he had natural breathing and died peacefully. It was dark midnight, silence all around. She found her husband's face pink and bright, surrounded by a very bright, dark pink light covering the walls near his bed. She was not frightened but became absorbed in that light, and sat there for three hours alone, near his bedside, not knowing where she was until the doorbell rang.

When death happens, it happens suddenly and quickly. There is no doubt about what is taking place. Sikhs always arrange for the end of life prayer, *Ardas* (supplication), whether in hospital/hospice or at home, as all their life-cycle rites are bound with religion. A chaplain or a *gurdwara granthi* (priest) performs this prayer as it has an element of pleading to God for merging the soul of the dying person with the Divine.

Moment to go

People may appear to choose the moment to die. Sanders states: 'On a more conscious level, some patients appear to exercise control over the timing of their deaths' (2007, p.66). Brayne and Fenwick state:

> *It is not unusual for someone to hang on to life against medical odds until a relative or friend arrives at their bedside, or until a special anniversary or birthday… In contrast, some people seem to make a deliberate choice to die alone. (2008, p.27).*

These experiences are similar to Sikhs. The author remembers that her grandfather did not breathe his last breath until her mother came around his bedside; he waited for her arrival the whole day. The author's husband waited until both their children left the room, and there are other instances of a similar nature. Death is a natural phenomenon and the dying process is a biological shutting down of the body's system. After death, there remains a physical body. According to Sikh beliefs, the soul is immortal and goes through the transmigration process judged by one's *karma*. It leaves the family grieving, sad and in despair, though Sikhs find consolation in reciting *gurbani* and listening to *kirtan*.

Euthanasia: ending or prolonging life

The term euthanasia is derived from the Greek word 'euthanatos', which means 'Good Death, Gentle and Easy Death' (Online Etymology Dictionary). A preliminary definition of euthanasia is a deliberate act aimed at ending a person's life, or hastening their death, for that person's benefit (Beauchamp and Childress, 1994). It is for this reason that euthanasia was also given the name 'mercy killing' (Bartels and Otlowski, 2010). It became the subject of debate for many years in Britain and is surrounded by religious, ethical and practical considerations. It is currently against the law in the UK.

Euthanasia is described as active and passive. 'Active euthanasia' involves a deliberate act to terminate life (Beauchamp and Childress, 1994) usually through the intentional administration of lethal drugs, to end an incurably or terminally ill patient's life. Passive euthanasia is withholding or withdrawing life sustaining treatment (ibid, 1994). The supporters of euthanasia use this term. This has become an established part of medical practice through the living will, if the patient has mentioned in it not to be resuscitated or put on a lifesaving machine.

Acts of euthanasia are further categorised as 'voluntary' when performed at the request of the patient, 'involuntary' with the intent of relieving the patient's suffering without their request, and 'non-voluntary' where treatment is given when the patient is incapable of indicating a preference. The term that is relevant to the euthanasia debate is 'active voluntary euthanasia' (AVE), which collectively refers to the deliberate act to end an incurable or terminally ill patient's life, usually through the administration of lethal drugs at his or her request.

The practice of euthanasia has been considered and proposed mainly for the persistent vegetative state of a person, severe dementia or Alzheimer's disease, with no capacity for any significant personal interaction, and in the case of agonising and unrelenting pain, enforced with the 'right to die'. It also covers problematic cases of disabled new-borns e.g. anencephalic or Down's Syndrome infants with duodenal atresia (intestinal blockage). The other main reasons for seeking euthanasia are a quality of life severely damaged by physical conditions such as incontinence, nausea and vomiting, breathlessness, paralysis and difficulty in swallowing, and psychological factors such as depression, fearing loss of control or dignity, feeling a burden, or dislike of being dependent. This raises further questions under what circumstances euthanasia can be justifiable.

There are arguments in favour of and against active voluntary euthanasia. Those who favour it mention respect for individual autonomy, and the right to decide about the circumstances of one's own life and death. In cases where palliation is ineffective, it would be unreasonable to deny anyone the right to make a dignified end to their suffering (Grey, 2000). The denial of a right to die is unfair and cruel. 'The denial of a right to die amounts to imposing a 'duty to live'- no matter what the abject condition of that life might be. This imposition is presumptuous and intolerable' (Grey, 2000, p. 274).

Neuberger suggests another reason: 'As far as one can tell, it is largely for reasons of property and the fear of gradually becoming destitute whilst paying nursing home fees, that it has become impossible to discuss the euthanasia issue properly in Britain' (1999, p.77). She further adds, 'yet many of those people had thought that the National Health Service would indeed look after them from cradle to grave.' (ibid). This has not happened. There is a lot of anger surrounding the issue of the cost of care of the elderly. One way to express that anger is by an increasing desire to allow euthanasia. This argument of cost is not a valid reason to introduce euthanasia. (Neuberger, 1999)

Arguments against legalising euthanasia:

Grey points out: 'Not everyone opposed to the legalization of euthanasia is opposed to the practice of euthanasia: we must therefore distinguish arguments against the practice of euthanasia from arguments directed solely against the legalization of the practice' (2000, p.274). Gormally gives seven reasons why euthanasia and assisted suicide should not be legalised (2000, pp.284-288). There is also a concern that to allow euthanasia, even if it is morally right, could lead to it being abused.

Sikh view on euthanasia

Euthanasia is a contentious issue. It has become a complex topic for many religions, including Sikhism. Sikh theology does not have any clear-cut answer. The *GGS* and the Sikh Code of Conduct have not discussed this question openly. One can deduce the answer from similar situations mentioned in Sikhism and the life stories of *Gurus*. For example, the Sikh *Gurus* rejected suicide and by extension, euthanasia, as an interference in God's plan. Sikhism believes birth and death is a prerogative of God. It is also about the meaning and value of human existence. Grey argues:

> *The related suggestion that ending life is the prerogative of the deity is equally unhelpful precisely because divine prerogatives are conceived so disparately by different religious authorities. It is not helpful to be told that an action transgresses the prerogatives of the deity unless we know what these prerogatives are.* (2000, p.278)

It is a matter of one's belief. It is considered contrary to Sikhism. *Gurbani* believes that only God controls death. 'Everyone comes here at the Lord's command, leaves in His Will and remains merged, too, in the Lord's.' (ਹੁਕਮੇ ਆਵੈ ਹੁਕਮੇ ਜਾਵੈ ਹੁਕਮੇ ਰਹੈ ਸਮਾਈ)

(*Guru* Nanak Dev, *GGS,* p.940). Therefore, it can be implied that hastening death or the early termination of life are disapproved of, on the basis that humans are defying God's Will as God has preordained how long one lives (*GGS*, p.1354). Since birth and death are in God's hands and the life given is the consequence of one's *karma,* no one has the right to take, assist or facilitate the end of any one's life in spite of unbearable suffering. Sikhism believes in the theory of *karma*; as a result, illness and bad circumstances are consequences of bad actions of previous lives and this life's *karma*. Therefore, it is necessary to suffer in order to make spiritual progress. There is also the question of the sanctity of life with the underlying ethos that it must be respected and preserved. Therefore, humans should not interfere with God's plan. This can have both a secular and religious basis. The Sikh view sees human life as a gift from God. It has a special value and dignity even if it is full of pain and suffering. Sikhism sees mortal life as part of a continuing cycle in which humans are born, live, die, and are reborn over and over again, a theory of transmigration. In each cycle of life and death, human beings make spiritual progression in order to attain their final aim of liberation and merging with the Ultimate Reality. The shortening of life by human actions, even though consented to by the suffering person, not only challenges the authority of God but also interferes with the working out of the laws of *karma* and delays the human being's journey to liberation.

It is important to assess the whole situation to make an appropriate decision. There are cases when resuscitation and the use of life-saving machines are absolutely necessary and appropriate. There are cases of terminal illness where all the treatments — medical and alternative therapies — are exhausted. In such cases, the author is of the opinion that passive euthanasia (rejection of resuscitation and artificially prolonging a terminal state) is justified in Sikhism. Sikhism allows the use of medicines for curing purposes and not necessarily those medical treatments that are only used for the extension of life, irrespective of quality of life. The patient has every right to decline such treatments. At least the person has a natural and dignified death, according to the Will of God. The role of healthcare professionals should be to care for the needs of the person whilst alive, and to seek his or her welfare whether they are caring or curing. It is important to die with dignity, according to one's faith and beliefs.

The family after the death has occurred

When someone dies, even if it is an expected death, the family is shocked and can be in despair. This is the time when they need support from the healthcare professionals and the chaplain. The family may support the healthcare professionals in the way they want to lay out the deceased, for example, by closing the eyes and straightening the limbs, and some families want to help them in cleaning, washing and dressing the body. Sikhs prefer that it should be done by the same sex to maintain the modesty of the patient. The chaplain performs *Ardas* at the request of the family. Families often ask questions about death and dying and the chaplain needs to be prepared to explain these in English and Panjabi. Some shed tears and need a shoulder to cry on to release their emotions, as it is only human. In many Sikh families, family members hug each other, not only to shed tears, but also to console each other in a silent way. Sikhism prohibits crying aloud and wailing. Some do cry aloud and create a scene in the hospital, which can be upsetting for some, but also disturbing for many patients on the ward.

Sikhs believe that upon death, one merges back into the universal nature (*GGS*, p.1244) leaving one's transitional home on earth, which is not one's permanent home (*GGS*, p.793), just as a drop of rain merges back into the ocean. According to Sikhism, Sikhs should accept God's *hukam* (order/Will) for what has happened and listen to *gurbani*. Kubler-Ross argues it is 'cruel and inappropriate to speak of the love of God' (1973, p.156) in those desperate hours. That is a matter of contention. One rule cannot suit all people, conditions and situations.

The family members are left alone after they have given their consent for a post-mortem/autopsy if needed. It is a difficult time for them. The families have to inform relatives and friends. The death has to be registered and the Green Disposal Form (a form for the disposal of the deceased's body) needs to be collected to arrange with the funeral director to collect the body from the home, hospital or hospice. The death certificate can be collected from the bereavement office 24 hours after death. In the case of a death which has occurred at home, the family's GP looking after the patient certifies the death. If that falls on a weekend or public holiday, then it can be collected on the next working day. This death certification is required for registering the death. If the person is in the hospital less than 48 hours before death and he or she has not seen the GP before being admitted to hospital, then the death is referred to the coroner and the body may have to go for a post-mortem. This can cause a delay in getting the death certificate. In these cases, civil law has the power to overrule any funeral, which has to be performed within 24 hours. Local governance provides more information.

Good Death

It has been argued that in non-Western societies 'good' deaths are those that demonstrate some kind of control over the events (Bloch and Parry, 1982). Those working in palliative care emphasise physical and psychological as well as religious or social perspectives. They often include good symptom control, maintaining autonomy and control, emotional support and comfort, family involvement, accepting death, setting practical affairs in order and resolving unfinished business (Payne, Langley-Evans and Hillier (1996), and Payne, Hillier et al (1996), BMA (1993), Pickett (1993).

Sikhs view a good death as when the person dies in his or her own home surrounded by the family and friends who could listen to their last words. Their silent presence gives the dying person a sense that they love and value the person. It also gives the vibrations of harmony. The person is not struggling but having a natural and easy end. The dying person is alert, calm and speaks gently. Some Sikhs want to go home from where they have come originally in India. This is a good and dignified death in Sikh culture. Religiously, it is a common tradition in Sikhs to have prayers near their end. In hospitals, this may include the recitation of *gurbani* when someone is dying to help the dying person to become in tune with God and detached from worldly affairs. It also helps the dying person to accept his or her departure. Those who are religious and believe in an afterlife are better adjusted, happier and less apprehensive about death (Beit-Hallahmi and Argyle, 1997, p.234). This is applicable to most Sikhs due to their religious beliefs. The idea of a good death is personal or is influenced by one's religion, beliefs and culture. Some Sikhs consider it a good death when someone dies suddenly or dies in their sleep, quietly and in a dignified manner, without any suffering. Death is followed by funeral and bereavement which are mentioned in the relevant chapters.

Conclusion

The end of life is a particularly worrying and anxious time for anyone. Most important is to be present with a dying patient with willingness, and to listen actively. Chaplains also care for emotionally upset family members. Consoling and giving them emotional support is a significant part of spiritual care, as expressed by a Sikh participant: "It is a kind, caring and supportive presence at critical times given with thorough understanding of our culture and religion". It is important that their spiritual needs are cared for. It is not only the responsibility of the chaplain, religious leader or priest but also any caring staff. Service providers should be skilled to give advice and support on religious and cultural rituals around dying and death. They are asked to come to perform rituals like initiation and naming for a dying baby and to give emotional support in case of death (Dyne, 1981). Sikhs are particular regarding the cleanliness of the patient, treating them with respect, and maintaining their privacy and modesty in order to make them feel valued and respected. Their religious, cultural and personal needs should be accommodated, and their choices respected. Near the time, it is important to ask the patients who they would like us to contact if they became very seriously ill. The bereaved and their families need support and advice. Patients of various faith traditions often have very specific religious needs, including Sikhs. The needs of patients, particularly at the end of life, must be met by healthcare organisations to fulfil human rights obligations irrespective of their religion and culture.

References

Bartels L, Otlowski, M. (2010). A right to die? Euthanasia and the law in Australia. *J Law Med.* 2010 Feb, 17 (4), pp. 532-55.

Basford, T.K. (1990). *Near death experience: An annotated bibliography.* New York: Garland.

Beauchamp, T. L. and Childress, J. F. (1994). *Principles of Biomedical ethics.* 4th ed. New York: Oxford University Press.

Becker, E. (1973). *The denial of death.* New York: The Free Press.

Beit-Hallahmi, B. and Argyle, M. (1997). *The psychology of religious behaviour, belief and experience.* London: Routledge.

Bloch, M. and Parry, J. (eds.) (1982). *Death and the regeneration of life.* Cambridge: Cambridge University Press.

Brayne, S. and Fenwick, P. (2008). *Nearing the end of life: A guide for relatives and friends of the dying.* Sue Brayne and Dr Peter

Fenwick in association with the Clinical Neuroscience Division, University of Southampton. Text c 2008 Sue Brayne work Ltd.

British Medical Association (BMA) (1993). Medical ethics today: Its practice and philosophy. *British Medical Association/British Medical Journal* Publishing Group, London.

Buckman, R. (1988). *I don't know what to say*. London: Papermac.

Buckman, R. (1994). *How to break bad news: A guide for health-care professionals.* London: Pan Books in association with Macmillan London.

Cobb, M. (2001). *The dying soul: spiritual care at the end of life.* Buckingham: Open University.

Fenwick, P. and Fenwick, E. (1995). *The truth in the light.* London\; Headline.

Firth, S. (2000). Approaches to death in Hindu and Sikh communities in Britain. In: Dickenson, D., Johnson, M. and Katz, S. eds. (2000) *Death, dying and bereavement.* London: Sage Publications.

Gormally, L. (2000) *Euthanasia and assisted suicide: seven reasons why they should not be legalised.* In: Dickenson, Donna, Johnson, Malcolm and Katz, Samson eds. (2000) *Death, dying and bereavement.* London: Sage Publications.

Grey, W. (2000). Right to die or duty to live: the problem of euthanasia. In: Dickenson, D., Johnson, M. and Katz, S. eds. (2000) *Death, dying and bereavement*. London: Sage Publications.

Guru Granth Sahib. (n.d.) Amritsar: *Shiromani Gurdwara Prabandhak Committee* (Standard version of 1430 pages in Panjabi).

Kearney, M. (2007). *Mortally wounded: Stories of soul pain, death and healing*. New Orleans: Louisiana: Spring Journal Books.

Kübler-Ross, Elisabeth (1973). *On death and dying*. London/New York: Tavistock/Routledge.

Moody, R. (2005) *Life after life: the interpretation of a phenomenon-life after death*. San Francisco, California: Harper Books (original work published in 1975).

Neuberger, Julia (1999). *Dying well: A guide to enabling a good death*. Cheshire: Hochland & Hochland Ltd.

Payne, S., Hillier, R, Langley-Evans A, and Robert T. (1996). Impact of witnessing death on hospice patients. *Social Science and Medicine,* 43 (12), pp. 1785-94.

Payne, S., Langley-Evans, A. and Hillier, R. (1996). Perception of a 'good death: a comparative study of the views of hospice staff and patients. *Palliative Medicine,* 10 (4), pp. 307-12.

Pickett, M. (1993). *Cultural awareness in the context of terminal illness*. Cancer Nursing 16 (2), pp.102-6.

Rait, S. K. (2013). *A guide to being a Sikh chaplain*. Great Britain: S.K. Rait.

Sanders, M. A. (2007). *Nearing death awareness: a guide to the language, visions, and dreams of the dying*. London: Jessica Kingsley Publishers.

Sikh Rehat Maryada (The Sikh Code of conduct) (1950). *Shiromani Gurdwara Prabandhak* Committee. Amritsar, Punjab, India.

Websites

Death Registration. [online] Available at: <https://www.gov.uk/after-a-death/register-the-death>. [Accessed 24 Nov.2018].

Dying Matters (2020) *Being with someone when they die.* [online] Available at: https://www.dyingmatters.org/page/being-someone-when-they-die [Accessed 29 Mar. 2020]

Euthanasia (2018). *Origin and meaning of euthanasia* by Online Etymology ... [online] Available at: https://www.etymonline.com/word/euthanasia [Accessed 24 Nov. 2018]

Chapter 9

Bereavement

Introduction

This chapter concentrates on bereavement, covering mourning and grief for adults, its experiences, and effects and coping mechanisms. It provides background information to offer a context within which Sikh customs and rituals of mourning and bereavement are explored. It also covers the pattern, stages and theories of bereavement.

Bereavement

Bereavement is the state or condition caused by loss through death, and the result of major psychological trauma. Stroebe and Schut (1998) see it as the situation of a person who has recently experienced the loss of someone significant through that person's death. All human beings, irrespective of their religion and culture, have to go through this process in their own chosen way. When we lose someone we care about and love, we are deprived of their companionship. The deprivation is, by definition, bereavement (Attig, 2011). Parkes (2000) describes bereavement as a psychosocial transition: a process of adaptation to change. He suggests that three things are needed during this transition: emotional support, protection through the period of helplessness, and assistance in discovering new models of the world appropriate to the emergent situation. Such changes are easier said than done. It is the period after a loss during which grief is experienced and mourning occurs. The amount of time spent in a period of bereavement depends on the degree of attachment with the deceased, capacity to adjust to the emerging neo-normal life and the supportive network. It is the time spent anticipating the loss, and the significance of the loss. It can be viewed as a personal journey from the head to heart, to soothe the emotions, and to convince the heart that the loved one has departed forever, not to come back. It is a time to think about how to rebuild life without the deceased. In most cultures, it begins with mourning.

Mourning: Mourning is the initiation of the process by which people begin to adapt to a loss. It usually indicates the means of coping with loss and grief, and the ways in which individuals and societies incorporate this process into their new reality (Corr et al, 1997). Stroebe and Schut (1998) expand the views of Corr et al, that mourning refers to social expressions or acts expressive of grief, which are shaped by the practices of a given society or cultural group. Although there are similarities across cultures, religious and/or cultural traditions, ritual influence makes mourning practices distinct. It is normal for the bereaved person to observe social customs, which is a shared social response for coping with one's own loss. It is standard in Sikh culture for the family, relatives, friends and congregational members to sit with the mourner during this period. The funeral is the last ritual of mourning for Sikhs in the

UK. Funerals are central to the grieving process. They allow the bereaved to share their grief and to take part in an established social and personal ritual of saying goodbye. Egan suggests: 'Many pastoral carers possess the skills to do short-term and brief counselling with the bereaved and with families. Pastoral carers, by the nature of their role, frequently offer more ready access to such people, especially as a first point of contact' (2014, p.8). Grief is another associated term with bereavement.

Grief: Grief is an internal experience to loss, more related to emotions, and has a wider coverage than human death. It covers physical, social and symbolic losses such as death (physical loss), divorce, redundancy (social losses), relationships, independence, identity, control or self (symbolic losses). It is the response to something the person has lost or been deprived of.

> *Grief is essentially an emotion that draws us towards something or someone that is missing. It arises from awareness of a discrepancy between the world that is and the world that 'should be'* (Parkes, 2000, p.326).

Grieving is nearly always complicated. It is a personal experience under one's own circumstances. Ordinarily, grieving involves nothing less than relearning the world of our experience, 'it is a natural human reaction and we do it whether we are the person who is dying or whether we are the bereaved' (Attiq, 2011). 'It is a process of extreme pain, with all kinds of attendant emotions - and there is no way out of it. It is impossible to emerge normal from the death of a loved one without grieving' (Neuberger, 1999, p.137). It incorporates according to Stroebe and Schut (1998): '...diverse psychological and physical symptoms and is sometimes associated with detrimental health consequences'.

Bereavement, its impact, experiences and coping mechanisms

Bereavement is a personal journey where the bereaved explore their grief. There is no fixed time for it. It depends on one's own relationship with the deceased, ability to cope with the changing circumstances and their support network.

Impact: Most bereaved people feel torn apart, numb, confused, anxious, helpless and completely lost. Many show a range of physical symptoms such as headache, loss of appetite, insomnia, tiredness and feeling weak. They become anxious about the tasks they have not done before. Loss of someone creates emptiness and a vacuum impossible to fill. It impairs concentration and memory. The observation of supporting a bereavement group suggests that most bereaved people, irrespective of their religion, beliefs and culture, lose appetite, sleep is often disrupted, and sleeping patterns change. They want to shut themselves away from the world and find it hard to get out of the house. Their life changes completely, they feel helpless, sad and desolate. They become disorientated and disorganised. The previously shared responsibilities become solo efforts and many find it hard to cope, at least initially. Some feel angry with God, with hospital staff, and occasionally with themselves for not looking after the deceased properly and with those who have not attended the funeral. One woman said that she was so angry with God for not responding to her prayers, she blamed Him (God) for taking away her husband's life. As a result, she stopped going to the church and completely lost trust in her faith. Another woman suffering with cancer burst into tears and said: "I was very religious. My husband died at a young age. Soon after, I was diagnosed with cancer and I could not walk. I have a young son and I worry for him. I lost my trust in God, feeling He is not fair". A Sikh woman relating her story said they worked extremely hard to settle in this country and had no time to relax. Her husband died soon after his retirement and left her alone, finding it hard to cope with life, which they dreamed to enjoy together.

Loss affects mental, physical, social and emotional conditions. Most of us go through bereavement at some stage in our lives. This can give us a much more natural, less denying approach to the whole subject of death and dying (Neuberger, 1999), believing that it is a natural process of life.

Experiences: The experiences of the bereaved are many and varied. Those who have seen death and its aftermath closely for the first time ponder on many things unheard of before. One Sikh woman said that she heard her husband's voice calling by her first name three days after his death. Another Sikh woman recounted that she had never experienced hallucinations before, but after her husband's death, it routinely happened every night, and she watched them with her open eyes trying to make sense of them. Another woman related her experience of seeing her mother standing in the doorway of her bedroom. Her mother had died 30 years ago, and this was the first time she had come back in her dream. One woman expressed her feelings anxiously that she saw green parrots with red beaks sitting symmetrically in rows, looking pretty. She associated it with two things, one was a consoling message for her, and the second one may be a sign of an afterlife for her husband.

Not everyone has a uniform experience of bereavement. For some it may be a relief and release. One Sikh woman said: "you do not know how relieved I was when my alcoholic husband died". Another Sikh man told how relieved he was to lose his wife who was in a coma for a year. However expected a death is, and under whatever circumstances, it always comes as a shock to those left behind in spite of their feelings of relief for the deceased.

It is important to leave the bereaved alone sometimes, giving them time to process their grief in their own way.

We need to understand that grief is the way the human body and mind eventually work through appalling loss, and that we need to experience it, however horrible, without anti-depressants, without being made to feel as if we are abnormal, overreacting, lacking self-control. (Neuberger, 1999, p.139).

Bereavement is a normal state and everyone experiences it at some stage of their life. It is a result of the closeness with someone who is no longer alive. Death comes to everyone eventually and its experience makes humans ponder on the nature of death and its consequences.

Coping mechanisms: Bereavement is an individual's way of reacting to the new situation for which there is no preplanning. It is a personal journey to explore one's own feelings and to find ways to cope with the situation created by loss. Neuberger states:

Loss through bereavement, especially loss of a spouse or other lifetime partner, represents a major change not only in the bereaved person's 'inner world', but also in all the external relationships of which he or she is a part. How people experience and handle loss will be affected by their own emotional histories and often by the extent to which their early experiences have affected their ability to cope with loss. If there are previous unresolved losses in a person's life, bereavement may be a time when these earlier pains resurface (1999, p.141).

It is time to relieve those pains. It is very common among Sikhs to talk about other deaths in the family, their experiences can prove a learning resource for the bereaved. The bereaved tries to find ways to cope with the situation and makes efforts to build a new normal life. There is no right or wrong way; it depends on what one wants to do and how one feels comfortable. How a person makes his or her journey through grief depends on one's own coping strength and mechanisms, commitment to faith and beliefs, physical and mental health, existing support network, family circumstances and financial status. One has to become reconciled with the reality of the loss, believing that it is irreparable and that life has to be lived without the deceased. One also has to experience pain and feelings associated with bereavement while reorganising life and make oneself learn to live around what has happened, though it is not easy. There may be an eventual rechannelling of emotional and mental energy into something one would like to do or develop.

Physically coping: The bereaved person needs to be encouraged to take self-care. If someone is living alone, persuade him or her to have proper meals if they are not eating well. Similarly, a disruptive sleeping pattern makes them tired. Supporting them with things that can help to foster better sleep and relaxation helps not just physically but also psychologically. It is a shared view that a bereaved person does not want to go out. Taking them out for short walks, to a movie, or to their religious place of worship is of immense help to them. Try to get them involved in activities which energise their spirituality, for example, walking, meditation and yoga. Developing hobbies and interests or taking up volunteering, studying, sports, art and craft or anything that interests the bereaved is good for personal growth and self-satisfaction. One has to be cautious not to overdo things as this often affects health adversely. Many bereaved people find it extremely hard to go on holidays alone. Guided tours or going with family and friends are helpful until they gain their self-confidence. When the grief becomes abnormal, one should seek help from a bereavement counsellor. They are trained to pick up the signs of abnormal grieving patterns and help a bereaved person to find a way of expressing their grief, often monitoring to see if they are making progress. It may become difficult to resolve grief properly without skilled intervention.

Emotionally coping: The bereaved must be allowed to grieve and mourn actively. They should be given the opportunity for some introspection in order to come to terms with accepting the loss, and to carry on living with the best of memories. Shedding tears is good for a grieving person in order to help to ease the internal tension and enable the flow of any suppressed emotions. This can be of some consolation for the bereaved person. Initially, it may be better to take it gently, and perhaps join a bereavement support group to share experiences with someone who has been through a similar ordeal. This will not only help to relieve painful emotions, but also to make some social contacts, giving one the opportunity to be more aware and realistic.

Supportive relationship: Family and friends can offer all-round support to the bereaved. They can ensure the well-being of the bereaved, making sure they are eating on time. They can help them to make their own routine and to sleep well. Families and friends are in the best position to give emotional support and comfort during the period when they are broken and helpless. They can help them by listening with empathy, and without disruption. Encourage them to talk about death and grief openly to process and relieve their emotions. This in turn supports the bereaved to take stock, review their lives, and to explore their new normal life. Family or friends can accompany them to attend bereavement support groups and death cafes. The silent presence of someone in the house who cares is a valuable support for the bereaved; to help them when they need help, listen to them with compassion, and to provide empathy when they want to talk. This includes supporting the bereaved through normal stages of their grief, encouraging them with the thought that they are not alone, and gradually nursing them into a more normal life. Some people do not know how to help the bereaved. Many people lack experience of death and are unsure how to converse with a grieving person. It is important to engage a grieving person in conversation, and if you know the deceased well, talk about their valuable contributions. This comforts the bereaved, knowing that the deceased is valued. Sometimes it is better to say nothing when unsure, but it is important to acknowledge their loss by saying: "I am sorry to hear such sad news". Just holding a hand (depending on cultural traditions) and leaving it to the bereaved whether they want to share their feelings, talk or cry, are helpful and consoling for the bereaved. Special days such as birthdays, wedding anniversaries, holidays and social functions are the worst time to be alone. The presence of the family can be very helpful on these occasions.

Religious coping: It is important to be aware of the religious, spiritual and, cultural values that the bereaved hold. These can help the bereaved to cope with life's vicissitudes. It is traditional in the Sikh community to visit the bereaved family to offer their condolences in person and show their support. Religious Sikhs pray and recite *gurbani* to normalise their lives.

> *For most religious groupings other than Christians in Britain, it is the sense of communal support, in the shape of ritualized grieving, that does bring comfort to the bereaved, and gives people a sense of belonging when a sense of isolation and of loneliness are the most common of emotions.* (Neuberger, 1999, p.161).

Alcohol-assisted coping: Some bereaved people mentioned that they felt the urge to drink alcohol in order to relax and sleep. Such a coping mechanism may be helpful in the short term but can become a maladaptive behaviour if it develops as a long-term routine.

Employers: They also have a role to play in facilitating the grieving process through giving people compassionate leave to grieve, time to attend bereavement support groups, and to let them return to work, even when they are grief-stricken, if they show their desire. Giving employees support, treating them gently and listening to them helps a great deal and creates close bonds with other colleagues.

Bereavement models and stages

There appear to be two models of bereavement, one is 'let it go' and the other is 'continuous bond'. 'Let it go', as Freud (1917) endorsed, is disengaging from the deceased. It has been the primary model of grief for most of the 20th century. The mourner has to let go of the past. Successful mourning required the bereaved to detach themselves emotionally from the deceased. Klass (1996) and Walter (1994) contended this view of detachment and advocated the 'Continuous Bond' theory. 'Continuous Bond' is a new model for understanding bereavement that emphasises the maintenance of continuing bonds with the deceased. Its theory revolves around the idea that people may maintain a continued relationship with those they have lost. They may find it changed but can still find a place to situate the relationship in their lives. This phenomenon is not considered problematic, and in fact, the deceased can provide resources for enriched functioning in the present (Klass et al, 1996). Stroebe & Schut define continuous bond as "the presence of an ongoing inner relationship with the deceased person by the bereaved individual" (2005, p.477). There is also a current definition expanding the scope of continuous bond. It is:

> *an ongoing, inner relationship that allows for a diverse set of possible expressions that range in the degree of interaction between the bereaved and the deceased, the degree of proximity to the deceased, the possibility of a direct connection to the deceased, the agency ascribed to the deceased, and the degree to which the relationship is framed as being in the past versus continuing to evolve in the present and future.* (Root and Exline, 2014, p.4)

The factors with which the deceased is bonded with a living person are dreams, memories, talking about them, and through cherished objects and hobbies. The bond may shift so that it is not as central to the lives of the bereaved and take on a new form with time. However, the connection remains. (Klass et al, 1996, p.350)

Bereavement stages: Kübler-Ross (1970) analysed the responses of the dying and categorised their reactions in terms of five stages: denial, anger, bargaining, depression, and acceptance, also known as DABDA. Parkes and Bowlby (1970) suggested four phases or stages of grief. These are shock and numbness, yearning and searching, despair and disorganisation, and finally reorganisation and recovery. These four phases of grief preceded the work of Elisabeth Kübler-Ross. Later Worden (1982) suggested four tasks in order to accept the reality: work through the pain; adjust to a new environment; emotionally relocate the deceased; and move on. Stroebe and Schut (2001) developed a dual process model (DPM) of bereavement as an alternative to the linear stage-based model. It provides an analytical framework for understanding how people adapt to the loss of a significant person in their lives. The key part of the dual process model is the concept of oscillation. According to the authors, healthy grieving means engaging in a dynamic process of oscillating between loss-oriented and restoration-oriented coping. A griever will oscillate between confronting the loss and avoiding the loss. It is a combination of accepting and confronting it.

Bereavement Models and stages in Sikhism

Bereavement Models: Sikhism believes in detachment in the lived life and after death. Continuous Bond theory does not fit into this concept. Sikhism does not believe in erecting memorials, creating tombs or holding memorial events, which is contrary to this theory. Religiously, Sikhs should be detached, and this fits more appropriately with the 'let it go' theory. In practice, it may not always be possible. It often happens that the bereaved wants to talk about the deceased, wants to hold their objects, misses them at weddings and family occasions, and misses the intimacy. Some may internalise their memories. These types of behaviour reflect the elements of continuous bonds with the deceased in practice. Sikhism permits widows to remarry as that can help emotionally to move on and to make life normal, though Panjabi culture frowns upon women if they remarry.

Bereavement stages: There has not been any research conducted on the bereavement stages and phases of the Sikh bereaved. It can only be suggested, based on observations as an insider, that most use Worden's suggestion of four tasks in order to accept the reality; work through the pain; adjust to a new environment; emotionally relocate the deceased, and move on (1982). Sikhs accept the reality of death but they are also humans, and may respond with shock to a sudden and untimely death, in spite of Sikh teachings of accepting the Will of God (*bhana manana*).

Bereavement time: There are no hard and fast rules for coping swiftly with loss, and there is no fixed pattern of grief or definite timescale to adjust to a new life. It is difficult to set any time limit on the bereavement period. Some hospices suggest two years, whereas when talking to the bereaved, it is common that they normally suggest two to five years. It took the author seven years to build her neo-normal life. It is a time of processing extreme feelings and coming to terms with a newly emergent life and building the capacity to cope with it. Allowing sufficient time is the only way; there is no shortcut to it, as it is much more dependent on the closeness with the deceased, individual circumstances and coping mechanisms.

Sikh customs and rituals of bereavement

Bereaved in Panjabi means 'taken away' (*khoh laina*) and bereavement is defined as '*sog*', which means processing of the feelings of loss when someone is taken away forever through death. This one term is applied to express both mourning and bereavement in Panjabi. Sikhs are mainly a religious community and faith guides their way of life. They follow mourning rituals according to their cultural and religious norms to manage a life crisis with a sense of meaning. Death is life's culmination and its crowning point when people think and talk about the achievements of the deceased, giving both sense and worth. 'It is nevertheless an immense mystery, a great question mark that we carry in our own marrow' (De Hennezel, 1997, p xi). For Sikhs, it is not a mystery or question mark, but a reality of life. Death is not horrible, miserable, or something to be scared of. It is the natural course of life.

Mourning: Sikhs consider death as a morbid word and instead they use the term 'passed away'. Religious Sikhs use words like gone to heaven (*parmatma de ghar gaye*) or has gone to God (*rab nue pyare ho gaye*) signifying the continuation of life and the Sikh belief in life after death. In Sikhism, death is a natural cycle of human life. 'One who is born has to die when their turn comes' (*GGS*, pp. 63, 474). Mourning is the beginning of the bereavement process. Sikhs mourn together during this period and this lasts for ten days. In the Punjab, the funeral is held on the same day before sunset or within 24 hours after death. After the funeral, mourning begins and it is usual for Sikh families to have *sadharan path* (recitation of the

GGS) and *bhog,* the finishing ritual held on the tenth day. Sikhs are a diasporic community in the UK. They have to obey the legal requirements of the country they live in. They are also, by nature, flexible, adapting and constantly compromising with traditions different from their own, as long as theological essence is maintained. Firth says that mourning days in the UK tend to fluctuate, as these are dependent on the funeral arrangements.

> *In Britain there may be delays of seven days or more waiting for space in the crematorium, and longer if a post-mortem is required. This causes major disruption in the mourning patterns, which would normally begin immediately after the body has been disposed of, and in Britain it has to begin before.* (2000, p.339)

This suggests that mourning begins straight after death when the family is able to make social and religious arrangements. The mourning family informs their relatives about the death and prepares for the commencement of the *sadharan path.* There is no surety or guarantee that the family may be able to fulfil the required number of days of mourning. This arrangement not only decreases or increases mourning days, but also changes the standardised pattern. Eisenbruch (1984b) states that when it is impossible to carry out traditional rituals that have great meaning and serve to comfort the bereaved, the stress of bereavement is amplified. Whilst bereavement and grieving are often described as individual states or processes (even if they are shaped by society in some form), they are often differentiated from mourning, which refers to shared social practices. (Currer, 2001)

The mourning process begins in a collective and shared way. Sikhs prepare a space, usually in the largest room, for the visitors, by removing furniture and covering the carpets with white sheets. It is normal to switch off the television and radio. Relatives and friends visit the mourning family as soon as possible to pay their condolences. The main mourner wears white clothes and those who visit the family normally cover their head in a white scarf (*dupatta*). This is a cultural obligation and not a religious injunction. It is an indication in the Panjabi community that death has occurred in the family so that people living nearby can behave in a sensitive manner. Relatives and close friends bring cooked food for the family, at least for the first few days. It is a cultural tradition to help the family not to have to cook in their distressing times and also to realise the business of the family in making mourning arrangements.

Those who visit the family hug the mourner of the same sex with the exception of close relatives who hug every member of the mourning family. Visiting the mourning family is an obligation in Sikhism, whether they are relatives, friends or members of the congregation. This is the time when extended family members, relatives, friends and other acquaintances console and support the mourning family. They sit and talk about the life and contributions of the deceased made to the family and the community; any previous deaths that had occurred in the family and how they coped with grief. They also talk about the nature of death and detachment. This collective mourning serves five purposes. First, the mourner talks and sometimes sheds tears, which relieves their emotions and eases internal tension. Second, most people who visit either hug or hold hands; touch has already proven therapeutic. Third, *path* (readings from the Holy Scripture) recited first thing in the morning and last thing in the evening is consoling, as it explains the reality of human life and encourages accepting the Will of God. Fourth, these valuable conversations not only make the mourner feel comforted, but also provide some ideas to consider when the mourner is spending time alone. Fifth, the funeral is the time to say a final goodbye to the deceased and the mourner feels supported at that sad occasion by all those gathered. Sikh funerals are open to all the congregational members and anyone who knows the deceased. The funeral and the aftermath rituals follow religious dictates, and hymns chosen are focused on death and detachment. Firth suggests that religions 'comfort and reassure the mourners by helping to make sense of death and personal loss' (2000, p.338). Attig (2011) views mourning as covering two aspects: the changing relationship with the dead and the behaviour during the mourning period (including practices prescribed by societies and cultures).

Langar (vegetarian food, an essential part of the Sikh prayers), tea and soft drinks are available on the funeral day to everyone who attends the last rites. Normally *Langar* is served to all when religious rituals are completed at the end of the funeral, though in the UK it is sometimes provided before the funeral, depending on the funeral time. The close family often eat after the funeral irrespective of time.

Eating together brings the beginning of normality, according to the Sikh faith traditions.

The Sikh *Gurus* discouraged certain social practices of mourning which display excessive grief. The Sikh faith strictly forbids lamenting, wailing, crying aloud, pulling hair, ceremonial weeping, beating the chest and other parts of the body and organised mourning practices (Sikh Code of Conduct, 1950). There may be occasional emotional outbursts at funerals in Britain. Sikhism is not against shedding tears as many interpret the literal meaning. Shedding tears is a normal human behaviour in times of shock and loss. It helps to relieve the pain and stress created by death or loss. Shedding tears by oneself or on the shoulders of someone close is a normal response to soothe the emotions and not against any religion. There is no denying the fact that death is a shock to the system and it is painful, however detached we are. 'It is lonely, soul destroying, difficult and depressing' (Neuberger, 1999, p.154). Devoted Sikhs console themselves by reciting *gurbani*. Most religious Sikhs conform to *Gurus'* teachings of detached living and accepting God's will.

There is also an extended mourning time of forty days prescribed by Panjabi culture. It is a time for private mourning or a close family to mourn. It gives the mourners private space to sort out their family affairs, prepare the probate and read the will if it is written. The house is cleaned and rearranged. The family decides what to do with the belongings of the deceased and whether to give away items or to keep them. Some family members hold on to one or more items in the memory of the deceased. Many Sikh families go to the Punjab to scatter the ashes, though it is not a religious requirement. It definitely gives time to mourn in the company of relatives and friends of the deceased in India. All these religious rituals and cultural traditions help to soften the grief. Firth suggests religious and cultural rituals:

provide shape and meaning to the process of mourning, which lasts for a clearly defined period in many cultures, providing 'milestones' during the period of mourning, allowing the bereaved a gradual time to let go of the deceased and adjust to the changes in their lives psychologically, as well as to changes of status socially (2000, p.338).

Family support assumptions: It is a general assumption that Sikhs support their own families. There is no doubt that they tend to stay in touch with their extended families and maintain connections with the Sikh community through *gurdwaras*. There is always a huge gathering at the Sikh funerals, however, how many people offer active support after the funeral is a subject of exploration. When talking to Sikhs regarding the support given to the bereaved during the time following the funeral, the general consensus was that attending the funeral was an obligation. The newer generations who are born and brought up in the UK, influenced by Western culture, education, and values are gradually losing their traditional values, expecting older people to live independently. For some, filial responsibility and respect for older people are not always high on their priority list. Some may have to move away from their parents to find work. In most Sikh families, both the husband and wife work and have little spare time to look after their elderly parents and extended families. Religious and cultural changes are beginning to show their impact locally. There are elders and widows who suffer loneliness and hardship following the death of their life partners. They are accustomed to living in a culture of dependency where decisions are made for them by others or in consultation with family members. Members of this particular group also find it hard to avail themselves of support mechanisms already in place due to language and cultural barriers.

After bereavement follows the time when the bereaved person starts thinking about reorganising and rebuilding their life ahead. Family members support those living in the family, and their routine remains the same. They talk about death and the deceased openly and are aware of its effects on those left behind. Most Sikhs are dependent on their own family network and *gurdwaras*. It is found through observations and discussion with the bereaved that mourners who live within an extended family appear to recover quicker than those who live alone. Those who live alone, are disabled, and/or are spiritual (with no faith) have nowhere to go. There are also difficulties in accessing support mechanisms like bereavement support groups and death cafes due to language and cultural barriers. There is a dire need to create facilities for the Sikh community, taking care of their religious and cultural needs of consoling, comforting and supporting. *Gurdwaras* are central to the lives of Sikhs and they do excellent work by providing a venue for socialisation for the lonely and feeding them without any cost (*langar*). Some find that *gurdwaras* help meet their needs. Some feel Sikhs need neutral venues where confidentiality is maintained and professional support is available. *Gurdwaras* are run by traditional Sikhs and are under the tight control of management committees. Their inability to grasp the changing needs of the Sikh community living in the UK and Sikhs' over-dependency on these institutions is depriving the community of many healthcare facilities.

Conclusion

The death of someone we love is a devastating event; it is shocking and one of the most stressful experiences in life. Funerals are central to the grieving process. They allow the bereaved to share their grief and to take part in an established social and personal ritual of saying goodbye. It is hard to recover within weeks or months, as it is natural for the bereaved person to think about the deceased and reflect upon the life they had together. There are many questions that come to mind during this time, such as one's purpose of life, death and its reality, life after death, and the role of the soul and spirit. It is the time to ponder over life ahead, to assess one's strengths and weaknesses, finding and building support mechanisms, and above all, finding ways to reintegrate one's life to make it workable. It is also a time of realisation that life is going to be changed and cannot remain as before. One has to be prepared for the changes, not only in life, but also in relationships, problem solving, and learning new skills. It is a time to look at the realistic situation beyond emotions. Time does help people to learn a degree of acceptance. Life will never be the same again, but people can learn to live around their loss. The traditional Sikh bereavement traditions have changed in the UK, which affects grieving and lone living. Widowers often only discover themselves as an individual after going through a period of loss. Many Sikhs do not know themselves until they are alone, and that is why it is a time of rediscovery.

References

Attig, T. (2011). *How we grieve: relearning the world*. Rev. ed. Oxford: University Press.

Bowlby, J., & Parkes, C. M. (1970). Separation and loss within the family. In E.J. Anthony & C. Koupernik (Eds.), The child and his family (pp. 197-216). New York: Wiley

Corr, C.A., Nabe, C.M. and Corr, D. (1997). *Death and dying, life and living*. 2nd ed. Pacific Grove: CA Brooks/Cole.

Currer, C. (2001). *Responding to grief: dying, bereavement and social care*. New York: Palgrave.

De Hennezel, M. (1997). *Intimate Death: How the dying teach us how to live*. New York: Knopf.

Egan, K. (2014) Pastoral care today: widening the horizon In: Flanagan, B. and Thornton, S. eds. *The Bloomsbury guide to pastoral care*. London, Bloomsbury.

Eisenbruch, M. (1984b). Cross-cultural aspects of bereavement 11: ethnic and cultural variations in the development of bereavement practices. *Culture, Medicine and Psychiatry*, 8 (4), December, pp. 315-37.

Firth, S. (2000). Cross-cultural perspectives on bereavement In: Dickenson, D., Johnson, M. and Katz, S. J. eds. (2000) *Death, dying and bereavement*. London: Sage Publications.

Freud, S (1917). Mourning and melancholia. In: Freud, S. *Collected papers*. Vol 4. London: Hogarth.

Guru Granth Sahib (n.d), Amritsar: *Shromani Gurdwara Prabandhak* Committee (contains 1430 pages written in Panjabi).

Henley, A and Schott, J. (1999) *Culture, religion and patient care in a multi-ethnic society: a handbook for professionals*. London: Age Concern Books.

Klass, D., Silverman, P.R. and Nickman, S.I. (eds) (1996). *Continuing Bonds: new understanding of grief*. Washington, D.C.: Taylor & Francis.

Kübler-Ross, E. (1970). *On Death and Dying*. London: Tavistock.

Neuberger, J. (1999). *Dying well: A guide to enabling a good death*. Cheshire: Hochland & Hochland Ltd.

Parkes, C. M. (2000). Bereavement as a psychosocial transition: processes of adaptation to change. In: Dickinson, D., Johnson, M. and Katz, J. S. (eds). *Death, dying and bereavement*. 2nd ed. London: Sage Publications.

Root, B. L. and Exline, J. J. (2014). The role of continuing bonds in coping with grief: overview and future directions. *Death Studies*, 38: 1-8, 2014.

Stroebe, M. S., & Schut, H. (2001) *Meaning making in the dual process model of coping with bereavement.* In: Neimeyer, R. A. (ed.), *Meaning reconstruction & the experience of loss*. Washington, D.C.: American Psychological Association. pp. 55-73

Stroebe, M., and Schut, H. (2005). To continue or relinquish bonds: a review of consequences for the bereaved. *Death Studies*, 29, pp. 477–494.

Walter, T. 1994). *The revival of death*. London: Routledge.

Worden, J. W. (1982). *Grief counselling and grief therapy: A handbook for the mental health practitioner.* New York, NY: Springer.

Websites

Morrow, A. (2019). *The four phases and tasks of grief.* [online] Available at: https://www.verywellhealth.com/the-four-phases-and-tasks-of-grief-1132550 [Accessed 23 Feb.2019].

SGPC (2019) *Sikh Code of conduct* [online] Available at: https://old.sgpc.net/sikhism/code_of_conduct.asp [Accessed on 10 Oct. 2019].

Stroebe, M. & Schut, H. (1998). *Culture and grief: bereavement care.* [online] Available at: https://www.tandfonline.com/doi/abs/10.1080/02682629808657425 [Accessed 10 Oct. 2019].

Bibliography

Dyne, G. (1981) *Bereavement visiting.* London, King Edward's Hospital fund for London.

Chapter 10

Conclusion

Conclusion

Sikhs are not a homogenous community, especially at present when they are migrating globally. They have become a diasporic community, and the cultural values of indigenous countries are naturally becoming influential, especially on generations born and brought up in those countries. The most influential factors impacting upon Sikhs are their Sikh way of life, culture, modernity and their ability to adapt and integrate wherever they go. Amidst all this, their binding force is their Holy Scripture and Sikh *Rehat Maryada* (code of conduct and conventions). These have shaped and standardised life-cycle rites and rituals which are followed consistently by Sikhs living anywhere in the world. The other binding factor is *gurdwaras*, their place of worship. It has always been a Sikh priority to establish a *gurdwara* wherever they go. The Sikh place of worship plays a crucial and significant role in providing a platform not only for religious worship and prayers, but also for secular discussions and social gatherings. It also works as a community hub and a way to promote togetherness for old and lonely and isolated individuals. Chaplaincy visitors must be vigilant about respecting confidentiality.

Sikhs are a faith community and they make efforts to maintain their religious values and traditions. They strongly believe that Sikhism is a distinct religion possessing all the requisites of distinctiveness. *Guru* Nanak established a spiritual community: his monotheistic belief of the single Divine power, fraternal unity of all human beings, and equality are key teachings. Sikhs believe that his farsighted thinking made his teachings valuable to the whole of humanity. The *GGS* offers spiritual guidance not only to Sikh adherents but also to all human beings. Sikhism is the fifth largest world religion, having 26-30 million followers despite the severe atrocities and mass killings they had to suffer since its inception. This made their life unstable leaving hardly any time and opportunity for them to spread the message and teachings of their founder *Guru* Nanak to the world, of recognizing all people as equals, transcending the distinctions of gender, social background, and economic status, race and ethnicity.

Sikhism is a monotheistic religion and Sikhs believe in one God and the unity of God. God is beyond human comprehension or description, the soul is considered to be the spark of God and the medium of connection between humans and God (*Atma*, soul and *Parmatma,* supreme soul). *Guru* Nanak taught Sikhs to respect other religions and promoted religious freedom with the human right to follow their own path to God. His ethical values inspired Sikhs with a strong work ethic, sharing with the less fortunate, and being thankful to God by remembering His *naam*, who has given them human life, believed to be superior to any other form of life and other resources to live on this earth. It is important for Sikhs to remain under God's *hukam* (order), believing that whatever is happening is under His order and is for the best interest of them. His succession of nine *gurus* not only promoted his teachings but also found ways to put them into practice. The tenth *Guru* Gobind Singh terminated human lineage and made *Guru Granth Sahib* the eternal source of spiritual guidance, giving the scripture the status of a living *Guru*. Since then, the scripture remains the highest authority of the Sikhs, offering guidance on all situations in life and motivating personal transformation.

Sikhs believe in the doctrine of transmigration and *karma* theory and these play a significant role and affect their attitudes to death quite substantially. Each soul goes through many cycles of birth and rebirth depending on their *karma* in the past and present life. Death is not, therefore, a frightening thing for Sikhs, but the ultimate aim is for each soul to reach perfection and to be reunited with God.

Most healthcare professionals believe that South Asians look after their loved ones. Traditionally, South Asian communities live in extended families and maintain close relations. The family care for their own in the Sikh culture and many of them still maintain these values. Sikhs feel proud to depend on their family. Most elderly Sikhs still live in a dependency culture, heavily relying on their families. Sometimes it is to maintain the family *izzat* (honour, respect), showing that their families care. The situation in Western countries is gradually changing, influenced by Western education and culture, independent living, social and geographic mobility and women working full time. It is important to bear in mind that individual circumstances may differ, making it necessary to check with patients in order to give them patient-centred care and ensuring that they are properly looked after in their times of need and distress.

Sikh patients include all who would enter 'Sikh' as their religion on hospital admission forms, as well as those identified by the suffix of 'Singh' (male) and 'Kaur' (female). It is important that admission staff and chaplains take a brief history of the patient, particularly focussed on faith, beliefs, communication problems, relationships, diet and personal care. As some patients are not listed, they miss out on chaplaincy contact and visits, particularly when they are not fully aware of this service or they are hesitant to avail it. According to the audit of needs conducted by the author, Sikh patients need chaplaincy services, at least as much as any other patients, but they are hesitant to demand them, mainly because of language and cultural barriers, and the fear of annoying hospital staff. In the author's experience, Sikhs need chaplaincy services desperately, as many older people are living on their own. They often do not get an adequate service in their most difficult times such as end of life, palliative care and bereavement, due to the service not being properly structured and mainly dependent on volunteers. This deprives them of regular and consistent support because of their working pattern. At the time of writing this book, when there is a spread of Coronavirus disease (COVID-19), a virus which is highly infectious with no viable treatment, Sikh patients have hardly any chaplaincy support, especially in this most difficult time when their families are not even allowed to visit and *gurdwaras* are closed due to lockdown policy. Most volunteers are not allowed to work, especially the over 70s, who are not working due to government's advice and guidance. Many patients want to see someone who knows their culture and speaks the same language, as well as who understands the makeup of the Sikh community. They must make do under the circumstances with the current standard of service and often die alone without last prayer, an essential part of their life journey. Speaking from personal experience, only one referral for Sikh prayer was received as a result of offering digital services during this time of Covid-19. It is important that chaplaincy departments carefully assess staff resources, their expertise and skills, and risk-assessments, by having team meetings also involving willing and well-trained specialist volunteers. The next step is to plan the service by keeping in view government guidelines and also guidelines and values followed by their local trusts. The planning process is necessary for effective service delivery. The service can be delivered in different modes, for example face to face, by telephone, video chat, and other similar techniques. It is necessary for chaplains to build close relationships with the patient's nurse and ward staff. The multidisciplinary and referrals meetings can be arranged virtually.

Chaplains spend a lot of time visiting patients on the wards. One of the main purposes of ward visits is to listen to patients in order to discern their needs. This has other purposes, such as auditing needs, knowing the patient, and building and gaining their trust to accompany them on their journey. Sikhs often do not open up and talk in a relaxed manner to any chaplains other than their own, who can speak their language and understand them. In the author's experience of talking to Sikh patients, they do not hesitate to complain to a chaplain of their own faith about hospital staff and facilities unsuitable for them. Some patients feel that other staff tend to ignore them. On occasion, they feel marginalised in hospitals when they are in desperate need of help, support and care. There is a need of patient-centred care based on their individual needs rather than demand. Volunteers are the main resource of this service in NHS hospitals and occasionally in hospices and care homes. It becomes particularly difficult for Sikh volunteers in NHS hospitals to deal with many difficult situations due to lack of status, wider knowledge of chaplaincy work, resources and expert supervision. Sikh patients often think that a volunteer can fix everything instantly, not knowing the politics of chaplaincy and the bureaucracy of large organisations. Volunteers sometimes have to face challenging situations being the sole representative of chaplaincy services for the community they serve.

Most Sikh patients need pastoral care, as they want to talk to someone they trust and who can communicate with them effectively. This needs cultural competency, along with language literacy, in order to make sense of their stories. The majority of Sikh patients are elderly, over 60, and many of them do not speak English fluently based on author's audit, some speak little or no English. This is the group who are more likely to require chaplaincy services, especially end of life care. The Equality Analysis suggests the use of interpreters for chaplaincy services. It is not always easy to have an emotional conversation through a third party. It may be beneficial to use experienced and well-trained chaplaincy volunteers as sessional paid workers for less cost, with the advantage that they know the patient and have language and chaplaincy skills, giving them an incentive and opportunity to develop in the profession.

The term 'Spiritual Care' is regarded as the more inclusive term of choice and is recommended in the 2015 chaplaincy guidelines, being a neutral term and acceptable to most, including medical staff and other healthcare professionals. Spirituality as understood today is recognised as a complex and multidimensional element of the human experience (Anandarajah and Hight, 2001). Andrew Todd quoting spiritual care from Swift's research (2009) in 'Responding to diversity: chaplaincy in a multi-faith context', as 'an ill-defined and contested term to be found in healthcare literature, especially relating to nursing practice' (2011, p.97). As a concept unique to each person, it is incapable of being categorised and subjected to a universally accepted definition due to the diverse and differing beliefs, values and meanings in the lives of human beings (Goodhead and Hartley, 2018). Despite this, it is widely recognised that spiritual care is an essential, integral aspect of high-quality care. Sikhs believe that spiritual care not only nurtures the soul but also lifts and energises the human spirit. Spirituality and religion are integrated in Sikhism. Spiritual care is a need of most patients, therefore it should be person-centred with a wide scope of pastoral, spiritual and religious aspects, encompassing cultural and existential issues, and delivered in the language understood by the patient. Another form of Sikh spiritual care is to keep patients connected with the Sikh calendar. Those embarking on visiting Sikh patients should give them greeting and prayer cards marking festivities, such as the birthdays of the *Gurus* and other religious and cultural festivals.

Sikhs, being a faith community, mainly ask for religious and pastoral care. In order to provide religious and pastoral care to Sikh patients, it becomes essential for care providers to have religious and cultural competency around all the life-cycle rites that are tied with Sikhism. The Scriptures are written in Panjabi, and prayers and supplication are too. *Ardas*, one of the most adaptable interventions that a chaplain can make in a fraught ward situation and with a wide variety of patients, is in Panjabi. End of life care includes reciting prayers, supplication, administering holy water, and listening to the last words of the dying, which all require language skills. Bereavement customs are also closely tied with religion and culture. Pastoral care draws its resources from the essence (extract, gist) of religion/beliefs and culture. Meaningful religious, spiritual and pastoral care can only be given by experienced chaplains having proficiency in the Panjabi language and good knowledge of Sikh religion, Sikh community, and Sikh culture.

The 2003 guidelines gave a fair and extensive treatment to minority faiths. The 2015 guidelines recommended a framework for various diversities and minority faiths. These guidelines tried to cover almost every aspect of chaplaincy services and highlighted to resolve minority faiths by appointing generic chaplains. It is disappointing that two national chaplaincy guidelines (2003 and 2015) seem to overlook the real barriers of the numerical criterion and harmony between strategy and practice in developing chaplaincy services for minority faiths and the growing population of no faith. Minority faiths have hardly had any voice at a decision-making level due to the lack of professional expertise. Generic posts are not even offered to qualified chaplains from minority faith backgrounds, according to the author's experience. Many job descriptions are written in a way to attract lay chaplains or chaplains other than Christians, but discreetly mention that it is an essential criterion to lead worship service (obviously Christian), which is evident from advertisements.

Nothing has changed since 2003, except extending services to Muslim communities and recruiting volunteers from minority communities. It may be more helpful if the new guidelines propose some recommendations on staffing ratio, paid proportionate hours for suitably qualified chaplains from minority faiths, and additional hours for research to create resources. NHS Trusts and chaplaincy managers blame funding, but in reality, there is more to it than that. They receive funding to serve the whole community in their catchment area, and not just majority communities. The author argues that uneven distribution of funding and the mind-set of chaplaincy managers are the main barriers to chaplaincy equality, making it essential to scrutinise how many Trusts are translating strategic guidelines in practice to ensure equality. It is evident in recruitment practices that the numerical criterion has been rigidly followed; it is also reflected in the chaplaincy literature that the first preference is for chaplains from a Christian faith, and if the head of department is Anglican, the first preference goes for Anglicans or for other Christian denominations. At present, Christians and Muslims are the dominant religions.

Sikhs should also own some responsibility by being proactive, demanding, giving their feedback, explaining their needs, supporting volunteers by sending 'thank you' cards, and giving suggestions on how chaplaincy services can be improved. It is important for those accessing the services to feel that chaplains always reflect presence. Attendance, participation and contribution in meetings are other tools to draw the attention of service providers. Self-sufficiency is a prominent cultural characteristic of Sikhs, and they take pride in it, which perhaps sets them at a disadvantage when demanding more particular and personalised treatment from hospital staff. Sikhs should be encouraged to demand the service as their right as a taxpayer as suggested by a participant in the pastoral care focus group.

Volunteers play an invaluable role in supporting chaplains, and to some extent, they complement their work. Stoter says, 'The role of the volunteer is not to replace professional input or to save money, but to enhance the care given (1995, p.140). At present, Sikh volunteers are the sole service providers with hardly any valuable or reliable support. The chaplaincy profession is a 'no go area' for them. They are not encouraged, supported or given incentives to prepare for professional roles. At present there are two key issues: 1) chaplains are not being recruited from smaller faith communities, and 2) if recruited, they are being excluded from professionalisation. Henley and Schott rightly commented:

> For healthcare to be truly accessible to everyone, the needs of cultural and religious minorities run as a continuous thread through all health planning, policy making, management, education and practice. Minority needs should not be seen as 'different' or 'separate' or considered only in relation to certain issues or services (1999, p.228).

The service should be adequately staffed, regulated and funded, as well as responsive to patients' needs. Traditionally, bed occupancy figures for each faith community have been the main criteria that determined the total number of sessions available and the proportion of these sessions applicable to each faith community. There are two problems in securing a realistic set of criteria: 1) lack of information on patients' religious affiliation; 2) difficulty of quantifying the time spent in supporting people at times of deep personal distress, prolonged serious illness and sudden or long-awaited bereavement. The small number of people from ethnic minorities in an area may not be sufficient to justify a sessional appointment. However, as recommended in the 'Fair for all' guidance, steps must be taken to ensure that the spiritual needs of individuals and family groups from ethnic minority faith communities are met, and that any necessary language support is provided (Scottish Guidelines, 2002).

It may be beneficial for hospitals and other healthcare institutions such as hospices and care homes to organise community engagement meetings to educate and engage communities by giving information on their chosen healthcare topics. This is a way forward to involve communities so that they can make informed decisions and participate in caring for their loved ones and their own communities. Chaplains and volunteers can become an equal partner in these efforts, having close links with their faith/belief communities. This approach may also encourage non-Christian communities to use the services of hospices and care homes. Hospices and care homes provide useful services and they need to create the capacity to accommodate the needs of minority faith communities. Raising awareness and promoting their services is the first step to move forward and the techniques used should be analogous to their way of life.

Healthcare chaplaincy adopted and accepted multi-faith chaplaincy through a combination of many factors: change in demography; the political agenda of community cohesion; the Human Rights Act 1998, with a key link with the European Convention of Human

Rights; the Race Relations (Amendment) Act 2000 to promote race equality; the Race Relations Act 2013, which focussed on discrimination in employment and brought in religion and belief. The Equality Act 2010 combined anti-discrimination laws, and brought in various diversities, making it a single document. It combined the writings and efforts of chaplaincy workers and academics with the contributions of forward-thinking NHS Trusts, health bodies, and organisations. The central theme for most of them is equality. Equality is about creating a fairer society, where there is respect and a sense of being valued. There is a feeling of inclusiveness and not being treated differently. Services should be planned in such a way that the needs of all communities are taken care of. There should be a genuine commitment as opposed to lip-service.

With chaplaincy services being overwhelmingly Christian, it is natural to derive chaplaincy terms from Christianity, for example, chapel, chaplain, and pastoral care. Society has changed and the nature of the community has become much more diverse. These changes call for secular terms to be adopted which are suitable to the changing nature of community and acceptable to all communities. In Sikhism, the term spiritual care is not understood by many people, especially when its interpretation is not unanimously accepted in the NHS. A compromise could be 'Religious and Spiritual care' for chaplaincy, and the word chaplain can be termed according to the status of the chaplain, such as Religious and Spiritual Care Manager (*Dharmic* and *Ruhani dekh bhal* manager ਧਾਰਮਿਕ ਅਤੇ ਰੂਹਾਨੀ ਦੇਖਭਾਲ ਮਨੈਜਰ),

Religious and Spiritual Caregiver for chaplain (*Dharmic* and *Ruhani dekh bhal karamchari* ਧਾਰਮਿਕ ਅਤੇ ਰੂਹਾਨੀ ਦੇਖਭਾਲ ਕਰਮਚਾਰੀ), Religious and Spiritual Care Volunteer (*Dharmic* and *Ruhani dekh bhal Niskam Sevak* ਧਾਰਮਿਕ ਅਤੇ ਰੂਹਾਨੀ ਦੇਖਭਾਲ ਨਿਸਕਾਮ ਸੇਵਕ) and compassionate care (*Rehimdil dekh bhal*) for pastoral care.

In conclusion, it is appropriate to reiterate that as the NHS is a publicly funded service, it should be made equally accessible for all, irrespective of religion, belief, culture, or numbers. Recruitment practices should be unbiased and fair, reflecting local religious, beliefs and cultural makeup. The NHS chaplaincy workers should have their own independent identity. Their loyalty should be towards the NHS and Trust population for whom they work and are paid by. The NHS provides a free service to the citizens of the UK, irrespective of their faith, belief, or tradition. It should equally apply to chaplaincy services, as minority faiths and people with no faith also contribute towards public funds. Systems need to be questioned and policies examined in the light of valuing humanity and equal rights, to remove the barriers between the privileged and the excluded, the majority and the minority.

References

Anandarajah, G. and Hight, E. (2001). Spirituality and Medical Practice: using the HOPE questions as a practical tool for spiritual assessment. *American Family Physician* Vol 63, No. 1, pp. 81 – 88

Goodhead, A. & Hartley, N. (2018). *Spirituality in Hospice Care* (London: JKP)

Henley, A. and Schott, J. (1999). *Culture, religion and patient care in a multi-ethnic society: A handbook for professionals*. London: Age Concern London (reprinted in 2001, 2002.

Stoter, D. J. (1995). *Spiritual aspects of healthcare*. London: Mosby.

Swift, C. (2009). *Hospital chaplaincy in the 'Twenty-first Century: the crisis of spiritual care in the NHS*. Farnham: Ashgate.

Todd, A. (2011). Responding to diversity: chaplaincy in a multi-faith context In: Threlfall-Holmes, M. and Newitt, M. (2011) *Being a chaplain*. London: SPCK.

Appendices

Sikh and Panjabi terms, Assessment tools, *Mool Mantar*, Short *Ardas*, Greeting and Prayer Cards and the important days in the Sikh calendar

Appendix 1

There may not be a direct comparison between Sikh and Panjabi terms with Judeo-Christian terms and that makes it difficult to find accurate and suitable alternatives in Sikh *Dharam*. Translating from one language to another is not always easy and accurate. An attempt is made to give near enough similar words/vocabulary and explanations.

Sikh and Panjabi terms explained

Panjabi	English
Adh marg	The ceremony of breaking the pot for bathing the dead body, halfway towards the cremation ground
Adhyatamvad	Spirituality
Adhyatmic	Spiritual
Adhyatmic dekh bhal	Spiritual care
Adhyatmicta	Spirituality
Adi Granth	Original version of Guru Granth Sahib
Advaitvad	Non-dualism
Akalis	Organisation for the Sikh rights
Akhand path	Continuous recitation of reading the whole of the GGS to be finished in 48 hours
Amrit	Holy water, empowering water
Amritdhari	Initiated person
Anand karaj	Sikh wedding
Antim sanskar	Funeral

Ardas	Supplication, invocation
Atma	Soul
Bandi Chhor Divas	Day of prisoners' release from Gwalior Fort, celebrated annually by Sikhs on the next day after Diwali
Bani	Hymns/verses
Barahmaha	Hymns related to twelve months
Betaba	Disclaimer
Bhagats	Devotees, saints
Bhai	Spiritual person/priest. In ordinary sense, brother
Bhakti	Devotion
Bhana manana	Accepting the will of God
Bhog	Concluding ceremony
Boliyan	Couplets that are sung in Punjab
Budha Marna	A ceremony of celebrating the death of an old man by waving a whisk over the hearse of an old person's dead body and decorating with festoons and balloons
Chardi kala	High spirit, highly spirited person, optimism
Chaur/chauri	Metal or wooden holder consists of a yak tail hair or artificial fibre
Dastar	Sikh turban
Daswandh	Tithe - donating one-tenth of the income in donation
Daya	Humility, compassion

Dharam	Duty in the narrow sense
	Religion, moral duty and the way of life
	Religion, spirituality and philosophy combined
Dharamsal	School of religious learning
Dharmic	Adhering to dharam
Divas	Earthen oil lamps
Diwan	Congregational gathering
Driśaṭānt	Parables- simple story used to illustrate or teach a moral or spiritual lesson
Dupatta	Female head cover/scarf nearly 2 metres long and one metre wide
Duvidha	Confused, unable to make a decision
Five Ks	Sikh symbols of Sikh identity
Gatra	Sheath
Geet	Punjabi folk songs
Ghar	A musical clef or key, in ordinary language, it is 'house'
Gidha	Clapping
Granth	Anthology
Granthi/bhai	Sikh priest
Gulgalay	Sweet made of wheat and jaggery
Gurbani	Hymns of GGS
Gurdwara	Place of Sikh worship

Gurmantar	The recitation of the word 'vaheguru', the wonderful Lord
Gurmat	Teachings of the Gurus
Gurmukh	God oriented and spiritually aware person
Gurmukhi	Script to write Panjabi
Gurpurabs	The religious festival commemorating the birth and death anniversaries and special events in the lives of the gurus
Gursikh	Sikhs of the gurus
Gursikhi	Sikh Dharam, teachings of the gurus
Gurti	Panjabi cultural tradition of giving honey to a newly born child
Guru	The spiritual guide
Guru Granth Sahib	The Holy Scripture of Sikhs
Guru Maryada	Sikh religious traditions, conduct and practices
Gutka	Liturgy
Gyan	Knowledge
Halal meat	Ritualistic slaughter by slow bleed
Halwa	Sweet pudding made of semolina, ghee, sugar and dry fruit
Hamdard	Compassionate, empathy
Hankar	Ego
Harmandar Sahib	The Golden Temple in Amritsar, Punjab

Hola Mahalla	A festival when Sikhs demonstrate their martial skills in simulated battle in Anandpur, a city in Punjab
Hukam	God's Will/order/command
Izzat	Honour, respect
Jaggery	Cane sugar, lumped brown sugar
Janamsakhis	Life stories of the Sikh gurus
Jarda	Sweet yellow rice
Jhatka	Animal slaughtered in one stroke
Jonies	Form of lives
Jooth/Juth	Food shared with the same spoon and drinking from one's drink makes it jooth/jootha
Kacchera	Cotton, knee-length undergarment - fairly long, reaching down to the knees and tight at the bottom worn by initiated Sikhs
Kafan	White sheet to cover the deceased - 4.75 metres long
Kakkars	Sikh symbols of identity
Kam	Lust
Kameez and salwar	Panjabi traditional suit - contains ladies' long shirt and baggy trousers
Kangha	Wooden comb
Kara	A steel bangle
Karah Prasad	Sacramental offering made of flour, sugar and butter in equal quantity - Sikh holy food

Karma	Sikhs believe in the doctrine of karma with its cycle of reward and punishment for all thoughts and deeds. Each person's life in this world is determined by their behaviour in their last life and what they do now influences the next life and so on. Sikhs believe that cycles can be altered by good actions in this life and by God's grace.
Karmai	Engagement
Katha	Religious stories
Kaur	Complementary part of the name, indicating female gender belonging to Sikh faith
Kes	Hair
Keshadhari Sikhs	Turbaned Sikhs not initiated
Khalsa	Initiated Sikhs with the spirit of faith and valour to fight for justice and human rights
Khalsa Panth	Khalsa order
Khand	Realm of spiritual progression
Khanda	Sikh symbol
Khoh laina	Taken away
Kirpan	A long or small curved symbolic sword from a few inches to three feet long
Kirt karna	Work ethos, honest earning
Kirtan	Singing devotional hymns with musical instruments
Krodh	Anger
Kurahit	Bad deeds

Kurta pyjama	Kurta pyjama consists of a top tunic called the kurta and bottoms called pyjama. The word kurta can be used generically to refer to the garment for both men and women.
Ladoo	Indian sweet mainly used for happy occasions
Langar	Community kitchen, communal meal
Lavan	Circling performed in front of the GGS and congregation
Lobh	Greed
Mahalla	A number which denotes the name of the composer Guru
Malpua	A sweet which is creamy and fried like a pancake
Manji	A system of religious organisation, type of raised bed
Manmukh	Self-centred person
Mela	Festival
Milni	A ceremony of introduction between the family of the bride and bridegroom in a Sikh wedding
Miri	Temporal authority
Moh	Attachment
Moksha	Liberation
Mool Mantar	Fundamental creed that literally means root formula
Naam	It means not only the word or utterance but is an encapsulation of divine reality. Naam is for Guru

	Nanak the total divine self-expression, rather than merely God's title or epithet.
Naam Japna	Remembering God and doing good deeds
Naam simran	Reciting the name of God, keeping the divine in mind and sustained remembrance of the divine. Naam simran is a constant spiritual practice not in isolation but as the grounding for: 'Highest is the truth, but higher still is truthful living'.
Nimarita	Humility
Nishan Sahib	A triangular Sikh flag
Pag	Turban
Palla	Long scarf
Palla Frowna	Similar to a 'giving away ceremony', where a father ties the end of his daughter's scarf to the groom's scarf
Pangat	Sitting in row irrespective of caste, creed and status
Parkash	Opening of the GGS first thing in the morning
Parkash utsav	Birth ceremony of Sikh *Gurus*
Parmatma	Supreme soul-God, supreme authority
Parna	A length of plain cloth used as a loin cloth, usually two metres long
Parvah	To consign
Patasha	Sugar bubble
Path	Recitation of Gurbani
Path Bhog	Finishing ceremony of the recitation of GGS

Phulke	Very thin large chapatis
Phuri	Sitting on a straw mat in mourning for a certain period
Pind	The ritual of donating lumps of rice flour, oat flour or solidified milk for ten days after death
Piri	Spiritual authority
Pitr	Ancestors
Prabhat pheri	Religious procession that takes place in the early hours of the day before sun rises
Purdah	The practice of certain Hindu and Muslim societies of screening women from strangers
Pyaar or pyar	Love
Raags	A pattern of melodic notes
Ragis	Religious musicians
Ruh	Soul
Ruhani sevak	Spiritual volunteer
Sadh sangat	Congregation of spiritual and humble people
Sadharan path	A non-continuous recitation of entire GGS
Sagan	Small token of money
Sakhis	Parables
Samadhi	Contemplation
Sandesh	Edict
Sandhara	A gift given by a brother to his sister - includes Panjabi saree/suit, bangles, henna, ladoo and swing

Sangat	Congregation
Sangrand	The first day of the lunar month
Sant bhasa	Language used by saints
Santokh	Contentment
Saropa	A scarf or a length of cloth bestowed on someone as a mark of honour, generally by a gurdwara's president
Sat	Truth
Sati	Immolation on the husband's pyre
Satsang	Congregation of faithful people
Seva	Voluntary and selfless work
Sevadar	Volunteer
Shabad	Psalms/religious verses, sung or recited
Shradh	Feast for dead ancestors by feeding priests and giving them donations
Sikhi	Sikh Dharam
Sikhiya	Sermon - talk on a religious or moral subject based on scripture
Singh	Complementary element of the name indicating male gender belonging to Sikh faith
Sog	Processing the feelings of loss as a result of death. It covers both mourning and bereavement
Sufis	Mystics
Sukhasan	Position of rest for the GGS for the night

Sutak	Keeping a woman aloof after childbirth nearly for forty days
Tabla	A set of drums
Transmigration	The continuation of life after death dictated by the laws of karma
Updesh	Sermon
Vaheguru	Wonderful Lord
Vak/hukamnama	A hymn randomly selected from the GGS on a daily basis. Also a guiding message when required on different occasions
Varna Ashram dharma	Stage of renunciation
Veil	Garment for women to cover their face to protect or conceal from strangers
Viah	Wedding ceremony
Wand chhakna	Share with the needy and less fortunate
Word	Word in the sense of Divine revelation is given much importance as it has come directly from God, remains forever and is unalterable in Sikhism.

Note: Some suggested terminology fit for the changing chaplaincy services.

Panjabi	English
Anek prakar dian sevava vich sanjh pauni	Multidisciplinary care
Dharmic ate adhyatmic dekh bhal or Dharmic ate Atmic dekh bhal	Religious and spiritual care
Dharmic ate Ruhani dekh bhal Karamchari	Religious and spiritual care worker
Dharmic ate Ruhani dekh bhal Manager	Religious and spiritual care manager
Dharmic ate Ruhani dekh bhal Niskam Sevak	Religious and spiritual care volunteer
Rehamdil dekh bhal	Pastoral care
Sikh ruhani carer	Sikh spiritual carer
Sikh ruhani niskam sevak	Sikh chaplaincy volunteer

Appendix 2

Assessment Tools

Table 1: HOPE
H – Sources of hope, meaning, comfort, strength, peace, love and connection What is important to you in your life: are there values that help you to make the most important decisions in your life? Where do you find your hope, strength, comfort and peace? What do you hold onto at difficult times? What sustains you and keeps you going? For some people, their religious or spiritual beliefs act as a source of comfort and strength in dealing with life's ups and downs. Is this true for you? If the answer is "No", consider asking "Was it ever?" If the person answers "yes" here, you may want to ask: "what changed?"

O – Organised religion

Are you part of a religious or spiritual community?

How important is that for you?

Do you believe in a higher being or deity, for example, God, Allah, Buddha?

How does your religious belief give you strength and hope?

What aspects of your beliefs or religious practices do you find most helpful to you personally e.g. prayer, worship, meditation, scripture?

Have you any concerns around dietary requirements, gender, washing and clothing? How can we help you?

P – Personal spirituality and practices

Do you have personal spiritual beliefs that are independent of organised religion? What are they?

What do you consider of prime importance in terms of your own sense of value, dignity and self-worth?

Are there aspects of your spirituality that are important and helpful to you personally e.g. leisure activities, family, music, nature, prayer, meditation?

How can we help?

What can we provide?

E - Effects of spirituality on care we provide

How has this illness affected you and your family's life?

Have your beliefs/spirituality been a help during the course of your illness?

If family/work/leisure are central, are there issues around worry for the future/grief/loss/finance?

Is there anything I can do to help you access the resources that might help you at this time?

Are there any other issues around family relationships that trouble you, or worries about family?

Are you worried about any conflicts between your beliefs and your medical situation, care or decisions?

How can we support you?

Table 2: CSI-MEMO
CS – Do your religious/spiritual beliefs provide Comfort, or are they a source of Stress?
I – Do you have spiritual beliefs that might Influence your medical decisions?
MEM – Are you a Member of a religious or spiritual community, and is it supportive to you?

O – Do you have any Other spiritual needs that you would like someone to address?

Table 3: FAITH
F– Do you have a Faith or religion that is important to you?
A – How do your beliefs Apply to your health?
I – Are you Involved in a church or faith community?
T – How do your spiritual views affect your views about Treatment?
H – How can I Help you with any spiritual concerns?

Table 4: FACT
F – Faith (or Beliefs): What is your Faith or belief? Do you consider yourself a person of Faith or a spiritual person? What things do you believe that give your life meaning and purpose?
A – Active (or Available, Accessible, Applicable): Are you currently Active in your faith community? Are you a part of religious or spiritual community? Is support for your faith Available to you?

Do you have Access to what you need to apply your faith (or your belief)?
Is there a person or a group whose presence and comfort you value at a time like this?

C – Coping (or Comfort); Conflicts (or Concerns): How are you Coping with your medical situation?
Is your faith (your beliefs) helping you Cope?
How is your faith (your beliefs) providing Comfort in the light of your diagnosis? Do any of your religious beliefs or spiritual practices conflict with medical treatment?
Are there any particular Concerns you have for us as your medical team?

T – Treatment plan: If the patient is coping well, then either support and encourage or reassess at a later date as the patient's situation changes. If the patient is coping poorly, then 1) depending on relationship and similarity in faith/beliefs, provide direct intervention: spiritual counselling, prayer, Sacred Scripture, etc., 2) encourage the patient to address these concerns with their own faith leader, or 3) make a referral to the hospital chaplain for further assessment.

Table 5: SPIRIT

S – Spiritual belief system: Do you have a formal religious affiliation? Can you describe this? Do you have a spiritual life that is important to you?

P – Personal spirituality: Describe the beliefs and practices of your religion that you personally accept. Describe those beliefs and practices that you do not accept or follow.

In what ways is your spirituality/religion meaningful for you?

I – Integration with a spiritual community: Do you belong to any religious or spiritual groups or communities? How do you participate in this group/community? What importance does this group have for you? What types of support and help does or could this group provide for you in dealing with health issues?

R – Ritualised practices and Restrictions: What specific practices do you carry out as part of your religious and spiritual life? What lifestyle activities or practices do your religion encourage, discourage or forbid? To what extent have you followed these guidelines?

I – Implications for medical practice: Are there specific elements of medical care that your religion discourages or forbids? To what extent have you followed these guidelines? What aspects of your religion/spirituality would you like to keep in mind as I care for you?

T – Terminal events planning: Are there particular aspects of medical care that you wish to forego or have withheld because of your religion/spirituality? Are there religious or spiritual practices or rituals that you would like to have available in the hospital or at home? Are there religious or spiritual practices that you wish to plan for at the time of death, or following death? As we plan for your medical care near the end of life, in what ways will your religion and spirituality influence your decisions?

Sources and References

Ambuel, B., and Weissman, D.E. (1999). Discussing spiritual issues and maintaining hope. In: Weissman, D.E., and Ambuel, B. (Eds.). *Improving end-of-life care: A resource guide for physician education*, 2nd Edition. Milwaukee, WI: Medical College of Wisconsin.

Anandarajah, G., and E. Hight (2001). "Spirituality and Medical Practice: Using the HOPE Questions as a Practical Tool for Spiritual Assessment". *American Family Practice* 63, pp. 81–88.

LaRocca-Pitts, M. (2008). "FACT: Taking a Spiritual History in a Clinical Setting". *Journal of Health Care Chaplaincy* 15, pp1–12.

LaRocca-Pitts, M. (2009). 5 Tool Review: Outlines five spiritual history tools (*CSI*-MEMO, FICA, HOPE, FAITH, and SPIRIT). *Australian Journal of Pastoral Care & Health*. Vol.3, no. 2, December 2009.

Maugans, TA. (1997). The spiritual history. *Archives of Family Medicine 5*, pp.11-16.

Puchalski, C. M., and A. L. Romer (2000). "Taking a Spiritual History Allows Clinicians to Understand Patients More Fully". *Journal of Palliative Medicine* 3, pp. 129–37.

Appendix 3

Mool Mantar, short *Ardas*, greeting and prayer cards

Mool Mantar

Mool Mantar is a root formula which is at the beginning of the GGS. There are different views on *Mool Mantar* as to where it ends. Professor Sahib Singh, an authority on the GGS, suggested until *gur prasad* (1972, p. 7). Some extend it to '*Nanak hosi bhi sach*'. The most accepted view is that of Professor Sahib Singh. The original text along with transcription and English translation is given below:

Panjabi	Transcription	Translation
੧ੳ	*Ek Oan kar*	God is one
ਸਤਿਨਾਮ	*Satnam*	Whose existence is true
ਕਰਤਾ ਪੁਰਖੁ	*Karta Purakh*	Creator
ਨਿਰਭਉ	*Nirbhau*	Without fear
ਨਿਰਵੈਰੁ	*Nirvair*	Without enmity
ਅਕਾਲ ਮੁਰਤਿ	*Akal Murat*	Timeless and formless
ਅਜੂਨੀ	*Ajuni*	Beyond the cycle of birth and death

ਸੈਭੰ	Saibhan	Self-existence
ਗੁਰ ਪ੍ਰਸਾਦਿ	Gur Prasad	Realised by Divine Grace

Cole and Sambhi paraphrased:

> 'This being is One; the Truth; immanent in all things. Immanent in creation. Without fear and without enmity. Not subject to time. Beyond birth and death. Self-manifesting. Known by the Guru's grace'. God is a transcendent being, eternal and self-existent. God is beyond space, and beyond time. (1990, p.111).

Ardas (supplication)

ਅਰਦਾਸ (Short *Ardas* in Panjabi version)

ੴ ਵਾਹਿਗੁਰੂ ਜੀ ਕੀ ਫਤਹਿ॥

ਸ੍ਰੀ ਭਗੌਤੀ ਜੀ ਸਹਾਇ। ਵਾਰ ਸ੍ਰੀ ਭਗੌਤੀ ਜੀ ਕੀ ਪਾਤਸ਼ਾਹੀ ੧੦ ।

ਪ੍ਰਿਥਮ ਭਗੌਤੀ ਸਿਮਰਿ ਕੈ ਗੁਰ ਨਾਨਕ ਲਈਂ ਧਿਆਇ।
ਫਿਰ ਅੰਗਦ ਗੁਰ ਤੇ ਅਮਰਦਾਸੁ ਰਾਮ ਦਾਸੈ ਹੋਈਂ ਸਹਾਇ।

ਅਰਜਨ ਹਰਿਗੋਬਿੰਦ ਨੋ ਸਿਮਰੌ ਸ੍ਰੀ ਹਰਿਰਾਇ।

ਸ੍ਰੀ ਹਰਿਕ੍ਰਿਸ਼ਨ ਧਿਆਇਐ ਜਿਸ ਡਿਠੇ ਸਭਿ ਦੁਖਿ ਜਾਇ।

ਤੇਗ ਬਹਾਦਰ ਸਿਮਰਿਐ ਘਰ ਨਉ ਨਿਧਿ ਆਵੈ ਧਾਇ।

ਸਭ ਥਾਈਂ ਹੋਇ ਸਹਾਇ।

ਦਸਵਾਂ ਪਾਤਸ਼ਾਹ ਸ੍ਰੀ ਗੁਰੂ ਗੋਬਿੰਦ ਸਿੰਘ ਸਾਹਿਬ ਜੀ !

ਸਭ ਥਾਈਂ ਹੋਇ ਸਹਾਇ।

ਦਸਾਂ ਪਾਤਸ਼ਾਹੀਆਂ ਦੀ ਜੋਤ ਸ੍ਰੀ ਗੁਰੂ ਗ੍ਰੰਥ ਸਾਹਿਬ ਜੀ ਦੇ ਪਾਠ

ਦੀਦਾਰ ਦਾ ਧਿਆਨ ਧਰ ਕੇ ਬੋਲੋ ਜੀ ਵਾਹਿਗੁਰੂ।

ਪੰਜਾਂ ਪਿਆਰਿਆਂ, ਚੌਹਾਂ ਸਾਹਿਬਜ਼ਾਦਿਆਂ, ਚਾਲ੍ਹੀਆਂ ਮੁਕਤਿਆਂ, ਹਠੀਆਂ, ਜਪੀਆਂ,

ਤਪੀਆਂ, ਜਿਨ੍ਹਾਂ ਨਾਮ ਜਪਿਆ, ਵੰਡ ਛਕਿਆ, ਦੇਗ ਚਲਾਈ, ਤੇਗ ਵਾਹੀ, ਦੇਖ ਕੇ

ਅਣਡਿੱਠ ਕੀਤਾ, ਤਿਨਾਂ ਪਿਆਰਿਆਂ ਦੀ ਕਮਾਈ ਦਾ ਧਿਆਨ ਧਰ ਕੇ, ਖ਼ਾਲਸਾ ਜੀ

ਬੋਲੋ ਜੀ ਵਾਹਿਗੁਰੂ।

At the end of *Ardas*, the name of the patient for whom it is performed and its purpose should be stated.

ਅੰਤਿਮ ਅਰਦਾਸ (**Last prayer**)

ਤੁਧ ਆਗੈ ਅਰਦਾਸਿ ਹਮਾਰੀ ਜੀਉ ਪਿੰਡੁ ਸਭੁ ਤੇਰਾ॥

ਕਹੁ ਨਾਨਕ ਸਭ ਤੇਰੀ ਵਡਿਆਈ ਕੋਈ ਨਾਉ ਨ ਜਾਣੈ ਮੇਰਾ॥ (੩੮੩)

ਜੇਹਾ ਚੀਰੀ ਲਿਖਿਆ ਤੇਹਾ ਹੁਕਮੁ ਕਮਾਹਿ॥

ਘਲੇ ਆਵਹਿ ਨਾਨਕਾ ਸਦੇ ਉਠੀ ਜਾਹਿ॥ (੧੨੩੯)

It is important to say these above-mentioned words at the beginning of *Ardas* if doing this for a patient who dies in hospital.

English transcription and translation of *Ardas* (Supplication)

Ardas

Ek-Oankar. Waheguroo Ji Ki Fateh

God is One. All victory is of the Wondrous Guru (God).

Sri Bhagouti ji Sahai

May the respected sword (God in the form of the Destroyer of evil doers) help us!

Vaar Sri Bhagouti Ji Ki Paatshaahee Dasvee

Ode of the respected sword recited by the Tenth Guru.

Pritham Bhagouti Simar Kai, Guru Naanak Layee Dhiyae

First remember the sword (God in the form of Destroyer of evil doers); then remember and meditate upon Guru Nanak.

344

Angad Gur Te Amar Das, Raamdaasai Hoye Sahai

Then remember and meditate upon Guru Angad, Guru Amar Das and Guru Ram Das: May they help us!

Arjan Hargobind No Simrou Sri Har Rai

Remember and meditate upon Guru Arjan, Guru Hargobind and Respected Guru Har Rai.

Sri HarKrishan Dhiyaa-eeai Jis Dhithi Sabh Dukh Jaye

Remember and meditate upon respected Guru Har Krishan, by having the sight of whom, all pains vanish.

Teg Bahadur Simareeai Ghar No Nidh Avai Dhai

Remember and meditate upon Guru Tegh Bahadur; and then nine sources of wealth will come hastening to your home.

Sabh Thai Ho-e Sahaai

Oh Respected Gurus! Kindly help us everywhere.

(This is the end of the section written by Guru Gobind Singh Ji, the rest was compiled after the Guru's time.)

Dasvaa Paatshaah Guru Gobind Singh Ji Sabh Thai Ho-e Sahaai

May the kind, the respected Tenth Guru Gobind Singh assist us everywhere.

Dasa Paatsaaheea Di Jot Sri Guru Granth Sahib Ji, De Paath Deedaar Daa Dhiyaan Dhar Ke Bolo Ji Waheguroo

Think and meditate upon the divine light of the Ten Kings contained in the respected Guru Granth Sahib and turn your thoughts to the divine teachings of and get pleasure by the sight of Guru Granth Sahib; Utter Wahe Guru (Wondrous God)!

Panja Piyariya, Chauhaa Sahibzadiya, Chaliya Mukhtiya, Huthiya, Jupiya, Tupiya, Jina Nam Jupiya, Vand Shakiya, Deg Chalaaee, Teg Vaahee, Dekh Ke Andhith Keetaa, Tinhaa Piariyaa, Sachiaariyaa Dee Kamaaee, Da Dhiyaan Dhar Ke Bolo Ji Waheguroo

Think of the deeds of the Five Beloved Ones, of the four sons (of Guru Gobind Singh); of the Forty Martyrs; of the brave Sikhs of indomitable determination; of the devotees steeped in the colour of the Name; of those who were absorbed in the Name; of those who remembered the Name and shared their food in companionship; of those who started free kitchens; of those who wielded their swords (for preserving truth); of those who overlooked others' shortcomings; All the aforesaid were pure and truly devoted ones; Utter Wahe Guru (Wondrous God)!

(Manpreet Singh, 2011)

Ardas in easy-to-understand English is also given in the Sikh Code of Conduct.

Greeting and prayer cards

Greeting cards:

Vaisakhi

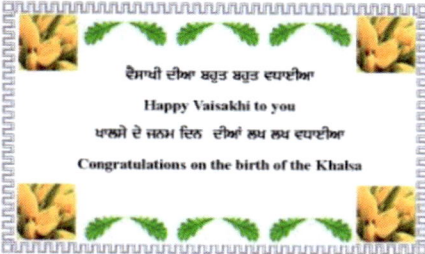

	With the Compliments of:

Guru Nanak's birthday

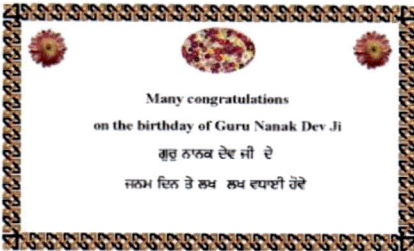

	With the Compliments of:

Diwali

	With the Compliments of:

Prayer cards

ਸਤਿਗੁਰ ਮੇਰਾ ਸਦਾ ਦਇਆਲਾ,
ਮੋਹਿ ਦੀਨ ਕਉ ਰਾਖਿ ਲੀਆ॥
ਕਾਟਿਆ ਰੋਗੁ ਮਹਾ ਸੁਖੁ ਪਾਇਆ,
ਹਰਿ ਅੰਮ੍ਰਿਤ ਮੁਖਿ ਨਾਮੁ ਦੀਆ॥੧॥
ਅਨਿਕ ਪਾਪ ਮੇਰੇ ਪਰਹਰਿਆ,
ਬੰਧਨ ਕਾਟੇ ਮੁਕਤ ਭਏ॥
ਅੰਧ ਕੂਪ ਮਹਾ ਘੋਰ ਤੇ,
ਬਾਹ ਪਕਰਿ ਗੁਰਿ ਕਾਢਿ ਲੀਏ॥

My God is always merciful
Who saved a humble person
like me
I felt comfortable when I was
cured of my disease
I was blessed to recite God's
name
God ignored my countless sins
I was freed from any bonds
From a deep dark pit
God has pulled me out
(GGS: 383)

ਤੇਰੀਆ ਸਦਾ ਸਦਾ ਚੰਗਿਆਈਆ॥
ਮੈ ਰਾਤਿ ਦਿਹੈ ਵਡਿਆਈਆਂ॥
ਅਣਮੰਗਿਆ ਦਾਨੁ ਦੇਵਣਾ,
ਕਹੁ ਨਾਨਕ ਸਚੁ ਸਮਾਲਿ ਜੀਉ॥

You are benevolent (Gracious)
I praise thee night and day
You give us without asking
Oh God, Guru Nanak has
grasped your reality (GGS: 73)

ਮੇਰੇ ਗੁਣ ਅਵਗਨ ਨ ਬੀਚਾਰਿਆ॥
ਪ੍ਰਭਿ ਅਪਣਾ ਬਿਰਦੁ ਸਮਾਰਿਆ॥
ਕੰਠਿ ਲਾਇ ਕੈ ਰਖਿਓਨੁ
ਲਗੈ ਨ ਤਤੀ ਵਾਉ ਜੀਉ॥

It is God's nature
Not to think about my virtues
and vices
God gives us unconditional
love
And saves us from disasters
(GGS: 72)

ਤੇਰੀ ਟੇਕ ਤੇਰਾ ਆਧਾਰਾ,	You are my refuge. You are my shelter.

ਤੇਰੀ ਟੇਕ ਤੇਰਾ ਆਧਾਰਾ,
ਹਾਥ ਦੇਇ ਤੂੰ ਰਾਖਹਿ ॥
ਜਿਸੁ ਜਨ ਊਪਰਿ ਤੇਰੀ ਕਿਰਪਾ,
ਤਿਸ ਕਉ ਬਿਪੁ ਨ ਕੋਊ ਭਾਖੈ॥੨॥
ਓਹੋ ਸੁਖੁ ਓਹਾ ਵਡਿਆਈ,
ਜੋ ਪ੍ਰਭ ਜੀ ਮਨਿ ਭਾਨੀ ॥
ਤੂੰ ਦਾਨਾ ਤੂੰ ਸਦ ਮਿਹਰਵਾਨਾ
ਨਾਮੁ ਮਿਲੈ ਰੰਗੁ ਮਾਨੀ ॥੩॥

You are my refuge. You are my
shelter.
You save me with your support
That being upon whom you
bestow your grace
Will never face any problems
Those are the comforts and
appreciations
Which appeal to my God
You are always generous and
compassionate
I am happy in reciting your
Name
(GGS: 383)

References

Cole, W. O. and Sambhi, P.S. (1990). *A popular dictionary of Sikhism*. London: Curzon Press.

Singh, Sahib (1972). *Sri Guru Granth Sahib Darpan*. Hoshiarpur: Raj Publishers.

Websites

Singh, M. (2010). *Ardas* English Translation. [online] Available at: https://manpreet159.wordpress.com/sikhism/ardas-english-translation/. [Accessed on 27 April 2020].

Appendix 4

The important days in the Sikh calendar

The Sikh Calendar: Gurpurab and Festival Dates (Fixed)

Gurpurabs / Festivals	Sikh *Gurpurabs* and Festivals	*Nanakshahi*	CE
Parkash Utsav	Guru Gobind Singh Sahib	23 Poh	5 Jan
Parkash Utsav	Guru Har Rai Sahib	19 Magh	31 Jan
Gurgadi	Guru Har Rai Sahib	1 Chet	14 Mar
Nanakshahi New Year	Nanakshahi Era 535	1 Chet	14 Mar
Hola Mahalla	Hola Mahalla Nanakshahi*	1 Chet	14 Mar
Jotijot	Guru Hargobind Sahib	6 Chet	19 Mar
Parkash	Guru Nanak Sahib *	1 Vaisakh	14 Apr
Khalsa Day – Vaisakhi	Khalsa Panth Creation	1 Vaisakh	14 Apr

Gurgadi	Guru Amar Das Sahib	3 Vaisakh	16 Apr
Jotijot	Guru Harkrishan Sahib	3 Vaisakh	16 Apr
Gurgadi	Guru Tegh Bahadur Sahib	3 Vaisakh	16 Apr
Parkash	Guru Angad Sahib	5 Vaisakh	18 Apr
Parkash	Guru Tegh Bahadur Sahib	5 Vaisakh	18 Apr
Parkash	Guru Arjun Sahib	19 Vaisakh	2 May
Parkash	Guru Amar Das Sahib	9 Jeth	23 May
Gurgadi	Guru Hargobind Sahib	28 Jeth	11 Jun
Martyrdom	Guru Arjun Sahib	2 Harh	16 Jun
Parkash	Guru Hargobind Sahib	21 Harh	5 Jul
Miri-Piri Day	Guru Hargobind Sahib	6 Sawan	21 Jul
Parkash	Guru Harkrishan Sahib	8 Sawan	23 Jul
First Parkash	Guru Granth Sahib	17 Bhadon	1 Sep

Jotijot	Guru Amar Das Sahib	2 Asu	16 Sep
Gurgadi	Guru Ramdas Sahib	2 Asu	16 Sep
Jotijot	Guru Ramdas Sahib	2 Asu	16 Sep
Gurgadi	Guru Arjun Sahib	2 Asu	16 Sep
Gurgadi	Guru Angad Sahib	4 Asu	18 Sep
Jotijot	Guru Nanak Sahib	8 Asu	22 Sep
Parkash	Guru Ramdas Sahib	25 Asu	9 Oct
Jotijot	Guru Har Rai Sahib	6 Katik	20 Oct
Gurgadi	Guru Harkrishan Sahib	6 Katik	20 Oct
Gurgadi	Guru Granth Sahib	6 Katik	20 Oct
Jotijot	Guru Gobind Singh Sahib	7 Katik	21 Oct

Gurgadi	Guru Gobind Singh Sahib	11 Maghar	24 Nov
Martyrdom	Guru Tegh Bahadur Sahib	11 Maghar	24 Nov
Martyrdom	Elder Sahibzadas	8 Poh	21 Dec
Martyrdom	Younger Sahibzadas	13 Poh	26 Dec

Definition of Terms

Parkash – birth

Gurgadi - ascension to Guruship

Jotijot - death

Moveable dates which change every year

Three events are still celebrated according to the lunar calendar, meaning that their dates change every year. Guru Nanak's birthday has been traditionally celebrated on Katik Poornamashi. Although the correct birth date according to the majority of *Janamsakhis* has been established as Vaisakh 1 (April 14), it continues to be celebrated on Katik Poornamashi until such time as it is changed to Vaisakh 1. In 2011 Katik Pooranmashi was on November 10.

Year	Parkash (birth) of Guru Nanak	Hola Mahalla	Bandi Chhor Divas
2011	Nov 10	Mar 20	Oct 26
2012	Nov 28	Mar 09	Nov 13
2013	Nov 17	Mar 28	Nov 03
2014	Nov 06	Mar 17	Oct 23
2015	Nov 25	Mar 06	Nov 11
2016	Nov 14	Mar 24	Oct 30
2017	Nov 04	Mar 13	Oct 19
2018	Nov 23	Mar 02	Nov 07
2019	Nov 12	Mar 21	Oct 27
2020	Nov 30	Mar 10	Nov 14

Source:

The Sikh Calendar: *Gurupurabs* **and Festival Dates.** Available from: <www.allaboutsikhs.com › sikh-festivals › the-sikh-calendar-gurupurab>. [Accessed on 27/04/2020].

Book Reviews

A Comprehensive Guide to Religious and Spiritual Care in NHS Hospitals and Hospices by Dr Satwant Kaur Rait

This book is an informative read into the beliefs, rituals, and practices of Sikhism. It is interesting to read all the aspects of chaplaincy including death and dying and bereavement. It is a good resource for healthcare chaplains wishing to increase their knowledge when caring for Sikh patients as well as other professionals working in a health care setting.

Jo Bewley, General Manager, Adult Therapies, Leeds Teaching Hospitals NHS Trust

As a young Sikh woman who works in the arts and cultural sector, the field of chaplaincy is completely new to me, and Dr. Rait's book provides a comprehensive, sensitive, and multi-faceted guide to not only spiritual care, but the values that Sikhs hold dear. I myself was enlightened on the meanings of several traditions and superstitions, as well as educated on the benefits, both to patients and wider society, of chaplaincy. The book is written from Dr. Rait's emotional, academic and religious experiences, bringing together her expertise in working with faith communities and challenging existing boundaries and definitions. It is a step towards making chaplaincy a multi-faith term that can comfort and advise people from all backgrounds, as well as making the Sikh faith accessible and interesting to a wider audience. This is the first time that a book has challenged the notion of pastoral care by breaking it down into comprehensive sections and applying these to healthcare settings. Dr. Rait has laid the groundwork for a generation that will go on to criticise, explore, and expand on the topic of spiritual and pastoral care. Using this book as a foundation, the various areas of the topic can be researched further and more in depth by chaplains and academics alike. Rites and rituals, bereavement, the role of a chaplain, and the changing scope of chaplaincy in healthcare are all explored through Dr. Rait's interpretations of existing literature and primary research.

Manpreet Kaur Dhadda (M.A. Culture, Creativity & Entrepreneurship)

About the Author

The author, Dr Satwant Kaur Rait, is a Sikh by faith, and so has an insider's knowledge of the Sikh religion, culture and community. She worked as a librarian in Delhi and in four local authorities in the UK and acquired a PhD in Library Science. She was on the bench for nearly twenty years and has many books and articles to her name. In her retirement, she became an honorary Sikh chaplain in 2009 in Leeds Teaching Hospitals following her husband's illness and realising that there is a gap in chaplaincy services for minority faiths. Having a professional background and having worked for many years in shaping service provision and delivery; she began her new career with auditing the needs and gathering the experiences of patients and their families using NHS services. Mark Cobb's (2005) book and support from other chaplaincy colleagues helped her to learn, grow, and gain confidence, and, within two years, she collected enough material to write a basic guide, acquired from her own experience with the needs and concerns of patients, for the use of new entrants in this field. As a result, *A Guide to Being a Sikh Chaplain* was published in 2013. She was keen to learn and studied for a postgraduate certificate (2011) and an M.A. in Chaplaincy in Health and Social Care (2015). Her belonging to a minority faith often deprived her of any opportunity for further development. Her M.A. thesis on pastoral care for Sikhs was published as a journal article in 2017; this encouraged her to self-develop by exploring Sikh chaplaincy as a topic of research and school of thought. She carried on working as an honorary chaplain in spite of many barriers. In 2016, she also started working as a spiritual care volunteer along with supporting a bereavement group in St. Gemma's, a local hospice, to test her own ability to provide services to patients of all faiths and none. In August 2017, she was appointed as a visiting Research Fellow at the University of Leeds and in 2019, she began to work as a trained facilitator in patient education on cancer, with Sir Robert Ogden Macmillan Centre in Leeds. During the Covid-19/Coronavirus pandemic, she offered her services by telephone on a voluntary basis to LTH and the wider community in Leeds. This period of more than a decade working as a volunteer gave her opportunities to observe chaplaincy politics, treatment, and training given to volunteers, as well as the attitudes of recruiting managers. This made her better equipped to revise and expand her previous book, covering all components of spiritual care with understanding.